BANKERS' AND PUBLIC AUTHORITIES' MANAGEMENT OF RISKS

Also edited by Zuhayr Mikdashi and published by Macmillan

INTERNATIONAL BANKING: Innovations and New Policies (*introduced by Charles Iffland and Pierre Languetin*)

Bankers' and Public Authorities' Management of Risks

Proceedings of the Second International Banking Colloquium held by the Ecole des Hautes Etudes Commerciales de l'Université de Lausanne

Edited by
Zuhayr Mikdashi
Professor of Banking and Financial Systems
University of Lausanne

Preface by Francis Léonard
Professor and Dean, Ecole des HEC
University of Lausanne

and

Introduction by Markus Lusser
Chairman of the Governing Board
Swiss National Bank

MACMILLAN

First published 1990

Published by
THE MACMILLAN PRESS LTD
Houndmills, Basingstoke, Hampshire RG21 2XS
and London
Companies and representatives
throughout the world

Printed in Hong Kong

British Library Cataloguing in Publication Data
International Banking Colloquium (2nd: Ecole des hautes études
commerciales de l'Université de Lausanne)
Bankers' and public authorities' management of risks
proceedings of the Second International Banking
Colloquium held by the Ecole des hautes études
commerciales de l'Université de Lausanne.
1. International banking.   Risks
I. Title   II. Mikdashi, Zuhayr
332.1′5
ISBN 0–333–49699–X

Contents

List of Tables

Notes on the Contributors

Georges Blum has been General Manager and Member of the Executive Board of the Swiss Bank Corporation at Head Office in Basle since 1984. He began his career with the Swiss Bank Corporation in 1961 at the Legal Division of the Lausanne Office. Ten years later Dr Blum became Vice President in the Lausanne Office. He was named its Senior Vice President in 1980, after having spent two years at the General Management Head Office in Basle in the Domestic Credits Division. In 1982 he was appointed Central Manager and Member of the Executive Board of the Commercial Group in Basle. He is also on the Board of Director of a number of financial and industrial companies.

E. Gerald Corrigan became the seventh President and Chief Executive of the Federal Reserve Bank of New York in 1985. He is also Vice Chairman of the Federal Open Market Committee (FOMC), the Federal Reserve Board principal body responsible for establishing national money and credit policies. He also served as Chairman of the Systems Pricing Policy Committee. Dr Corrigan's career at the New York Fed began in August 1968, when he joined the domestic research division as an economist after teaching economics at Fordham University in 1967–8. From 1968 to 1976, he served in a variety of staff and official positions at the New York Fed. In 1979, he left the New York Fed to become special assistant to Federal Reserve Board Chairman Paul Volcker in Washington, DC. In August 1980, he became president of the Federal Reserve Bank of Minneapolis. He is also a member of the Council on Foreign Relations and the Trilateral Commission.

Lamberto Dini has been Director General of the Bank of Italy since 1979 and is Chairman of the Deputies of the Group of Ten and a Member of the Board of Directors of the Italian Exchange Office. He was an official of the International Monetary Fund from 1959 to 1975; he was elected Executive Director by Italy and Spain until 1978 and then by Greece, Portugal and Malta until 1980. Dr Dini has been Governor for Italy of the Asian Development Bank between 1979 and 1982. He is also Vice President of the Monetary Committee of the European Economic Communities; Alternate Governor for Italy of the International Monetary Fund; Alternate Member of the Board of Directors of the Bank for International Settlements; and Alternate Governor for Italy of the Inter-American Development Bank.

Gaston Gaudard has been Professor of International and Regional Economics at the University of Fribourg since 1966 and Professor of International Economic Exchanges at l'Ecole des HEC since 1979. He is also a Member of the Board of Directors of the Swiss Bank Corporation in Basle. Dr Gaudard is President of the Social Sciences Division of the Swiss National Scientific Research Fund in Berne. Between 1975 and 1979 he was Rector of the University of Fribourg. He is the author of more than a hundred works and scientific articles.

Rainer E. Gut has been the Chairman of the Board of Directors of Credit Suisse in Zurich since 1983. In 1971 he was named Chairman and CEO of Credit Suisse's US investment banking affiliate Swiss American Corporation. In 1975 he became a Member of the Executive Board at the Head Office of Credit Suisse in Zurich. After two years he was named Speaker of the Executive Board. A year before being appointed to his present position he became President of the Executive Board. His other business appointments include: Chairman of the Board of Directors of Financière Crédit – First Boston in Zug; of Electrowatt, Zurich, and of Centralschweizerische Kraftwerke in Lucerne; a Member of the Board of Directors of Ciba-Geigy Ltd, Basle; Daimler-Benz Holding, Zurich; National Bank of Switzerland, Berne; Nestlé SA, Vevey; Swiss Reinsurance Company, Zurich; Swissair, Zurich; First Boston, Inc., New York; and Sofina SA, Brussels.

Kazuaki Harada is the Managing Director and Chief Economist of the Sanwa Bank and also the Senior Managing Director of Sanwa Research Institute in Tokyo. He joined the Sanwa Bank in 1956. After being a Visiting Officer at the Ministry of International Trade and Industry from 1962 to 1965 he joined the London Branch of Sanwa as an economist. In 1971 he became a Deputy General Manager of the Nagoya Branch of Sanwa and two years later he was named General Manager of the Hachioji Branch. Among his research works are: 'Flows of Funds in Japan', 'Effects of the Financial Deregulation on Japan's Economy' and 'Commercial Banks' Strategy for the Following Ten Years'.

Kurt Hauri has been Director of the Secretariat of the Swiss Banking Commission since 1986. He worked in the Swiss Finance administration from 1962 to 1986. In 1976 Dr Hauri became Vice Director and Chief of the Legal Services. He was named First Director in 1984. During the period 1977–86, Dr Hauri presided over the Study Group on the Revision of the Banking Law.

Robert Holzach was named Honorary Chairman of the Board of the Union Bank of Switzerland in 1988. He is also Chairman of Swiss National Insurance Co. and of Reinsurance Union Co. and a Member of the Board of Directors of major firms in Switzerland and the Federal Republic of Germany. He joined the Union Bank of Switzerland in 1951 after completing his legal training. In 1962 he was named Manager of the Commercial Department. Appointed General Manager in 1968, he headed the Administrative Division. From 1976 to 1980 Dr Holzach was responsible for the Staff Departments of the General Management and for coordination within the General Management. In 1980 the General Assembly elected him to the Board of Directors of which he was Chairman until 1988.

Yasuo Kanzaki was elected Executive Vice President of the Nikko Securities Co., Ltd in Tokyo in 1986. He had joined the Nikko Securities Co. in 1955 and continued his career with appointments in both the Research and Foreign Divisions before being named Manager of the International Finance Division in 1969. In 1974 he was appointed Managing Director of the Nikko Securities Co. (Europe) Ltd. Five years later he became General Manager of the International Finance Division and the next year was elected a Member of the Board of Directors. From 1982 to 1985 Mr Kanzaki was Managing Director before being named Senior Managing Director.

Pierre Languetin was the Chairman of the Governing Board of the Swiss National Bank and a Member of the Board of Directors of the Bank for International Settlements until 1988. He began his career in international economic relations at the OEEC (now OECD) in Paris. In 1955 he was appointed to the Trade Division of the Federal Department of Economic Affairs and in 1966 he became a permanent delegate of the Federal Government for Trade Negotiations and Head of the Swiss delegation at the European Free Trade Association (EFTA) in Geneva, with ambassadorial rank. Mr Languetin was commissioned by Switzerland to negotiate accession to the International Energy Agency (1974) and served on the organisation's Board of Directors from 1974 to 1976. In 1976, he joined the Governing Board of the Swiss National Bank. Currently, he is a Member of the International Committee of the Red Cross in Geneva and President of the Institut de Hautes Etudes en Administration Publique (IDHEAP) of the University of Lausanne.

Francis Léonard is a Professor of Business Administration and Dean of Ecole des Hautes Études Commerciales (the School of Management and Economics) of the University of Lausanne. He is also advisor to European and North American companies. After graduate and postgraduate studies in commercial and financial sciences at the University of Liège, he held diverse managerial functions in several companies and, in particular, in the Nestlé group (1962–73). Eventually, after having graduated from IMEDE Management School and the University of Lausanne (PhD degree in business administration), he served as a faculty member at the International Management Institute (Geneva), then, in parallel, at Ecole des HEC of the University of Lausanne. Francis Léonard is author of articles, cases and books on industrial marketing (products and services), in particular in its international dimension. He has organized and run various seminars in different European countries and in Brazil.

Markus Lusser has been the Chairman of the Governing Board of the Swiss National Bank since 1988. This function is linked with the assumption of duties as Head of Department I (staff sectors) in Zurich. After law studies Dr Lusser entered the office of the Swiss Bankers' Association in Basle in 1959 where he acted as Secretary and Deputy Director; in 1976 he was appointed its Director with full responsibility. In addition, he was in charge of the secretariat of the Association of Swiss Holding and Finance Companies from 1959 to 1979. Moreover, he participated actively in realizing various joint undertakings of the Swiss banks such as SEGA (Swiss Clearinghouse AG): he was Secretary of the Board of Directors from 1970 to 1980; Swiss Cheque and Eurocheque; and Eurocard Switzerland SA: he was Chairman of the Board of Directors from 1978 to 1980. He was elected a Member of the Governing Board of the Swiss National Bank and Head of Department in Zurich in 1980 and in 1985 he was appointed Vice Chairman of the Governing Board and Head of

Department II (capital markets, business transactions with the Federal Government, issuing banknotes and administration of gold reserves) in Berne.

Zuhayr Mikdashi has been Professor of Banking and Financial Systems, and of Petroleum Economics at the Ecole des HEC since 1976. He has been a consultant to the World Bank in Washington, DC, the UN, and other intergovernmental agencies and financial groups. Among his principal publications are: *A Financial Analysis of Middle Eastern Oil Concessions: 1901–65* (1966); *The Community of Oil Exporting Countries – A Study in Governmental Cooperation* (1972); *The International Politics of Natural Resources* (1976); *Transnational Oil – Issues, Policies and Perspectives* (1986); and editor of *International Banking – Innovations and New Policies* (1988).

Moeen A. Qureshi was appointed in 1987 Senior Vice President, Operations, at the World Bank in Washington, DC. Before joining the International Monetary Fund in 1958, Dr Qureshi served as Department Chief of the Planning Committee, government of Pakistan. In 1970 he joined the International Finance Corporation as Economic Advisor and was appointed Vice President four years later. Concurrently he was appointed Vice President Finance at the World Bank in 1977, and in 1981 he became Senior Vice President Finance. Mr Qureshi, in his current position, leads the World Bank's Operations Complex on the basis of strategy and policy. He is the principal decision-maker on the interpretation of Bank operational policies. He also decides most adjustment lending operations.

H. Onno Ruding was sworn in as a Minister of Finance of the Netherlands in 1982. Dr Ruding is Governor of IMF/World Bank and of the Asian Development Bank, the African Development Bank Group and the Inter-AmerBank Group. He has been the Chairman of the Interim Committee of the International Monetary Fund since 1985. In 1985/86 he served as the Chairman of the Group of Ten. Dr Ruding served in the Ministry of Finance as Head of Division of International Monetary Affairs from 1965 to 1970. In that capacity he was a Deputy Member of the Monetary Committee of the EC. After six years as a Joint General Manager heading the securities underwriting, new issues and corporate finance department of the Amsterdam–Rotterdam Bank in Amsterdam, he was appointed an Executive Director of the International Monetary Fund in Washington DC in 1977. In 1981, Dr Ruding became a Member of the Board of Managing Directors of the Amsterdam–Rotterdam Bank.

L. William Seidman became Chairman of the Federal Deposit Insurance Corporation in 1985. At the time of his presidential appointment, he was dean of the College of Business at Arizona State University, where he founded the Institute of Business Leadership. He served as Co-Chairman of the White House Conference on Productivity in 1983 and 1984. Mr Seidman was Vice Chairman of the Phelps Dodge Corporation from 1977 to 1982. He was President Ford's Assistant for Economic Affairs from 1974 to 1977. From 1968 to 1974 he was Managing Partner of Seidman & Seidman, Certified Public Accountants. He was Special Assistant for financial affairs to the Governor of Michigan from 1963 to 1966. At Arizona State he was responsible for the operation of the University's Economic Outlook Center and its widely-acclaimed statistical report. In Arizona, he was also Chairman of the Governor's Commission on Interstate Banking. He is the founder of The Washington Campus, a consortium of universities organized to help students and corporate executives to understand the operations of the White House, the Congress and the regulatory agencies.

Walter Seipp is Chairman of the Board of Managing Directors of Commerzbank AG in Frankfurt am Main since 1981. He began his career with Deutsche Bank AG in 1951 and became an Executive Vice President in 1970. Four years later Dr Seipp became Member of the Board Managing of Directors of Westdeutsche Landesbank Girozentrale and in 1977 he was appointed Deputy Chairman of the Board. He is Chairman of the Supervisory Board of Karstadt, Europe's number one department store, and of Rheinische Hypothekenbank, West Germany's biggest mortgage lending bank. In addition, Mr Seipp is a Member of the Board of the Federation of German Banks whose capital market committee he chairs. He is also on various international committees, including the Board of the International Monetary Conference, for which he served as Chairman in 1987–8.

Jacques Thierry has been Chairman of the Board of Banque Bruxelles Lambert in Brussels since 1986. After having been in training with BNCI and Union Bank of Switzerland in Zurich, Mr Thierry was appointed Swiss Representative of Banque Lambert, Brussels, in

1952. Four years later he became Executive Director of Compagnie d'Outremer pour l'Industrie et la Finance. In 1960, Mr Thierry continued his career with Banque Lambert as a Managing Partner. He was named Vice Chairman, Executive Director of the Compagnie Bruxelles Lambert and Vice Chairman of the Supervisory Board of Banque Lambert in 1972. After three years, upon the merger of Banque de Bruxelles with Banque Lambert, he was appointed President and Chief Executive Officer of Banque Bruxelles Lambert SA. At the time of the merger he was also President of the Executive Committee of Banque de Bruxelles. Since 1987 Mr Thierry has been Chairman of the Board Artois Piedboeuf Interbrew.

Shigeru Uemura has been Vice Chairman of Daiwa Securities Co. Ltd in Tokyo since 1988. He began his career with Daiwa Securities Co. in 1953 at its Foreign Department. In 1964 he became Executive Vice President of Daiwa Securities America Inc. He returned to Tokyo as a Deputy General Manager of its Underwriting Department four years later. His career at the Tokyo office was interrupted by two years spent as President of Daiwa Europe NV from 1976 to 1978, and three years, from 1982 to 1985, as Chairman of Daiwa Securities America Inc. In 1985 he was appointed Managing Director of Daiwa Securities and two years later Head of its International Division. He was named Head of International operations in 1987.

Philip Wilkinson is a Deputy Chairman of National Westminster Bank plc and Chairman of NatWest Investment Bank and County NatWest. He joined NatWest Bank in 1943 and after a wide-ranging career was seconded as a Director of the Orion Banking Group in 1972. After several appointments inside the NatWest group, Sir Philip was appointed Deputy Group Chief Executive in 1980. In 1982 he became a Director of International Westminster Bank and NatWest Group Chief Executive in 1983, before reaching his actual position in 1987. He is Deputy Chairman of HandelsBank NatWest and also a Director of National Westminster Bank USA. In 1983 he became a Council Member of the Confederation of British Industry and for the two next years he was Chairman of the Chief Executive Officers of the Committee of London & Scottish Clearing Bankers. He was appointed a non-executive Director of British Aerospace plc in 1987.

Acknowledgements

A select number of personalities from public authorities and from the international banking community examine in this book major risks encountered by the global banking system and reflect on means of mastering them. Their analyses and evaluations constituted the basis of intensive exchanges at the Second International Banking Colloquium on 4–5 November 1988, hosted by the Ecole des Hautes Etudes Commerciales (HEC) – viz. the School of Management and Economics – of the University of Lausanne. On that occasion, some one hundred top policy- and decision-makers from all continents participated in an informal, frank and exhaustive discussion of issues of primary importance to all concerned with the safety and stability of the banking sector.

The contents of this book testify to the exceptionally high quality of exchanges held at the Colloquium. It ends with the editor's paper which focuses on major issues raised by representatives of the world banking sector at the Colloquium. Though he retains sole responsibility for its contents, the author would like to acknowledge with gratitude the valuable comments offered by some of these representatives on a preliminary draft of the terminal paper.

Several persons assisted me in my capacity as Programme Director of the Colloquium and editor of this book. A special tribute is owed to those who have offered so generously their precious advice and time. In this respect, I should like to record my profound gratitude to Dr Markus Lusser and to Mr Pierre Languetin – respectively Chairman and former Chairman of the Governing Board of the Swiss National Bank, to the Dean of the Ecole des HEC, Professor Francis Léonard, and to Professors Charles Iffland and Alfred Stettler.

My sincere thanks are owed to Ms Eva Wennerth for her valuable help in carrying out efficiently, with the fine support of the administrative staff of the Ecole des HEC, all assignments entrusted to her, notably in relation to the logistics of the Colloquium and those of the book's manuscript.

ZUHAYR MIKDASHI

Preface

Francis Léonard

The banker's role has considerably evolved over time. After having been essentially an intermediary, the banker is increasingly, nowadays, an actor whose difficult job consists in analyzing the problems, perspectives and risks associated with different economic activities and of behaving as an entrepreneur.

THE BANKS AND MANAGERS' DEVELOPMENT

The traditional banks have always had a marked preference for on-the-job training: holding positions at different operational levels was usually the only conceivable way of learning one's job as a future manager and being progressively prepared for making strategic decisions. This could be easily accepted inasmuch the banker's function consisted essentially in linking suppliers and users of funds, and historically the attitude of other sectors such as the integrated distribution trade has been exactly the same: priority was given to on-the-job learning of selling, then buying activities whilst there was a certain reservation *vis-à-vis* academic education.

This approach was understandable since in a world which used to be more stable than turbulent, it was much more important to master adequately the internal aspects of banking techniques than to question them through anticipation of the evolution of the economic, political and social environment as is the case today. As far as universities were concerned, they lived too much in their ivory tower and their fields of interest – generally too abstract and speculative – could not meet the concerns of company managements confronted with practical realities.

CONSEQUENCES OF THE RECENT EVOLUTION OF FINANCIAL SERVICES

The industry of financial services is undergoing important changes in several respects:

- in terms of products, since it generates financial packages integrating various new instruments;
- in terms of new markets, be it only from a geographic point of view, since it is driven to get involved in ever more international activities;
- in terms of operating techniques since the adoption of the most recent developments in office automation, telematics, expert systems and other technological areas tend to give them, increasingly, certain characteristics of manufacturing industries.

To these new terms of economic efficiency let us add new facets of the relations between banks and their economic environment, a topic which will be abundantly covered in this book. In a nutshell, one can say that the banks must not only keep doing things right, but must also increasingly check that they are doing the right things.

What about people in this evolution and, in particular, what about their development? It has probably become a commonplace to say that the quality of human resources – at all levels – is a key factor of performance and growth of banking institutions. Banks are conscious of this which is illustrated by the fact that all major Swiss banks have resources – sometimes very impressive – staff, premises and equipment to implement initial and continuous training programmes for which they spend, on average, the equivalent of 1.5 per cent of the aggregate remuneration.

Parallel to the development of in-company training activities, interesting initiatives have been taken outside banking institutions, often out their instigation and with their active support. Internal and external training activities are clearly complementary. As in other economic sectors, the business firms of the financial services industry must use both of them jointly. Internal training is irreplaceable to transfer the indispensable knowledge at the operational level – and even beyond – and to modify attitudes, in particular to create a team spirit and to instil the company culture.

The need for a complementary education *outside* is imperative when the objectives are:

- to give managers and senior executives complementary knowledge and work methods to help them make *strategic* decisions;
- to give them a chance to meet other managers even from other industries and by so doing avoid a narrowing of their field of vision.

THE CONTRIBUTION OF ECOLE DES HEC

Given the existing or projected managers' development programmes, both internal or external to the establishments, are there unserved needs which the Ecole des HEC could satisfy by a specific contribution? We have a firm conviction at least as far as *permanent* education is concerned and, in particular, that of chief executive officers (CEOs) and other high ranking executives. We believe that these people are jeopardized by compartmentalization and therefore have a double need:

- on the one hand, the need to understand and anticipate the behaviour of other institutions which are also interested in money, particulary the central banks, the supervisory agencies, the specialized international agencies, etc.;
- on the other hand, to have points of reference for the interpretation – as a banker – of relevant economic, social, political, technological or cultural trends, which do not necessarily *to-day* have a *direct* link with banking activities but which could, later on, affect them considerably.

We, at the Ecole des HEC, think we can make a contribution as an academic institution already engaged in that direction because we can assemble competences, in particular for organizing meetings with eminent persons. The biennal International Banking Colloquium and our publications in the banking field are part of this enterprise.

Introduction

Markus Lusser

I really must say that you are an ignorant person, friend Grey-beard, if you know nothing of this enigmatic business which is at once the fairest and most deceitful in Europe, the noblest and the most infamous in the world, the finest and the most vulgar on earth. It is a quintessence of academic learning and a paragon of fraudulence; it is a touchstone for the intelligent and a tombstone for the audacious, a treasury of usefulness and a source of disaster, and finally a counterpart of Sisyphus who never rests, as also of Ixion who is chained to a wheel that turns perpetually (José de la Vega, *Confusion de confusiones*, 1688).

The double-edged nature of the stock market – of the financial markets in general – can hardly be described in more appropriate or more striking terms than in the above instruction of the 'philosopher' by the 'speculator'. The quotation is taken from the oldest discourse on the stock market known to me. The book reminds us that the sophisticated financial transactions are not an achievement of our time: forward transactions – to name but one example – were already mentioned in the statutes of Verona in 1318 and, together with options, were quite familiar to the trading community in the seventeenth century. The fact that de la Vega, a Portuguese of Jewish decent living in Amsterdam – the centre of the financial world at that time – published a book in Spanish seems to be a further indication that the degree of globalisation – at least as regards market participants – was quite considerable even then.

Globalisation of the financial markets, however, has only recently become a catchword. Under the influence of telecommunications and computers the outlines of a single, world-spanning financial market are emerging ever more clearly. The financial markets are not only growing closer in a geographical sense: the large number of new – or recently revived – financial instruments has closed the gaps between individual markets, enabling market participants to move easily – and swiftly – from one to another.

Today, José de la Vega would note with a sense of satisfaction that his description of the financial markets is as valid as ever. On sifting through the specialist literature he might be amazed by the extent to which this domain has indeed become a 'quintessence of academic learning'. And he would certainly note that in today's closely linked and fast-reacting financial markets the tension between the opportunity of being a 'treasury of usefulness' and the risk of becoming 'a source of disaster' has intensified.

The contributions in this book therefore deal with a highly topical subject: how can the risks inherent in the financial markets be reduced, or at least be controlled, while at the same time the usefulness of the markets is preserved? Most of the articles have been written from the point of view of the banks, the major group of suppliers on the financial markets. They reveal two sources of risk. The first are financial innovations, which make the 'risk management' of a bank – i.e. identifying, measuring and monitoring risks – at the same time more difficult and more complicated (Mikdashi Chapter 19). In particular, the process of disintermediation, that is, on the one hand replacing traditional bank credits by direct loans from the creditor to the borrower and on the other hand the use of contingent liabilities by banks confronts us increasingly with the tricky problems of risk selection and risk control (Blum, Chapter 14). Yet the international debt crisis – the difficulties of the highly indebted countries (Qureshi, Chapter 2) – is a constant and forceful reminder that traditional banking is not beyond committing errors either. At any rate, modern financial instruments not only require the banker to have a knowledge of technical details but also present a challenge to top management. Cases in point are: corporate philosophy (Seipp, Chapter 6); the role of the board of directors (Holzach, Chapter 15), and bank strategy (Gut, Chapter 7).

A second source of risk is globalization and the ensuing increase in competition (Kanzaki, Chapter 5). This applies in particular to the European banks that are now facing the single EC market of 1992 (Thierry, Chapter 8). But also on a worldwide scale fiercer competition lead to a narrowing of profit margins and a tougher selection process (Wilkinson, Chapter 4). Thus, there is an increasing probability that not all banks will remain in the market. Such fears and a measure of distrust with respect to the rationality of the speculative markets lead some authors (Holzach, Chapter 15; Dini, Chapter 3) to doubt whether further deregulation is advisable. It might, however, be argued against these doubts that the greater flexibility of financial transactions has severely limited policy options: interference with the markets quickly causes business to be shifted to 'more convenient' financial centres (Uemura, Chapter 13). This fact has been recognized by the authorities; they are no longer philosophical greybeards – to quote de la Vega once more – who have to be initiated into the arcana of the market. Evidence to this effect was provided, for instance, after the stock-market crash in October 1987. The authorities did not emulate earlier examples such as England's prohibition of 'puts' and 'refusals' in 1734, France's banning of *agiotage* in 1785 and the American Glass–Steagall Act of 1932. The small number of new reforms – instead of again pressing the markets into a regulatory corset – is rather aimed at strengthening their freedom of movement and, consequently, their efficiency.

The authorities' recipe for dealing with the risks of modern financial markets is not re-regulation but improvement and adaptation of supervision. The recipe contains three vital ingredients. First, traditional bank supervision is increasingly developing into 'functional' supervision, which focuses on the economic character of market participants and of transactions rather than on their legal appearance (Hauri, Chapter 17; Wilkinson, Chapter 4). Second, the authorities prescribe a more solid capital base for financial intermediaries (Kanzaki, Chapter 5). Third and finally, the globalisation of banking creates the need for a 'globalization of supervision', starting with cooperation between the responsible authorities (Gaudard, Chapter 18; Corrigan, Chapter 11) to achieve coordinated supervision of the banks and financial markets (Languetin, Chapter 16). The notion of an 'ideal' form of supervision – if this can be said to exist – should not, however, be allowed to blur our view of the transitional problems (Seidman, Chapter 1).

Finally, the central banks must ask themselves what they can do to enhance the stability of the financial markets and of the banking system. Today it is widely agreed that a monetary policy aimed at maintaining price stability and transparency prevents macroeconomic disequilibria and thus provides the best basis for sparing the financial markets from shocks (Languetin, Chapter 16). Only the coordination of national economic policy under the motto 'soundness' and 'austerity' (Lusser, Chapter 12) would create the environment in which the vision of a European central bank (Ruding, Chapter 10) or perhaps even a yen–dollar–ECU 'zone' (Harada, Chapter 9) could become reality.

List of Abbreviations

ALM	assets liabilities management
BA	bankers' acceptances
BIS	Bank for International Settlements
CB	convertible bond
CD	certificate of deposit
CP	commercial paper
CEO	Chief Executive Officer
CSFB	Crédit Suisse – First Boston
DIC	developed industrial countries
EC	European Community
ECP	Euro-commercial paper
EDP	electronic data processing
EMCF	European Monetary Cooperation Fund
EMS	European Monetary System
FB	foreign bond
FDIC	Federal Deposit Insurance Corporation
FFF	free financial fund
FOMC	Federal Open Market Committee
FSLIC	Federal Savings and Loan Insurance Corporation
GAO	(US) General Accounting Office
GCM	General Clearing Members
HEC	Ecole des Hautes Etudes Commerciales
ICCH	International Commodities Clearing House
IDHEAP	Institut des Hautes Etudes en Administration Publique
IMF	International Monetary Fund
LBO	leveraged buy out
L/C	letter of credit
LDC	less developed countries
LIFFE	London International Financial Futures Exchange
MMC	money market certificate
NIC	newly industrializing countries
NIF	note issuance facilities
RUF	revolving underwriting facilities
SICAV	Société d'investissement à capital variable (open-end investment companies)
SOFFEX	Swiss Options and Financial Futures Exchange AG
TSE	Tokyo Stock Exchange
UBS	Union Bank of Switzerland
UCITS	undertakings for collective investment in transferable securities
WB	warrant bond
VAT	value-added tax

1 Deposit Insurance and Banking Efficiency

L. William Seidman

The US banking system is facing its greatest challenges ever as it functions in an increasingly competitive and risky environment. Consequently, the topic of this discussion is particularly germane to American financial institutions, which no longer operate under interest-rate constraints, prohibitions against offering many types of services and products, or protection from non-bank competition. Our financial services industry now involves retailers and brokerage houses, as well as commercial banks, savings banks, savings and loan associations, credit unions, industrial banks, mortgage banks, and others, all competing for deposits and good loans.

The changes in our financial services industry have been accompanied by increased risk. Many American banks have been hurt on the bottom line, and record numbers have failed. The most obvious manifestation of increased risk is the deterioration of many US savings and loan institutions. In the early 1980s, thrifts were deregulated on both the asset and liability sides of their ledgers so they could purportedly better compete – and indeed survive the challenges from new competition and inflationary environment. Many of these institutions ventured into speculative financing that eventually led to their downfall. The savings and loan regulators were not prepared or allowed to control risk in this more complicated world. Ultimately, the cumulative effect of this imbalance between risk and supervision overwhelmed the ability of the industry and the thrift regulators to absorb the problems.

To draw lessons from the experiences of this decade, we need to examine the performance of the US banking industry, and then to determine the reasons for its condition. It is also useful to look at the deposit insurance system in the USA, especially the Federal Deposit Insurance Corporation (FDIC), the depositors' cushion against the disruption competition and risk can cause. An examination of our proposals for restructuring the American banking industry to facilitate fair competition and minimize risk will also help to address the subject of this discussion.

1

CONDITION OF THE US BANKING INDUSTRY

The US banking industry has experienced declining profitability and historically high rates of failure during this decade. This has occurred primarily for three reasons:

1. competition from other parts of our financial services industry combined with restrictive regulatory structures that limit bank's ability to provide competitive service to their customers;
2. economic problems in the south-west and farm-belt areas of the country;
3. increased reserving for Latin-American and other developing-country debt, which especially reduced bank profitability in 1987.

Non-banking Competition

First, non-banking competitors have made inroads into the traditional business areas once dominated by banks, aided by restraints in the regulatory system under which banks must operate. The result has been the slow erosion of profitability and increase of risk in bank portfolios. Return of assets of US commercial banks has deteriorated steadily throughout the 1980s, even before dropping to 0.12 per cent in 1987. Banks are moving toward riskier commercial real-estate lending and away from more conservative blue-chip commercial lending.

Non-bank competitors have captured increased amounts of what had been traditional banking business, while banks have been constrained from expanding into new areas. A two-way street has not been established. Since 1980 the annual asset growth rate of banks in the USA has been lower than for all other types of financial services institutions.

Economic Problems in the South-west

Another factor in the banking industry's lacklustre performance over the past few years has been depressed commodities prices, leading to severe economic problems in the south-west and in the farm belt.

Over 90 per cent of the banks that failed in 1987, for example, as well as almost 80 per cent of the unprofitable banks, were located in the western half of the USA. Roughly 85 per cent of last year's bank failures were caused, at least in part, by troubles in the farm and energy sectors, together with mismanagement. In 1987, 24 per cent of banks located in the western USA had losses, compared with only 8.5 per cent of the banks in the east.

Problems arising from the collapse of energy prices had a negative effect on the overall profitability of the banking industry. 36 per cent of the banks in the south-west, where real-estate loans that soured with the collapse of the energy boom played a major role in bank portfolios, reported net losses in 1987. If the relevant statistics for banks in the south-west are removed from consideration, industry profitability in 1987 almost doubles.

Developing-Country Loan Reserves

A further reason for low profitability in the US banking industry, especially in 1987, was significant reserving for losses on Latin America and other developing country debt. In the second quarter of 1987 alone, commercial banks lost almost $10.6bn, most of that attributable to this reserving process. In 1987, the amount set aside for anticipated losses on international operations amounted to $20.6bn, up $18bn from 1986.

Situation Improving

We are heartened that 1988 is looking better. In all three problem areas just mentioned – increased competition, regional economic conditions, and developing-country debt-losses – there are signs of improvement.

First, in the absence of new banking legislation this year, regulators and the courts have eased some restrictions on permissible banking activities, and have responded to the call to let banks compete.

Second, economic conditions in the western USA have begun to improve. The farm-belt economy is clearly improving and is contributing to a much stronger profit picture in 1988. However, significant problems continue in the south-west, and it will take time for economic improvements to be reflected in the banking system. Thus, failures are continuing this year (1988) at a record pace, although we expect that pace to slow in 1989.

Third, with respect to developing-country debt, the major bank lenders have reserves equalling 30 per cent to 50 per cent of their total developing-country debt. We do not see substantial additional reserving being made in this area in the immediate future. This will have a strong positive effect on major bank profitability. For example, if there had been no major developing-country reserving in 1987, aggregate bank net operating income would have been over $13bn – close to the level in 1986. Developing-country debt continues to be a matter of long-term concern, but the action taken by banks in 1987 will mean lower reserving and thus higher profits in the future.

We have already seen bank profitability improve dramatically in the first half of 1988. Commercial banks nationwide earned a record $10.5bn in the first half of 1988, bolstered by the best second-quarter earnings ever. For the four quarters ended 30 June 1988, bank earnings aggregated to $19.5bn, another record – despite sizeable losses at several large Texas banks.

Several factors help to account for this strength. As noted, banks reserved heavily last year, the economy has been generally strong, and the US banking industry seems to have recovered from much of the economic dislocation of the early 1980s. Certain non-recurring gains, derived from the sale of real estate, venture funds, data-processing units, and credit-card operations also contributed to the industry's reportedly high earnings.

With better asset quality, the expectation of stable interest rates, the return of Brazilian debt to performing status, and the steps taken in 1987 to fortify reserves, 1988 promised a return to profitability levels not seen since 1985.

As good as those trends are, if the problems in Texas could be separated from overall statistics, the banking industry would really be breaking records. One third of all banks with earnings losses for the first half of 1988 were in Texas. And 102 of the 186 banks which failed or received assistance during the first three quarters of this year were in Texas.

RECENT TRENDS IN US BANKS

The FDIC publishes various data concerning commercial banking performance in its *Quarterly Banking Profile*. Several interesting trends were emphasised by the data in our latest publication.

Changes in Portfolio Management

First, banks are increasingly turning to real estate and consumer lending for new business, and changing the way they manage their portfolios. The dollar volume of real-estate loans on their books now exceeds commercial loans outstanding. Real-estate loans had increased from 25 per cent of total loans in 1982 to over 34 per cent by 30 June 1988. Much of the growth in this area was in commercial real-estate lending, such as construction and development financing. With the growth of securitization, US banks were also moving further toward a transactional business, rather than a loan-and-hold business.

It is still too early to tell what these shifts in lending practices will mean for overall portfolio risk. For example, are banks being forced into more hazardous lending patterns as the most creditworthy commercial borrowers increasingly turn to money and capital markets themselves? Also, what happens if stress is put on a system that is relying on securitization more heavily than ever before? These are areas that certainly demand greater attention.

Slowing of Deposit Growth

Second, deposits at banks grew at only a 3.7 per cent rate over the last two quarters of 1987, and the first two quarters of 1988. That is significantly less than the growth rate needed to stay even with the economy as a whole after inflation.

The high growth of deposits at savings and loans, attracted by high interest rates, helps to account for this trend. Even more disturbing for banks, the relative slowing of deposit growth may mean that the public is turning to other financial services competitors to find investments. While it is not clear what this will mean to the US economy as a whole, this trend is certainly not good for the banking industry.

Consolidation

Third, we are seeing a marked consolidation taking place in the banking industry. As recently as year-end 1984, we had almost 14 500 banks. By mid-year 1988, the banking ranks had thinned by over 1000. Merger activity, bank failures and liberalized branching laws help to account for this trend.

Improved Outlook for Credit Quality

Fourth, for the first time in the 1980s, there has been a reduction in non-performing assets, and an improving trend in net interest margins. We believe that the credit quality outlook may finally be improving for the industry as a whole.

Looking a little further into the future, banks are facing increasing competition on both the asset and liability sides of their ledgers. Prudence, and attention to asset quality, will help to ensure that even if an economic slowdown does occur, the US banking industry will remain stable and prosper.

CONDITION OF THE FDIC AND FEDERAL DEPOSIT INSURANCE

Turning to the condition of the FDIC and federal deposit insurance – part of our system's cushion against the disruption competition and risk can cause – a bit of background may prove useful.

The FDIC (not to be confused with the Federal Savings and Loan Insurance Corporation (FSLIC), which insures the savings and savings-and-loan (S&L) industry), is an independent agency that was created in 1933 to protect bank depositors from the devastation of losing their savings, as had happened to hundreds of thousands when banks closed during the early 1930s. Until the 1980s, the FDIC had a fairly straightforward job, insuring deposits in our country's banks, and having primary supervisory responsibility over a majority of those banks, but only handling a few bank failures each year.

Conditions turned for the worse in the early 1980s. In 1981, just ten banks failed. By 1985, the numbers had increased to 116 failures and four assistance transactions, the latter involving the provision of financial assistance to prevent banks from failing. In 1987, 203 banks failed or received assistance, and, unfortunately, we are seeing a similar pace this year (1988). In the last year alone the FDIC handled more banking assets than it did in its first fifty years! As discussed earlier, most of these problems have been centred in the south-west and mid-west, and largely result from the collapse of the energy, real estate, and agricultural markets in those regions.

To handle the mounting problems in the banking industry, the FDIC's staff swelled from 3800 in 1983 to over 9000 this year. Only seven of those employees are political appointees, which is unusually low for an agency of our size. Most of the employees hired since 1983 service and market the $10bn in loans and assets which the FDIC has acquired from failed banks over the years. These assets include anything a bank might accept as collateral for a loan, ranging from office buildings and homes, to a parcel of Florida land that has now become a state park. To accomplish its various tasks, last year the FDIC spent the more-than-$3bn in revenue which it generated from insurance premiums and interest on its reserves of over $18bn – federal tax dollars were not used.

During the first nine months of 1988, we handled 168 bank failures and 18 assistance transactions. We expect over 200 failures and assistance transaction in 1988, including the first and third most costly failures the FDIC has ever handled: First Republic and First City.

Despite our having handled a record number of problems, the financial condition of the FDIC fund remains strong. The US General Accounting Office (GAO) approved the FDIC financial statements for 1987, which showed the FDIC fund had a net worth of roughly $18.3bn. Over $15bn of that net worth is in cash-type reserves.

1988 continued to be a busy one with the expectation of some decrease in the net worth of the fund this year, to about $15–15.5bn by year-end – the first such loss in FDIC history.

Never the less, we are able to deal with any banking problems we can foresee. With the number of banks on our problem list declining for two quarters now, our task should be a bit easier down the road. Bank failures should be down next year, and unlike 1988, there are no banks with over $2bn in assets on 1989's list. We expect the FDIC fund will increase by $500m in 1989. Of course, conditions can change, but this is our best estimate at this time.

THRIFT INDUSTRY PROBLEMS

While the FDIC has been under stress, the plight of the FSLIC is more severe. The thrift industry was originally a simple business designed to promote savings and to encourage home construction by providing low-cost funding. Not much could go wrong, and as a result, it required minimal supervision. As discussed earlier, increased competition and volatile interest rates changed that, and put the thrifts under increased pressure. In the early 1980s Congress deregulated much of the thrift industry, hoping this would be the answer to the industry's problems. But instead many thrifts loaned funds for risky real-estate ventures and other speculative activities, and the problems have become worse.

GAO has reported that the FSLIC had a negative net worth of $13.7bn at year-end 1987. And, according to one congressional estimate, the problems are getting worse at a rate of over $30m per day, or roughly $1bn a month. Estimates of the cost of handling the thrift industry's problems by closing the insolvent S&Ls now range from $50bn to over *$100bn*!

So deposit insurance can cost billions of dollars, which ultimately must be paid – or the US government's creditability will be impaired. We at the FDIC believe that the insurance system is at a watershed, and needs to be modified in the light of today's increasingly competitive and risky environment.

ROLE OF FEDERAL DEPOSIT INSURANCE

From a modest New Deal programme created in 1933 to bolster consumer confidence in the shaky banking system, federal deposit insurance has grown to become an important factor in the safety and soundness of America's financial system.

Deposit insurance was created as a reaction to the severe problems which the banking industry faced during the Depression. The FDIC's beginning was modest in scope. But even then it was not without controversy. Small depositors and small banks supported the plan, while larger institutions opposed anything that would help to put smaller banks on a more equal footing with them.

The role and form of deposit insurance as conceived in the 1930s have changed dramatically as the structure and risks in the banking system have evolved. Deposit insurance has become a significant factor in the total US financial system because it gives banks and thrifts an almost unlimited power to borrow on the credit of the USA. FDIC-insured bank- and thrift-owners are only required to put in 6 per cent of a bank's resources (capital), while FSLIC-insured thrift-owners only need to contribute 3 per cent. The rest is borrowed from depositors based on the credit of the US Government.

Any federally insured institution can gather deposits up to $100 000 without the depositors worrying about the institution's creditworthiness. Since the government no longer regulates the interest rates paid by these institutions, they are free to raise their rates to attract almost as much in deposit liabilities as they desire. At the same time deregulation, new technologies, and increased competition have combined to make the banking business a different and more risky business than ever before.

Let us look at a few of the recent changes in the operation of the deposit insurance system. Significant differences from the original concept are apparent.

Large Banks have Perceived Advantage

First, small banks complain about the insurance system. They contend that the deposit insurance safety net – the 'too large to default' doctrine – gives unfair advantage to large institutions by protecting their creditors from loss.

Protection of all depositors and bank creditors in failing large banks has distorted the deposit insurance system. However, no major industrial nation has allowed its largest banks to default because of an unwillingness to risk the consequences. The international competitive ramifications alone make it unlikely that this policy will be changed. So an insurance system designed originally to help small banks to compete with big banks now operates to favour big banks over small banks. Alas, as Caesar lamented, 'All bad precedents began as justifiable measures' (quoted in Sallust's *Conspiracy of Catiline*, 1st BC).

FDIC Now Lender of Last Resort

Second, the Federal Reserve Board, traditionally considered the lender of last resort in the USA, has become the lender of next-to-last resort. The deposit insurance system has become the last resort for rescuing failing banks, and thus protecting the stability of America's banking system. When First Republic went to borrow at the Federal Reserve's discount window last winter, deposit withdrawals at its banks increased. Depositors and creditors were aware of the Fed's policy of requiring the best collateral for its liquidity lending, so they too rushed to beat the Fed and get the best assets out they could. When the FDIC gave an unlimited guarantee to depositors and creditors, and a loan of $1bn, the run was stopped. So the FDIC has become the back-up source for banks that need to be protected even though they may be solvent. Clearly, this is a role not envisioned by the creators of federal deposit insurance.

No Protection for Bank Holding Companies

Third, the status of the bank holding company in the US banking system has been called into question by recent FDIC policy. The 'too large to default' doctrine has been applied to banks, not to holding companies.

In the Spring of 1988 the FDIC stated that it would handle First Republic so that all depositors and other general creditors of First Republic's banks would be fully protected – but these assurances were NOT extended to the holding company creditors or share-holders. This FDIC policy is critical when considering what new activities holding companies should be permitted, as well as such issues as whether it is appropriate to apply the proposed risk-based capital standards to holding companies.

Deposit Insurance Potentially Damaging

And fourth, our experience, especially in the south-west, has taught us that deposit insurance is a powerful tool, which if misused, has the potential to damage the financial system severely. This argument was raised by some at the creation of the deposit insurance system, but was rejected by the Congress.

As mentioned earlier, deposit insurance effectively gives banks and thrifts the ability to borrow on the credit of the federal government. It must be properly safeguarded or it can threaten the system. Deposit insurance is like a nuclear power plant. Operated properly, it is beneficial; but only appropriate safety precautions can keep it from going out of control. Once out of control, it can blow up, with great damage to the entire country.

One has only to look at the problems of the savings and loan industry to see the financial fall-out of a deposit insurance meltdown. And, lest we become satisfied with bank supervision as the answer, look at the losses the FDIC is incurring on failed Texas banks despite supervision by federal and state bank regulators.

We are having our financial Chernobyl this year in the south-west, and it is time to reflect on what we have learned. We need to look at how deposit insurance should be changed if it is to manage better the risks that have been manifested in the 1980s.

NEW FDIC STUDY

Thus, we are undertaking a complete review of deposit insurance and its role and operation in the current banking environment. Our study on this subject, *A Deposit Insurance System for the 90s and Beyond*, will be released later this month. We hope that our study will help to focus the debate on what we used to call deposit insurance reform.

The following are a few of the fundamental questions which we are addressing in constructing a better deposit insurance system:

Can Supervisory Mechanisms Control Risk-taking?

This is a key to the future of the system. If supervision does not work, the ability to borrow on the credit of the USA can destroy. As we enter an environment of greater powers for banks, how will supervision need to adapt to keep the system safe and sound? Are our present supervisory resources, such as examination procedures, off-site monitoring systems, and supervisory sanctions, adequate? And, once problem banks have been identified, are our present regulatory powers sufficient to deal with institutions that pose a high risk to the insurance fund? How can we avoid the cost of another south-west débâcle?

How Can the Market Be Used to Control Risk in Today's Environment?

Is depositor discipline really alive and well despite deposit insurance and big bank protection? Can we increase market discipline and promote safety by statutory and *de facto* limits on deposit insurance protection, changes in coverage to include only certain types of liabilities, or the introduction of private coinsurance? Should we control rates paid on insured deposits, or provide insurance only for individuals and not corporations?

How Far Should the 'Safety Net' Extend?

The FDIC's treatment of certain large Texas banks demonstrates our present position that we will not extend the 'safety net' to include holding companies.

How Can We Improve the Way We Handle Failing Banks?

Should large bank depositors be protected, and if so, by whom – i.e. our central banker, the FDIC, or by other banks as is the case in some other nations? How can we handle failed banks so as to treat large and small banks more equitably?

Do we price deposit insurance appropriately?

Would a system of risk-related premiums do a better job than our current system? Can we find a formula that will be practical, accurate and defensible?

Of course no look at deposit insurance would be complete without addressing the question of whether there should be a merger of the FDIC and FSLIC funds.

The difficulties of the thrift industry and the FSLIC are having negative repercussions on the banking industry. These problems are creating a higher cost of funds, forcing banks to compete in an unfair environment against insolvent institutions. Therefore, the resolution of the FSLIC's problems is important to the banking system and the entire financial system.

As we have said many times, we do not favour a merger under current conditions.

But to be fair, we need to be ready to deal with the suggestion that a merger is needed to save the system. If such a merger is to take place, how might it be structured?

There are four fundamental principles that must be maintained if a merger is to be acceptable. First, all insured deposit financial services institutions must be regulated by common standards and supervisors. Second, the new single-deposit insurance agency must be politically independent, and free to do its job of supervising insured institutions given its own budget constraints. Third, the agency must have the ability to deny insurance to an institution chartered by another body. And fourth, banks must not be forced to pay the bill created by the problems of their competitors, the S & L industry.

The future of our deposit-insurance system – both the FDIC and the FSLIC – depends on how we deal with these issues. We need an improved system if deposit insurance is to be viable in the 1990s.

A BLUEPRINT FOR THE FUTURE

It is certainly clear that the banking industry, and the FDIC, are functioning in a difficult, challenging and changing environment. Our goal must be to manage that change – and adjust our environments when necessary – to thrive with change and new risks.

Over a year ago, the FDIC decided to look at the competitive position of banking, and to decide whether structural changes in the banking environment were needed. This resulted in our major study dealing with these issues, entitled *Mandate For Change*. That study looked at a great many banking problems, and posed a number of practical solutions.

Our 1987 study made several recommendations:

1. To *streamline bank regulation*, *Mandate For Change* proposed that bank regulators focus on the bank itself, not on the bank holding company, or non-banking subsidiaries.
2. To *attract new capital investment* into banking, the study proposed that banks should be able to own, or be owned, by enterprises engaged in any legal business.
3. To *give banks additional powers in the marketplace*, our *Mandate* proposed that banking organizations be allowed to take part in any business activity, through a separately capitalized subsidiary or affiliate.

Streamlining bank regulation, attracting new capital, and granting banks additional powers are widely viewed as worthwhile objectives. The central issue is whether these objectives can be reached while protecting the 'safety and soundness' of banks and the banking system? Our answer is a definite yes!

The FDIC's study offers two keys to justify that conclusion. One key to keeping banks safe, yet allowing banks freedom to offer new products and effectively compete, is proper supervision. The other key is to insulate the activities of the supervised banks from any potential negative side-effects – risks – associated with either new activities or broader bank ownership.

This insulation can be achieved by placing new activities in a subsidiary or affiliate of the bank; restricting transactions between banks and these affiliates; and enforcing penalties against any abuse of the bank – in effect, protecting the bank with a 'firewall'. The 'firewall' can separate all the traditional attributes of a bank, including insured deposits, from the adverse consequences of any new business activity – or the actions of any new bank owner or investor. The need for banking regulators to supervise non-banking subsidiaries would be eliminated. Only functional regulation would be required.

This approach would allow banks greater competitive latitude. It would expand opportunities for banks to experiment and innovate. It would allow vast sources of new capital into the banking system, providing it with renewed strength. And it would allow banks, and the government, to carry a streamlined and less expensive regulatory burden.

Would enforcing a 'firewall-based system' require a vast new effort on the part of the federal banking regulators? We do not think so, based on our 55 years experience in regulating and protecting banks. After all, the 'firewall' concept is not really new. It is a logical extension of the regulatory and supervisory safeguards that already exist, and would require only minimal changes.

When *Mandate for Change* was released, these ideas were seen by some as an extreme and politically unrealistic view of what could be accomplished. And certainly we were not so naive as to believe that the study's recommendations would be embraced by everyone, and adopted by acclamation overnight. However, the FDIC has been pleasantly surprised to see how far events this past year have carried us toward the views we presented in our study.

Many of the conclusions we reached were reflected in banking legislation considered by Congress in 1988. And many of the *Mandate's* conclusions are being tested and proven in battle in the 'real world'.

This brings us to what is going on in the banking environment itself, despite slow progress under the Capitol dome. These 'real world' developments are moving, right now, in the direction the FDIC proposed in our *Mandate*. The FDIC's handling of recent bank failures, for example, shows the 'firewall' concept at work. We have demonstrated that banks and their parent bank holding companies can successfully be treated as separate entities.

Most recently, with respect to First Republic Bank Corporation, FDIC actions have shown that bank depositors are protected by the safety net offered by federal deposit insurance, while bank-holding-company shareholders and creditors are not.

In that transaction the FDIC limited the federal safety net to the banks. It also prevented the First Republic banks from supporting their holding company at the expense of the banks' creditors – namely the FDIC. The assets of First Republic's forty Texas banks were used to offset the liabilities of those banks, not to aid the holding company's creditors or shareholders. The point is that our handling of First Republic upholds the doctrine of corporate separateness, showing that, in the ultimate proving ground of the real world, the 'firewall' idea does work.

The FDIC does not stand alone in this view. We are seeing more examples of banks and bank holding companies being viewed and treated as separate units. One sign of this is in the credit markets, where the interest rates on debt issued by bank holding companies have generally become higher than rates on debt issued by banks. The markets understand that bank creditors have been protected, while bank-holding-company creditors have not.

Another example is that of the recent Basle accords, which called for international bank regulators to set risk-based standards for bank capital. On the international level, it was agreed that such standards should be set for banks, but should not be applied to bank holding companies. In other words, bank regulators should focus on regulation of the bank, and not the holding company, or non-banking subsidiaries. Here again, the 'real world' can be seen as moving in the direction supported by the *Mandate*.

Still, we have some distance to go. We need to loosen the restraints on the types of institutions that can own banks. As both healthy and troubled banks require additional capital in the years ahead, why preclude many of our most respected and well-funded institutions from participating in meeting those needs?

CONCLUSION

One American banker noted that there are *some* parallels between our past and the vast changes through which the banking environment is going these days. He compares these changes to:

• the world order before and after the Second World War;
• the USA before and after the Civil War;
• the banking system before and after deposit insurance.

The competition and risks facing banks and bank regulators are greater than ever before. But like many changes, the challenge is to manage the process while minimizing the disruption.

Longfellow advises us:

Look not mournfully into the past.
It comes not back again.
Go forth to meet the shadowy Future, Without fear, and with a
    manly heart.

I hope that is an apt description of the behaviour of bankers all over the world. If it is, the future looks bright!

2 The Banking System and the Indebted Developing Countries: Retrospective and Prospects

Moeen A. Qureshi

Six years after the debt problem emerged as a crisis of global proportions, I am not sure whether we should commiserate that the crisis is still with us, or rejoice that the financial system has avoided severe economic disruption. I believe that we have much to be satisfied with in the management of the debt crisis so far. Both the commercial banks and the international financial institutions have made substantial contributions to that end, but there is a great deal still to be done before we can claim a victory on the debt issue.

We have weathered the immediate threat to the stability of the international financial system, but have not yet resolved the problem of restoring growth in the debtor-countries. Failure to do so will diminish prospects for growth and stability worldwide. Here we face a particular kind of problem. It is in our long-term interest to work together to restore growth, and that will require both a concerted effort on the part of all concerned and a realistic sharing of the burdens.

BANKS AND INTERMEDIATION

Banks play a critical and privileged role in the modern economic systems. By facilitating transfers of resources, by intermediating between savers and investors, and by absorbing and spreading risk, they facilitate the complex flow of goods and services that characterizes today's international economy. The speed and efficiency with which the financial system is able to conduct these transactions contributes importantly to economic growth and the expansion of world trade. In fact, one important measure of the stage of a country's economic development is the sophistication of its financial system and its integration into world capital markets.

One of the challenges of international economic management is to assure continued provision of financial services to the highly indebted countries in order for them to achieve their growth potential and emerge from their current crises. The difficulties involved are considerable, and simply pouring more money into these countries is no solution. But continued access to funds intermediated through the international financial markets, risk-diversification, and the uninterrupted availability of finance for trade-flows will all be essential elements of their long-term recovery. The other key ingredients will be the continued pursuit of adjustment and economic reform in the debtor-countries and adequate support from the international community for the adjustment process.

Neither the banking community nor the international financial institutions nor indeed the governments of the creditor countries, can realistically draw away from the problems and issues that are raised in dealing with the indebted developing countries. In this respect, the future is not likely to be the same as the past. We shall have to use our ingenuity and creative talents to devise new and better ways to structure and package the financial intermediation, risk-diversification, and trade-support functions that the banking community provides to developing countries.

While the recycling of Eurodollars during the 1970s was probably a good and necessary reaction to the events of the time, I would like to note two flaws that were to become the seeds of its later downfall. First, syndicated lending was essentially balance-of-payments support, and the creditors exercised little if any control over the final uses to which the money was put. All too often, it went to fund projects and proposals that probably would not have passed reasonable project evaluation criteria, or it went to finance consumption rather than productive investment. Thus the borrowed resources did not contribute to creating new wealth that would be available to repay the loans, even at their subsequent diminished inflation-adjusted values.

This leads to the second flaw: both creditors and borrowers tended to ignore the basic accounting of debt. Simple models of debt-accumulation normally describe three phases. In the first, the debtor is a net borrower of foreign resources, which are used to finance investments yielding higher rates of return than the rate of interest after allowing for risk. This 'accumulation phase' continues while the economy grows rapidly, exploiting high-yielding investments. In the second phase, the country cannot or does not need to increase its net borrowing as the debt-service absorbs all its borrowing capacity, or because it is generating sufficient savings domestically. Its debt stabilizes. In the third phase, the growth of the economy is sufficient to generate enough resources to reduce debt, and eventually the former debtor may become a net creditor.

In general, the slower the rate of accumulation, the longer the period of accumulation can be. For some countries with modest rates of accumulation, low interest rates, and rapid rates of growth, the accumulation of debt can continue for a very long time. The converse is also true; the more rapid the accumulation, the shorter becomes phase one. In addition, countries with low initial levels of debt can attain rapid initial rates of debt growth without obvious impact on traditional creditworthiness indicators because grace periods and delayed disbursements mask the extent of borrowing in the initial years. Unfortunately, in the rush to increase lending by the banks and to obtain more financing by many developing countries, these simple guide rules were ignored. Countries sought – and in some cases were induced – to borrow very rapidly with little concern by leaders for the use to which the funds were put.

The sentiment captured in Walter Wriston's widely quoted statement that 'countries don't go bankrupt' probably created a false sense of security about sovereign lending and contributed to the rapid accumulation of debt. While technically correct, the statement is quite misleading. It is true that countries do not become bankrupt in the same sense as individuals do. They do not go out of business, do not get taken over by creditors, or fall prey to corporate predators (at least not in this century); but this does not mean that they do not default and stop making payments on their debt. They have done so in the past and are doing so today. And because bankruptcy regulations and courts do not exist internationally, once countries cannot pay the creditors have little recourse but to negotiate and eventually accept what can be negotiated. It is not feasible to try to attach sovereign assets or to contest all the wealth of a debtor-country. Cross-border lending is riskier than domestic lending, and it is more complex in the former case to resolve problems of excessive debt.

THE DEBT CRISIS

It is now (1988) six years since the debt crisis broke, a crisis which we had hoped would be solved by now. But we are at best nearly half way through. It is safe to say that the international financial system is no longer in jeopardy, although some important individual banks remain in danger. And that is no small accomplishment. The industrialized countries have experienced six years of steady growth with some exceptions here and there, and have managed to keep the doors open for exports from the developing countries. This growth, the continued rapid evolution of the financial markets in the developed countries, and expanding deregulation in most OECD countries have also opened new profit opportunities for commercial banks in their domestic markets. The banks have improved their capital base and now see a clear gain – at least in the near term – in withdrawing from their activities in the developing countries and pursuing new business opportunities at home. This does not bode well for the developing countries, who still need their intermediation and financial services. The withdrawal of the smaller, regionally-oriented banks from the international arena is probably not a serious issue. This is not their natural turf. But the same cannot be said for the large international banks, although their fatigue from the protracted and time-consuming debt-restructuring exercises is understandable.

We are at best half-way through the resolution of the debt crisis. The other half concerns the restoration of growth in the debtor-countries. That is the proper concern of the World Bank, but the renewal of growth in these indebted countries is also vital for the continued stability of the international financial system. These countries have followed, with varying degrees of success, programmes of stabilization and adjustment for six years. For most, per capita income has not improved, but unemployment and sometimes inflation have risen dramatically. They have seen their adjustment efforts contribute to slow the growth of their debt, but not lead to any palpable improvement in their well-being. As a matter of fact, per capita income has fallen 12 per cent in the highly indebted countries since 1980. Debt-service ratios have declined only marginally to an average of 33 per cent, while debt as a share of GDP has risen 20 points to 57 per cent.

Democratic governments are hard-pressed to justify the continuation of such measures to their beleaguered citizens, and radical forces are in the wings in many countries. They are suffering from severe adjustment fatigue and seek some solace. The world is too small to contemplate major economic disruption, stagnation, and the political turmoil which would follow if the major debtor-countries do not restore their growth rates. Just as we had a common interest in assuring the stability of the international financial system, so we too have a common interest in restoring growth in these debtor-countries. It is not wise for creditors to allow short-run profit-seeking, or current stock-price movements, to cloud their long-run interest, which must be based on a healthy and growing world economy. Financial institutions are granted special privileges in a complex world economy, but they also have a special responsibility to preserve the long-run stability and growth of that world economy. And this includes helping to restore the economic health of the debtor-countries.

THE FUTURE EVOLUTION OF FINANCING FOR THE DEVELOPING COUNTRIES

Because of the gradual drying-up of new commercial bank lending to developing countries, there is a growing feeling that the debt strategy in its current form is no longer sustainable. The banking community, which had a role in the making of the crisis, now risks exacerbating it by progressively trying to distance itself from contributing to its resolution. The official community does not have the financial nor the technical resources to service all the financial needs of the developing countries, nor should it. But more importantly, the debtors cannot succeed in restoring growth if they are deprived of access to the international financial system. Therefore, the objective must be ensure that the actions of the banks and international financial institutions provide the debtors with appropriate incentives, investment resources, and policy guidance to create the conditions for a resumption of sustained growth. It should be recognized, however, that while the international community must remain involved, most of the effort will have to come from the developing countries themselves.

Consider for a moment those countries – primarily in Asia – both rich and poor, that have enjoyed a decade of spectacular growth. They have managed their economies and their foreign borrowing well. They have invested wisely and expanded their manufactured exports. And they have retained their access to commercial credit markets. Commercial banks have recognized their excellent performance and expanded their lending activities accordingly. Some of those countries have been able to increase their debt while improving most of their debt indicators, and some have even begun to reduce their debt. This is reassuring, both because it shows that developing countries can implement policies that assure steady growth and because it demonstrates that commercial banks respond to good performance with greater access to productive financing. While the circumstances and situations of these successful countries differ, I believe that there are some common elements and certain key policies that are transferable. These include the active promotion of productive activities rather than subsidization of inefficient enterprises; the prevalence of competition and elimination of cost–price distortions; adequate domestic resource mobilization and price stability; and the encouragement of private investment. There are lessons to be kept in mind in determining the future course of the debt strategy.

TOWARDS A RETURN TO CREDITWORTHINESS

I understand that not all developing countries have the potential or the prospect of emulating the spectacular growth of the newly industrialized countries of Asia and I do not expect private financial markets to act as if they did. For the least-developed countries for example, the major responsibility will be on the countries themselves, on bilateral donor-governments, and the international financial institutions to design, implement, and support basic development programmes. In these countries, the commercial banks have a role – a supportive one – of providing trade credit and basic financial services. The other developing countries that are not highly indebted have proved their ability to manage their economies. In most cases they have received, and will continue to receive, the foreign lending they need and deserve.

For highly indebted middle-income countries, the future is more problematic. These debtor-countries are still in the 'accumulation' phase – that is, they need to borrow – but have run out of borrowing capacity before their economies were productive enough to make the transition to the second phase. In the isolated cases where this had occurred in the past, the creditors, the debtor, and usually the international financial institutions were able to negotiate a work-out involving domestic reform, debt relief, and some new financing. We must now forge a new consensus that will build on the relative strengths and comparative advantage of the debtors and move them into the second phase where they can stabilize their debt and improve their creditworthiness indicators. Until they reach the stage where they no longer need concerted rescheduling or new lending, they will not have free access to capital markets. Our objective is to reach that situation as soon as possible. Each must make his contribution; and I will now suggest what those would be.

DEBTOR RESPONSIBILITY

Basic policy reform in the debtor-countries is essential to the solution of their balance-of-payments problem and the recovery of growth. It provides the justification for the additional support sought by the country from the banks and international financial institutions. The policy changes must aim not only at moderating the demand for foreign financing in the short run, but also at initiating the structural changes necessary for the country to sustain satisfactory medium term growth rates without undue dependence on external savings. Specifically these reform programmes must include:

- the elimination of distortions in factor prices;
- fiscal and monetary policies aimed at stimulating domestic savings and resource mobilization;
- trade and exchange rate policies which encourage efficient production of tradeable goods (with particular attention to exports) and promote domestic competition;
- the reform of public-enterprise operations through improved management and, where appropriate, divestiture and privatization;
- allocation of public-sector resources to the most productive investments;
- efficient development of the financial sector and capital markets.

Without such efforts on the part of the debtors themselves, there is little that the international financial institutions or the commercial banks can do to promote sound economic growth. More lending under these circumstances would be tantamount to pouring good money after bad. It would not help the banks and it would not help the countries; it would only increase their future debt burdens. The evidence from indebted countries that have undertaken successful adjustment programmes such as Chile, Uruguay, Bolivia, and Mexico demonstrates that it is possible to recover and grow in a difficult world environment.

RESPONSIBILITIES OF THE MULTILATERAL FINANCIAL
INSTITUTIONS

The multilateral financial institutions have a major role to play, both
in providing policy guidance to help the debtors to design and carry
out their reform programmes and in providing a part of the new
capital required during the recovery period. Both the World Bank
and the IMF have devoted extensive resources to helping developing
countries with their policy reform programmes. Our advice has been
actively sought and usually followed.

The World Bank has, in recent years, expanded its programme of
financial support for the highly indebted countries. Commitments to
these countries have increased from an average of $4.5bn per year in
the financial years 1982–4, to $6.9bn per year in the financial years
1985–8, and we expect to reach about $8bn this year (1988). Overall,
about 25 per cent of the Bank's total lending programme has been
channelled to support structural adjustment. In some individual
countries, the proportion of such lending has reached 50 per cent. We
have streamlined and improved our procedures to be more efficient
and responsive to the needs of our member-countries, and have
increased our net exposure in highly indebted countries by about
$2.5bn per year to support their reform programmes and encourage
the resumption of productive investment. This increase of the Bank's
exposure in the highly indebted countries has been much greater than
that of commercial lenders, despite numerous reschedulings and new
money packages. Although lending in the highly indebted countries
has been primarily in the form of direct support to economic reforms
and adjustment, a shift to investment lending has been readily
undertaken where it was considered necessary to increase the debtors'
productive capacity, and to provide vehicles for co-financing with
other institutions.

In addition, the World Bank's B-loan programme (loans involving
cofinancing) – including direct participations and guarantees – serves
as a catalytic instrument to encourage more capital flows from commercial lenders. So far, these instruments have been used on a very
selective basis. We are studying ways in which the Bank's credit-
enhancement powers could be used more effectively to enhance the
access of countries undertaking adjustment to commercial funds. We
are also seeking ways to expand co-financing with export-credit
agencies to increase their involvement in indebted countries.

Through its advice and financial assistance, the Bank can make an important contribution to economic recovery in the indebted developing countries, but it cannot take on the entire burden of financing new investment, nor for that matter financing the net outflow of capital from these countries. The primary objective of the World Bank's lending is to support growth, not to finance the repayment of debts to other institutions.

RESPONSIBILITIES OF THE COMMERCIAL BANKS

Commercial banks should not ignore their long-term interests in providing financial services and intermediation to developing countries. The strengthening of banks' capital bases since 1982 is a healthy development, and one which will permit them to continue to play their traditional role. The withdrawal of commercial capital from debtor-countries is counter-productive in the longer run because it draws off resources urgently needed for investment in growth-promoting activities. It is also important that trade and inter-bank lines remain open and active to support trade- and growth-oriented adjustment programmes. Banks may not put in large amounts of new capital, but it is clearly in their interest to continue to maintain a posture of support while the debtors carry out their reforms. The commercial banks have shown themselves to be remarkably innovative in their response to demands for new financing. The 'menu' approach is a valuable framework that has offered a variety of potentially attractive options to banks operating under different regulatory and tax environment and responding to different business situations. It has also offered debtors alternative ways of packaging their debt, and even reducing the amount of debt outstanding through swaps and debt conversions. The World Bank fully supports the 'menu' approach and is providing assistance to our members in using it more effectively.

The menu has opened the door to a major new departure in the debt strategy: voluntary debt-reduction. This has so far been undertaken through debt–equity swaps, debt conversions, and some exit instruments. As you are aware, debt-service reduction has traditionally figured in domestic bankruptcy work-outs; its incorporation in sovereign lending is an important and welcome development. The emergence of the secondary market in developing-country debt as a result of increased provisioning, regulatory changes, and the desire of some banks to clear their portfolios of developing-country debt has created many more possibilities for imaginative treatment of the debt overhang. I do not wish to suggest indiscriminate or forced use of these options. That will not work. But within well-defined limits, debt reduction is likely to be a critical next step in the evolution of the current debt strategy. By judicious use of the instruments that are already available and of others that are being developed, banks can help debtor-countries reduce the stock of debt as well as the debt-service burden, thereby strengthening both the credit standing of their borrowers and their own loan portfolios.

In the case of most highly indebted countries, there is a large gap between the price in the secondary market and the face value of the debt which reflects expectations about the eventual performance of the debtor on the loans. The market price reflects an assessment of risk regarding the eventual repayment of debt. The existence of this market, although it is typically quite a narrow one, provides an opportunity for both creditors and debtors to devise means of using it to ease debt-service burdens, and restructure loan portfolios.

Clearly, in debt-service reduction schemes, the creditors take some form of loss. To an extent, this represents merely a recognition of a reduction in the value of loan assets for which provision has already been made in bank portfolios. In formulating approaches to debt reduction, the objective must be to use the 'discount' on the debt as a positive instrument to restructure that debt while minimizing the problems of 'free riders' and 'moral hazard'. While it does not seem very realistic at this time to think in terms of a new international institution which will be mandated to perform this task, it is perfectly feasible to envision an orderly process by which the creditors and debtors can negotiate, on a voluntary basis, mutually agreeable restructurings and debt-service reductions. Such a voluntary and market-oriented process could, of course, be supported with appropriate assurances and supervision by the international financial institutions. It would be in the interest of the creditors to support those approaches to debt reduction that place a premium on continued good economic performance. The role of the international financial institutions could be to ensure the sustainability and monitoring of country performance.

ORDERLY DEBT REDUCTION

The conditions for an orderly reduction in debt could exist where a debtor-country, the commercial banks and the multilateral financial institutions reach agreement on a monitorable reform programme that promotes growth and reduces demands on external resources. In some such cases, it is possible to visualize a script in which the international financial institutions and commercial banks could jointly support a financing package which includes a significant debt-reduction component, particularly for some of the medium-sized and smaller highly indebted countries. It might be possible, for example, for the international financial institutions and bilateral sources of financing, to provide the major part of the medium-term financing required to support the reform programme until the country's economy has improved enough to attract more commercial lending. As regards the commercial banks, they could:

(i) expand the 'menu' to include enough options to prevent, as a minimum, any net withdrawal of private capital from the country;
(ii) include debt-conversion options on the basis of a discount, thus involving a voluntary debt reduction. This may not appear to be an attractive option to all financial institutions, but in the case of some indebted countries, it may be the only viable and sustainable approach in the long term.

Such approaches should only be considered where the country is pursuing a determined adjustment programme that needs additional support and debt-service relief.

In these cases when the indebted countries are prepared to undertake strong corrective measures, and the commercial banks are prepared to make a significant contribution along the lines mentioned above, there is a strong case for support from the international financial institutions and creditor-governments to these commercial banks for their participation in debt reduction. The World Bank is reviewing ways of providing more active support to such voluntary and market-based approaches; for operations that involve significant debt reduction to the debtor, an argument can be made for some form of credit enhancement of the replacement instruments. This would engage some of the Bank's capital, but it could well be the best form of support for development that could be provided to the debtor-country.

There can be no doubt that such decisions would have to be made on a case-by-case basis and in support of a significant reform programme by the debtor. The World Bank would have to design its approach to credit-enhancement, taking into account its own financial and balance-sheet considerations, as well as the need to apply uniform criteria to its members.

The active support of the governments of major creditor-countries will be necessary for schemes of voluntary debt reduction to become established on any significant scale. A certain measure of regulatory 'accommodation' will be required to enable commercial banks to participate in innovative new menu options without excessive cost or penalties resulting from accounting or tax regulations. While it is reassuring to see a new level of cooperation and consistency among bank-regulatory practices consequent on the new BIS agreements, it is unfortunate that the immediate impact of the capital-adequacy guidelines, while desirable, is to make lending to the developing countries more difficult. Regulatory accommodation may also have to extend to acceptance of certain schemes designed to mitigate the 'free rider' problem in cases where there is an orderly debt-reduction programme.

In brief, the prospect of a sustainable and satisfactory debt strategy continues to rest on an effective process of adjustment and reform in the heavily indebted countries, a measure of flexibility and accommodation in the regulatory practices of the major creditor-governments, the continued participation of the commercial banks in devising concerted financial packages, and expanded support by the international financial institutions.

Working together, there are good prospects that the debt strategy can continue to evolve, not only to the long-run benefit of the financial system and the improved creditworthiness of the debtor-countries, but also by contributing to higher levels of international trade and growth in the global economy. If we do not act in concert, the issue is not survival or viability – either that of the financial system or that of the indebted countries – but rather, greatly impaired prospects of growth and well-being for debtors and creditors alike.

3 Multilateral Supervision for the New Financial System

Lamberto Dini

THE CHANGES IN BANKING, FINANCIAL INNOVATION AND THE EMERGENCE OF NEW KINDS OF RISK

The management of risk with the aim of earning profits while complying with the regulations in force is the very essence of banking. Bankers have always had to take decisions about the size and composition of their balance sheets, with particular reference to the risk/return features of assets. Traditionally, risk management involved both day-by-day assessment of customers' creditworthiness and strategic choices, which were conditioned to a varying extent by regulatory constraints on fund-raising and lending instruments as well as interest rates.

During the past three decades, however, the nature of the problems encountered has changed very rapidly. At the end of the 1950s, with demand for bank credit still high and liquidity in short supply, banks ceased to be passive takers of deposits and began to compete actively for funds. A few years later, negotiable certificates of deposit were introduced. At the same time a market was created in Europe for funds denominated in US dollars. The absence of reserve requirements and interest rate restrictions contributed to its uninterrupted growth in the 1960s and 1970s. Participation in these markets varied from one country and from one bank to another, but the general tendency was to rely increasingly on funds obtained wholesale at terms negotiated directly on the market.

With liabilities management, the nature of liquidity underwent a basic change: it no longer depended only on banks having reserves but also reflected their access to the market. This diversification and reduced stability of deposits increased the likelihood of maturity mismatching, thereby aggravating liquidity risk and giving rise to interest rate risk. Consequently, to meet the demand for medium-term credit with funds raised at short term on financial markets, banks had growing recourse to roll-over credits, with the result that interest rate risk was eliminated or, rather, transferred to final borrowers.

Risk management therefore increasingly involved the management of a wide range of short-term assets and liabilities. The money-market function became much more important and complex with the advent of floating rates in the early part of the 1970s. The growth of the international financial markets in the following years and banks' increasing participation, at a time of high and volatile interest rates and unstable exchange rates, resulted in the corresponding risks being a conspicuous feature of banks' balance sheets and stimulated a shift towards their formal and integrated management.

The diverse trends and events of the 1980s make it particularly difficult to analyze their links and effects on the management of risk in international banking. Two developments were exerting a growing influence at the turn of the decade: the application of EDP and telematics and the deregulation of banking and financial markets. The reduction in the time and cost of processing and transmitting information and the steady easing of the structural rigidities in banking regulations were major factors in the globalization of markets and the increase in competition. The dangers inherent in market volatility, the third factor carried over from the past, were clearly revealed in the early 1980s, when the sharp rise in short-term interest rates inflicted heavy losses on numerous banks in various countries.

Higher interest rates also exposed the vulnerability of the non-oil developing countries, which had borrowed hand-over-fist from banks during the 1970s at floating rates. Indeed, some observers consider the outbreak of the international debt crisis in 1982 as a watershed. The declaration by major debtor-countries that they were unable to honour their commitments, and the consequent rescheduling agreements gave material force to a risk that had until then been considered as little more than hypothetical, and in any case not significant.

A huge mass of bank loans was suddenly turned into assets that, to all intents and purposes, were locked in. Banks had to match these with medium and long-term funds and make special provisions. In addition to the direct consequences of this freezing of assets, there were others of a more general nature. In particular, banks sought to offset the tying up of a part of their loan portfolios by making the rest of their balance sheets more flexible and finding non-capital-intensive sources of income.

These forces are at the heart of the process of financial innovation and explain its off-balance-sheet bias. It was the interaction between the application of technology, regulatory change, market volatility and external imbalances that stimulated the demand for and supply of innovatory products. Individual operators sought to achieve two basic objectives with such products: to enhance their liquidity and to hive off interest rate and exchange risk.

The first of these ends has been pursued through products permitting securitization, whereby banks transform the risk arising from the possession of a non-negotiable financial asset – loans – into that involved in placing a negotiable financial asset – securities. Lending power is replaced by placing power. The success of instruments serving to redistribute interest rate and exchange risk is directly related to the extreme volatility of the prices of financial assets in both the short and the longer term.

Can financial innovation really modify risks or liquidity? In systemic terms the answer is obviously 'no', since neither the risks nor the liquidity of the economy as a whole can be modified by internal transfers. For individual operators, however, the answer may well be 'yes'. What many of the recently-introduced financial instruments can do is to alter the distribution among intermediaries of risks and liquidity, both of which are important for stability. This is all the more true because the sophisticated nature of these new instruments makes it difficult to record the related risks properly in intermediaries' information systems. Indeed, risks are often estimated on the basis of statistical series, a method whose shortcomings and dangers are obvious.

THE RELATIVE IMPORTANCE OF THE VARIOUS KINDS OF RISK IN THE 1980s

The spread of financial innovation and banks' active participation in the process have been accompanied by warnings of the danger of destabilizing repercussions. Attention has been drawn to the difficulty of correctly assessing the risk associated with new types of contract, which often involve insurance, in view of the lack of either practical experience of the problems or a satisfactory theoretical framework for analysis. It is widely accepted that risk assessment has also been complicated by the growing separation between final lenders and borrowers resulting from the proliferation of intermediate financial transactions, securitization and the disintermediation of banks. It has also been suggested that the availability of innovatory financial instruments may have contributed to the rise in the ratio of financial to real transactions and pushed up corporate gearing ratios – developments that could prove destabilizing in a cyclical downturn.

These and other risk factors have been thoroughly analyzed in the voluminous literature on financial innovation. Indeed, if a systemic crisis is caused by the new market mechanisms created by innovation, the writing will have been on the wall. Nonetheless, while the possibility of such a crisis cannot be excluded, it appears only fair to note that banks and other financial intermediaries weathered last year's stock-market crash with relatively small losses.

There are two aspects of the crash and its aftermath that I want to stress because of their bearing on the problems facing supervisors. First, a new and as yet not fully understood development, the fact that prices fell almost simultaneously and by similar amounts on all the leading stock markets, despite the pronounced differences in economic and market conditions in the various countries. This can be seen as evidence of the strength of the integration of financial markets and of the dominance of financial over real factors. However, we still do not have a rational explanation of the rush to get out of stocks in every market, mainly into bonds and with little or no currency switching. It would be going too far to talk of panic, but there appears to have been a dangerous herd effect. The second point is that the resilience which markets displayed probably owed more to the liquidity support provided by central banks than to any built-in stabilizing forces.

Even though the concern about the risks inherent in innovatory financial activities has not yet been followed by actual losses, there is no denying that international banking is passing through a phase marked by uncertainty and an increase in the number of failures. If one examines the losses incurred, one finds that they were directly related to traditional credit risk rather than to any of the new forms, although a part was also played by the radical change in condition in the banking market produced by internationalization and deregulation.

Both trends have resulted in banks and other intermediaries entering new and unfamiliar markets; they have also precipitated changes in competitive conditions. An additional indirect incentive to enter new markets has been provided by financial innovation, which to a large extent consists in the invention of contracts that are the result of unbundling and recombining features of existing financial instruments typical of the credit, insurance and capital markets. Accordingly, it has been a powerful force breaking down the barriers between the principal products, operators and markets, thereby undermining the justification for administrative segmentation and making operators' strategies more aggressively competitive.

With hindsight, it can be seen that even institutions with a record of prudent and conservative behaviour in their traditional habitats have often fared poorly in assessing risks in new markets. In trying to acquire a multinational status, banks have had to choose between the difficulty of penetrating foreign markets relying on their domestic organization and the risk of decentralizing decision-making to local units; cultural and information barriers have proved tougher obstacles than had been predicted.

The rush to lend to developing countries in the 1970s is telling evidence of the risks associated with indiscriminate internationalization in response to competitive pressures. In turn, the plight of some savings and loans associations in the USA exemplifies the risks associated with deregulation.

One specific aspect of internationalization deserves special attention – the creation of a unified European financial market. The process of integration is likely to be slower than expected by those who present 1993 as the start of a new era, but it will be much more far-reaching than what we have seen in international financial markets. The single market will consist of millions of consumers, affect the whole territorial network of banks and, in contrast with the move to interstate banking in America, bring together a wide variety of banking systems.

Individual banks' development of retail activities in several countries will not only entail the risk assessment problems I mentioned earlier, but will also impose considerable standardization on banks that are currently marked by pronounced disparities in terms of size, range of operations and costs. Banks will have to reorganize on a massive scale, which will add to the costs and strains they face.

RESPONDING TO THE 'NEW FINANCIAL WORLD'

I am not implying, of course, that we should try to halt, or even reverse, the process of deregulation and internationalization, since it can unquestionably have a positive influence on economic efficiency. The lesson to be learnt is another, and of a dual nature.

First, financial institutions must fully apply the principle of 'self-responsibility'. Managements must give top priority to ensuring that their organizations have effective systems for monitoring risk, with no gaps. Financial institutions cannot afford not to exercise integrated control over all the credit, market and operational risks they incur worldwide, and they will have to develop new instruments to cope with new risks as they emerge.

Second, I am convinced that the experience of the 1980s reinforces rather than diminishes the need for financial markets to be regulated, but at the same time it shows that existing supervisory systems have to be overhauled and improved.

Allocative efficiency benefits significantly from both global financial integration and the highly competitive environment created by lower transaction costs, easier access to markets and faster transmission of information. Rent positions are eroded, the scope for risk diversification is increased and the social cost of intermediation is reduced.

It would nonetheless be wishful thinking to believe that credit and financial markets can achieve optimal solutions on their own. In particular, there is no denying the evidence undermining the claim that stock markets are efficient in pricing securities. Share prices sometimes diverge quite considerably from underlying asset values; speculative bubbles and bandwagon behaviour prevent prices from reaching equilibrium values; and credit intermediaries have not always found market forces to be a reliable guide to an efficient allocation of resources.

Furthermore, the restructuring that banking systems must undertake may prove to be extremely costly in terms of the destruction of resources, especially when one considers the systemic risks inherent in financial intermediation and that the 'natural selection' would take place in a market that is far from being atomistic. It would thus be foolhardy to entrust it entirely to market forces.

A STRATEGY FOR BANKING SUPERVISION IN EUROPE

Innovation

The authorities are responding to the faster rate of change in the economic environment by speeding up the revision of prudential controls. While capital requirements were only adopted in the various supervisory systems over a period of several years, the preparation of instruments for dealing with market risks is proceeding apace and has been on an international footing from the start.

The capital ratios agreed in Basle by the G-10 countries already cover off-balance-sheet business, and therefore apply to most innovatory operations. Supervisory authorities are nonetheless convinced that the adequacy of capital should be assessed in relation not only to credit risk but also – and in some cases above all – to market risks, in particular position risk. In the immediate future, efforts will need to be concentrated on establishing appropriate ways to measure such risks and agreeing suitable capital requirements.

The regulation of position risk will probably see the first serious efforts in the leading countries to coordinate the prudential controls on banks and other intermediaries, in this case securities firms. Recent events have clearly shown that shocks are propagated extremely fast in an integrated system; that the size to which some securities operators have grown means that the problem of their control for the purpose of protecting system stability cannot be ignored; and that efforts to ensure uniform competitive conditions for the various categories of intermediary must be pursued.

There is increasing recognition of the desirability of some form of comprehensive regulation of financial intermediation, though the solutions proposed, or implemented, in various countries have so far differed widely in their attempts to reconcile the need to include all the most important activities while not making the system too rigid or extending the safety net provided for banks any more than necessary.

In Italy new legislation is being proposed with the aim of extending prudential supervision to all intermediaries which grant credit, invest customers' savings or trade in or underwrite securities. It is planned to vary the intensity of the controls according to the category of intermediary, depending basically on the extent to which the activity involves a delegation to make discretionary investment decisions on behalf of their customers.

Internationalization

The internationalization of banking raises problems not only for the banks that decide to enter new markets, but also for the supervisors who have to assess and control the risks they incur.

The theory of optimal currency areas can provide the basis for a more general philosophy: when trade within an area increases, the effectiveness of public control over only a part of that area decreases, but can be restored by extending the control to the whole area.

We are faced with a similar situation with regard to banking and other forms of supervision. Banks are going international, and this is bound to result in some European banks doing only a small proportion of their business in their countries of origin. Consequently, responsibility for the stability of banks and the relevant information on markets and individual borrowers will increasingly be in the hands of different national supervisors.

If supervision is to remain effective in Europe, the authorities will have to cooperate more and more closely and some form of institutional coordination will have to be put in place. The problem is complicated by the existence alongside banks of numerous other financial intermediaries with their own systems of supervision, which are organized differently from one country to another and whose activities are bound to overlap in the case of financial conglomerates and intermediaries undertaking several activities.

CONCLUSIONS

The 'new financial world' harbours risks that were previously unknown, or which existed, but in different or less threatening guises. The accelerated pace at which banking activity is being transformed by innovation, deregulation and internationalization is a cause for concern because the assessment of risk, which lies at the heart of banking, is necessarily based on knowledge and information that can only be acquired through long experience in a market.

While the new forms of financial contracts and the multicurrency nature of business almost certainly involve increased risks, actual losses in recent years have been concentrated in traditional lending operations. All three factors of change thus appear to have had their greatest impact on risk-taking in an indirect fashion, by inducing banks to enter unfamiliar markets, where errors of judgement are more likely, especially under competitive pressure.

The situation requires a two-pronged strategy, aimed at controlling the risks arising both from new operations and from traditional ones in new markets. This strategy should be adopted first and foremost by the intermediaries themselves by organizing their internal control systems to provide continuous and integrated monitoring and assessment of the risks to which they are exposed.

But supervisors – and law-makers – are also faced with important and complex tasks. Relying on the self-stabilizing properties of financial markets is a dangerous illusion. Accepting that the market should be left to take care of inefficiencies through a selection of the fittest would have unbearable costs when a fundamental restructuring of the banking system is on the horizon, as is the case in many European countries. Regulations will also have to be introduced to limit new risks, and supervisory authorities will need to be able to control the adequacy of capital to cope with them while seeking to create conditions that will encourage operators in their efforts to adapt.

Care will have to be taken to ensure that regulations do not result in some activities being protected and, more generally, that the playing field is acceptably level, especially as regards competition for securities business between banks and other intermediaries.

The systemic risks surfacing in some non-bank financial activities, the blurring of frontiers between intermediaries and the close integration of their activities call for a new and more comprehensive approach to supervision, which would eliminate dangerous gaps in prudential controls while avoiding a mechanical extension of the regulations applied to banks.

Finally, a new chapter in the international cooperation of control authorities needs to be written, especially in Europe, to cope with the danger of a widening rift between supervisory responsibility and the availability of the information required to exercise it, as a result of banks going international and supervisors remaining within their frontiers. This objective implies the need for a universally-recognized – and therefore authoritative – multilateral forum.

4 International Banks Bracing up to New Competition and Risks

Philip Wilkinson

Recent years have shown very marked changes in the competitive climate surrounding banking. It is difficult to distinguish any particular factors as being decisive, but we have seen major changes in technology, market structures, supervision, the availability of capital, and marketing. All these factors together have transformed the way the banks see their opportunities and problems. This chapter is divided into two main parts, the first concerned with the technicalities of new risk products and new financial instruments, and the second with wider elements of bank management.

NEW FINANCIAL INSTRUMENTS

The implications of the new financial instruments for the banking system have been profound, and the effects are still being felt. Indeed, the emergence of the new instruments has forced a restructuring of banks and in many cases a complete reconsideration of their basic strategy. The new financial instruments are mainly:

  (i) futures;
 (ii) options;
(iii) swaps;
(iv) Note Issuance Facilities and Revolving Underwriting Facilities;
 (v) Forward Rate Agreements (FRAs);
(vi) commercial paper.

There has been no single reason for the creation of new instruments, and they serve a wide range of purposes. A series of developments has created conditions which have transformed the financial instruments available in the market-place.

New Factors

It is difficult to identify any single factor as being the most important. Nevertheless, I am inclined to the view that changing technology may have had that role. In previous years we had seen the intensification of technological use in foreign exchange dealing rooms and in the treasury function. This created a large corps of people with experience in handling this kind of financial transaction, together with the technology to effect the calculations quickly, accurately, and on a massive scale. This technology could be used at extremely low marginal cost to support new markets. In some fields the concepts of the markets were previously well known, such as options or Forward Rate Agreements but it was simply impractical to run a market on a significant and controlled scale before the computer hardware to support it was available.

A second pressure was the marketing and competitive structure of the banking industry. With the globalization of international finance, many banks and innovative investment houses moved into other markets, taking their ideas with them. The nature of marketing in banking in some fields is through innovation. Those finance houses attempted to think of new products which they could take to their customers and use as the justification for being given their business.

The traditional relationship between a bank and its customer had been a one-to-one link, with the bank and the customer meeting across a table to negotiate a loan or other deal. But in the new structure the innovative finance house put itself between the bank and its customer, suggesting ideas to the customer, and expecting the banks to compete on price and quality to provide whatever financial instruments the customer wished. This new marketing structure thus accelerated the introduction of innovations, and at the same time forced more competitive pricing.

During the mid-1980s the margins on wholesale business were reduced significantly. This stemmed from many factors. There was excess capital in banking, in particular as the Japanese banks benefited from the enormous commercial success of Japan, and began to take their due place in the world banking scene. Corporate treasurers became increasingly concerned about price, and about being seen to obtain the best deal in the market-place. They began to measure their success in pricing in terms of basis points, or 0.01 per cent. The advent of new bankers in the market-place, and of extra capital in banking, gave them plenty of scope to test their bargaining.

During this period the banks were slowly coming under greater regulatory pressure, in particular as regarded their capital ratios. This, combined with the low margins on wholesale business, led them to look to new sources of income, and preferably ones which were not on the balance sheet, and thus were not (at that time) subject to capital ratios. New financial instruments provided an excellent means of achieving both fee income and off-balance sheet business.

Seeing the development of new markets, such as for example the futures markets in the USA, banks elsewhere supported the development of such markets as a means of achieving income, and possibly of generating customer business.

Taken together these factors were fully adequate to generate a period of major innovation in the banking markets, which has also to some extent transformed the relationship between banks and their major customers.

The New Instruments

What then are the qualities of the new instruments which led to their adoption? These innovations were of genuine importance in improving the quality of service available to the corporate sector and other financial customers. This improvement in service has been the underlying reason why the innovation has been sustained, and why the new instruments have become well established. There are five main benefits from these new instruments:

(i) They are cheaper. This condition may vary according to market circumstances, but instruments like commercial paper are likely to be cheaper than bank loans, partly because of their marketing structure, and partly because they bring into play a wider range of potential lenders or investors. Swaps, in particular, are by their structure almost certain to lead to a cheapening in the cost of finance to borrowers.

(ii) They make available a wider range of financial sources to the customer (or certain relatively unfamiliar markets may be tapped at a much lower cost than would otherwise be the case). This applies particularly to swaps, under which the participants borrow in the markets in which they have the greatest acceptability, and then swap the resulting financial commitments. A swap will not take place unless a financial gain is achieved, so all swaps lead to some combination of tapping wider markets and/or obtaining cheaper money. Thus, the archetypal swap between the World Bank and a Swiss corporation means that the World Bank obtains Swiss franc money to an extent which might not easily be available to it, together with low-cost fixed-rate Swiss-franc financing, while the Swiss corporation obtains dollars at a rate much lower than it would otherwise be able to obtain.

(iii) They provide instruments for hedging risk. These are the clear benefits of the futures markets, of the use of options, and of the use of Forward Rate Agreements. In the case of futures and Forward Rate Agreements, the customer is bound to a contract, so may forego a profit if the markets move in his favour. In the case of options, the customer pays a fee, and that is his greatest cost. If markets move against him, he may exercise the option and save himself the loss. If markets move in his favour, he may benefit from that movement, subject to the cost of the fee. With the recent volatility in interest rates and in particular in exchange rates, sophisticated companies have had to investigate far more closely the potential for hedging their risks;

(iv) They may involve maturity transformation, thus improving the mix of cost and availability of funds. This applies in particular to Note Issuance Facilities and Revolving Underwriting Facilities, which combine periodic raising of funds at short-term interest rates with a commitment to the long-term availability of funds. The customer thus has the assurance of long-term availability, while being able to obtain the funds at a price associated with the interest rates in the short-term markets.

(v) The new techniques may increase the liquidity of financial instruments, and thus widen the range of sources of finance. Again, this applies in particular to the various forms of securitization which mean that a wide range of investors will be able to provide the finance, and not just the traditional banks.

The Banks

The banks have thus had to adjust to a genuine and substantial change in the quality of instruments available to their customers. What are the business implications for banks of this sharp change in commercial conditions? To understand this point, it is necessary to realise that banks do not ask the precise question 'how should we cope with the new financial instruments?' They ask the questions 'how should we decide which markets to be in?' and 'how can we be profitable in those markets, given the entire commercial background?' In this regard, the dominant feature is in my view the extreme competitiveness of the wholesale markets, both the capital and banking markets. The first question a bank thus has to ask is whether it wishes to remain in those markets. Many substantial banks around the world appear to be deciding that they do not wish to be substantially in those markets, or if they are to be in those markets they intend to be only in particular niches where they may guarantee to make an adequate profit.

For banks which decide to remain in the wholesale markets, having a full capability in these new instruments is absolutely vital to remain credible there. Nevertheless, that is by no means the whole picture. The broad thrust of the competitive situation is that banks seek to differentiate themselves from others, and to obtain prominent or lead positions, through acquiring special skills and strong positions in certain markets. Thus banks are acquiring skills in project finance, taxation and financial engineering, for example, which they make available to customers. Likewise, banks with certain competitive advantages, such as placing power or computer skills, will endeavour to obtain market positions based on their special strengths. One should also not ignore the importance to banks of obtaining profits from their traditional business in the capital and wholesale markets, such as bond and share issues, stockbroking, and foreign exchange trading. Maintaining a profitable presence in these traditional markets is as vital a matter as making the appropriate impact in the new markets. Nevertheless, a fully effective presence in the new markets is essential if banks are to be credible participants in the modern wholesale markets, and the banks' use of these markets takes several forms.

Banks' Use of New Instruments

Banks may use these markets for their own funding, to reduce the cost of funds and/or tap additional markets. This function is analogous to the use made of those markets by the corporate sector and other customers. In view of the narrow margins now available in the wholesale markets, any cost reductions which banks can achieve through this means are valuable, and in this field banks are as determined and aggressive as companies in obtaining reductions in their cost of funds.

Banks will provide these instruments to customers, as a customer service. Thus in approaching a borrower, or approaching a customer regarding any traditional service, banks will expect to have to offer the most sophisticated combination of instruments so as to satisfy the customer's requirements most effectively.

As a follow-up to this service, banks may make markets professionally in these new instruments. This is a source of income. It also enhances the quality of the markets available to customers, providing liquidity to those instruments. If banks did not make these markets, then the pricing to customers of instruments would be less keen, since the instruments would not be so liquid. Banks make markets in options, swaps, and Forward Rate Agreements, as well as in more traditional instruments.

Banks also use the instruments to hedge their own risks, such as on the balance sheet. Moreover, in offering these new products to their customers, and in making a market in some of these products, banks are taking on risks which they had not done beforehand. These further risks also require protective action, and these instruments have to be used widely in hedging the bank against both traditional and non-traditional risks.

The banks may manage the infrastructure of a market, or help to police it as part of the financial infrastructure. An example of this is the backing given by the London clearing banks to the London International Financial Futures Exchange (LIFFE), through the ownership of the International Commodities Clearing House (ICCH) as well as their being founder General Clearing Members (GCMs) of the Exchange.

In some cases these new instruments are intrinsically riskier and there can be no perfect hedges. This is very much the case where the hedging strategy has to be based on assumptions about the volatility of the market, as is particularly the case in options. Moreover, hedging techniques may require assumptions about continuous pricing and the liquidity of the market, which may not be borne out in practice. The events of 19 October 1987 showed that many assumptions about volatility, continuous pricing, and liquidity, were considerably in error at the precise moment when they were called into question. Banks which have made mistakes in assessing the fundamental characteristics of instruments, or in supervising their exposure in these markets, have made substantial losses. Nevertheless, banks are forced to operate in these riskier markets if they wish to be credible in wholesale business. It is therefore of vital importance that the established banks with a long-term perspective should operate the strictest controls over the conduct of their own business.

Regulatory Costs

A significantly greater consideration for banks now, as they structure their entire business, is the regulatory cost. The agreement at the Bank for International Settlements on the convergence proposals for capital supervision, combined in Europe with the expected proposals from the European Commission, will create a mandatory framework for banks' prudential control. The ratios have already been set out in some detail as regards business on the balance sheet, and progress is being made regarding the ratios to apply to off-balance sheet business. Banks will be assessed on both credit risk and position risk. These ratios will have influence over the minimum prices which banks will need to charge so as to cover their capital costs. The application of these controls on a continuing basis to sophisticated activity in a wide range of wholesale and capital markets will require a corresponding strengthening of the banks' control systems. Moreover, this development will also affect the character of the management of the banks, in the sense that greater continuing emphasis will have to be placed on monitoring a bank's positions and the business it undertakes.

At present there is a slowdown in the pace of innovation, for two main reasons. First, the major innovations of the greatest commercial advantage have probably been achieved in recent years, and there is less to aim for. Second, the existing new instruments have created a range of problems for banks, as regards setting up the internal technological infrastructure, creating viable business units, and in particular in establishing and maintaining effective controls. The market is thus now going through a phase of consolidation, which coincides with the slower activity in some of these securitized markets, following Black Monday during October 1987.

BANK MANAGEMENT

The executive team in a bank has a wide responsibility – to see the attainment of a bank's goals whatever the external environment happens to provide. It is thus not possible to disentangle executive responsibility into neat compartments. Objectives have to be achieved whatever the intermingling and relative proportion of the issues raised by the outside environment. I should like now to mention many of the themes which have impinged upon bank management, and finally to draw some conclusions.

Marketing Structures

Marketing structures have changed both in the wholesale and in the retail markets. In the wholesale markets our customers have now acquired almost as much expertise as, if not more than, we have, and ensure both the strongest price competition and the best quality of service that can be provided for them. Many erstwhile customers, such as the Treasury Department of multinational oil companies, are now indeed banks in their own right, while at the same time many other treasury departments have full banking knowledge, if not yet the same legal structure.

At the retail level structures have also changed. We now have a plethora of magazines and newspaper articles informing customers of their 'best buys' in deposits, borrowing, and services. The advent of mail order, direct mail, and credit cards means that customer access may be achieved indirectly, without necessarily having the infrastructure of a bank branch and a basic bank account. The efficiency of modern telecommunications and even of postal services means that remote access to customers may be extremely effective in certain circumstances. Using these techniques some market participants may target particular customer segments, thus taking away the particularly attractive niches which had been the jam on the bread-and-butter of basic banking services to the majority of the population. There is the continuing possibility that somebody may discover a new technological way of providing basic services at a much lower cost, in which case an entire business structure might be undermined rapidly. Bankers no longer regard their customers as necessarily loyal. In the main they have been, but like retailers, bankers are forced to regard their customers as being potentially fickle, and with their loyalty having to be retained only by the bankers maintaining the most up-to-date service in price, quality, and indeed fashion.

Barriers are breaking down between countries as well as within countries, given the opportunities provided by the Single European Market and, for example, the advent of global plastic-card systems. Marketing is becoming extremely and increasingly important as a means of maintaining both the size of the customer base and the loyalty of the existing customers.

Technology

A further challenge to banks relates to technology. A major bank may be spending some £200m a year on buying computers and other technological systems. There is inevitably substantial risk in this process. The first risk is whether the system will work and carry out the function for which it has been designed. So far the banks have been mainly successful in this, any good luck being related to their care in the installations they establish. There are other risks. Will the system end up being commercially efficient, in being able to deliver a product or service in a way which meets the competition? Will the service remain technologically advanced for a significant period of time, or will it be outmoded within a matter of days, weeks or months? Does the system fit in with other systems and with other objectives of the banks, which might possibly have greater strategic importance? Banks are by now developing expertise within themselves, together with hard-headed commercial knowledge, so as to be able to deal with suppliers on both technological and commercial grounds. These days even suppliers are not entirely aware of where the market is going, and are forced to run just to stand still in terms of their ability to sell in the marketplace. Banking is about information, both in the sense that money is information, and in the sense of all the other areas of financial services which rely upon information and provide it. That is the area where technology is having the greatest impact. I doubt if any bank regards itself as having a surfeit of technical expertise. In this area the banks are having to move down a commercial path, spending a substantial amount of money on technology, which they hope is not only right for the purpose but also will work effectively.

Deregulation

Deregulation has increased the risks for banks in many ways. The general impact of deregulation is to make markets more competitive. Regulations nearly always have the effect of protecting certain areas of the market from a degree of competition, regulations which usually had some support from various public-interest motivations, and indeed in many areas actually did provide some such service. But as a side effect, in almost all cases regulation has the effect of protecting some market participants, a fact which many of them may not realise or be willing to admit at the time.

We saw this clearly in the case of 'Big Bang' in the London securities markets. Prior to Big Bang it was impossible for corporations to become members of the Stock Exchange, which was reserved to personal partnerships, while the accepting houses were also protected from hostile takeover. Stock Exchange members and the London merchant banks which were members of the Accepting Houses Committee were protected from direct competition. As a result, income was relatively high, and I am sure that many of them no doubt had the impression that their high level of income was a reflection of their innate skills, rather than being something provided partly on the one hand by the rules of the Stock Exchange and on the other hand by the benevolent authority of the Bank of England.

After Big Bang we saw the full unleashing of market forces, with London becoming the 'Wild West' of international securities markets, with no protection for any company or individual, and business going to those with the greatest commercial strength. London became the most internationally owned and the most international of the major securities markets around the world (see Table 4.1). We saw the classic effects. The medium-sized brokers faced difficulties, being as they say too small to be big and too big to be small. Likewise, only four of the British traditional merchant banks (Warburgs, Morgan Grenfell, Kleinwort Benson, and Hill Samuel) decided they could begin to compete on a global basis, and the rest hurried quickly to niches or to takeovers – as indeed happened in due course to Hill Samuel. The benefit of a fully competitive market is that the customer does well in terms of quality of service and price, but the producer has to work much harder since he or she is faced with full competition.

In the UK we have also seen the liberalisation of the retail banking market, with the granting of greater powers to the building societies, our traditional mortgage offerers, who may now enter virtually the full range of the banking markets. The Building Societies Act of 1962 contained severe restrictions upon their functions, but this has since been liberalised in the Building Societies Act of 1986. Some societies may form themselves into companies, when they may become vulnerable to takeovers, but the majority by number and amount are at present retaining their mutual status. This should give them enough resources to pursue their expansion plans, and should also protect

Table 4.1   The new city line-up: who bought into whom ahead of deregulation in London

Buyer	Stockbroker/ stockjobber	Holdings %	Remarks
UK Commercial Banks			
Barclays Banks	Barclays de Zoete Wedd (TBJ)	100.0	
Midland	W. Greenwell (TB)	100.0	
	Smith Keen Cutler (RB)	100.0	Midland Bank is ultimate parent
National West- minster Bank	County Bisgood (TJ)[1]	100.0	
	Fielding, Newson-Smith (TB)	100.0	
Royal Bank of Scotland	Tilney (RB)	100.0	
Merchant Banks			
Baring Brothers	Baring Far East Securities (SB)[2]	100.0	
	Wilson Watford (SJ)	100.0	
Brown Shipley	Heseltine Moss (RB)	100.0	
Guiness Mahon Securities	White & Cheesman (SJ)	100.0	
Hill Samuel	Wood, Mackenzie (TB)	100.0	
Kleinwort Benson	Charlesworth & Co. (SJ)	100.0	
	Grieveson Grant (TB)	100.0	
Morgan Grenfell	Pember & Boyle (SB)	100.0	
	Pinchin Denny (TJ)	100.0	
N.M. Rothschild	Smith Brothers (TJ)	33.7	Holdings may be increased to 34.5%
	Scott Goff Layton (MB)	33.7	Held 100% by Smith Brothers
Schroders	H. Wagg, Anderson, Bryce, Villiers (SB)	100.0	
SG Warburg (through Mercury Securities and Mercury International)	Rowe & Pittman (TB)	100.0	
	Mullens (SJ)	100.0	
	Akroyd & Smithers (TJ)	100.0	
Foreign Banks/Institutions			
Arbuthnot Savory Milln[3]	Savory Milln (TB)	100.0	

(continued)

Table 4.1   *continued*

Buyer	Stockbroker/ stockjobber	Holdings %	Remarks
ANZ Merchant Bank (Formerly Grindlays)	Capel Cure Myers (TB)	100.0	
Bache Group	P.B. Securities, Down, de Boer & Duckett (SB)	100.0	
Banque Arabe et Internationale d'Investissement	Sheppards & Chase (MB)	100.0	
Bank Cantrade	Nivison Cantrade (SB)	49.9	50.1% owned by R. Nivison
Banque Bruxelles Lambert	Williams de Broe Hill Chaplin (MB)	56.7	
Canadian Imperial Bank of Commerce	Grenfall & Colegrave (MB)	100.0	
Chase Manhattan Bank	Laurie Milbank (TB)	100.0	Both firms merged into Chase Manhattan Securities
	Simon & Coates (MB)	100.0	
Citicorp Investment Bank	J. & E. Davy (RB)	29.9	Will increase holdings to 100%
	Scrimgeour Vickers (TB)[4]	100.0	
Crédit Commercial de France	Laurence, Prust (MB)	80.0	
Crédit Suisse	Buckmaster & Moore (SB)	85.0	
	H. Rattle (SJ)		100% owned by Crédit Suisse Buckmaster & Moore Ltd (formerly B&M)
EXCO International	Laurie Milbank Money Brokers (TB)	100.0	
	Wico Galloway & Pearson (SB)	100.0	
	Walter Walker (SB)	100.0	Through Wico Galloway & Pearson

Table 4.1   *continued*

Buyer	Stockbroker/ stockjobber	Holdings %	Remarks
FBD Insurance	McGuire McCann Morrison (RB)	29.9	
Girozentrale Vienna	Gilbert Eliott (SB)	75.1	Will increase stake to 100% later
Groupe Paribas	Quilter Goodison (TB)	100.0	
Hambros Bank	Strauss Turnbull (SB)	29.9	Also owned by Société Générale
Hong Kong & Shanghai Banking Corporation	James Capel (TB)	100.0	
	Allied Provincial Sec (SJ)	20.0	Through James Capel; also 20% owned by Postel
Merrill Lynch	Merrill Lynch Giles & Cresswell (SJ)	100.0	
NCNB Corporation, USA	Panmure Gordon (MB)	29.9	
Orion Royal Bank[5]	Kitcat & Aitken (MB)	100.0	
Roach Tilley Grice[6]	Cobbold Roach & Co (SB)	50.0	
Security Pacific Bank	Hoare Govett (TB)	83.0	
	Campbell Neill (RB)	100.0	
	Charles Pulley (SJ)	100.0	By Hoare Govett
	Trevor Matthews & Carey (RB)	52.0	Hoare Govett has the option to increase stake to 100%
Shearson Lehman American Express	L. Messel (TB)	100.0	
Shingebis	Dillon & Waldron (RB)	29.9	Will increase holdings to 100%
Société Générale	Strauss Turnbull (SB)	29.9	Also 29.9% owned by Hambros Bank
	Société Générale Strauss Turnball (SJ)	51.0	
Union Bank of Switzerland	Phillips & Drew, Moulsdale (TB)	100.0	By Phillips & Drew
	Edwards Jones & Wilcox (SJ)	100.0	By Phillips & Drew

Table 4.1 *continued*

Buyer	Stockbroker/ stockjobber	Holdings %	Remarks
Other UK Institutions			
Charnley Davies Group (Insurance Brokers)	Giles & Overbury (SB)	100.0	
Fredericks Place Holdings	Spencer Thornton (SB)	100.0	FPH was formerly Hill Woolgar, an OTC House
Granville & Co (OTC House)	R. A. Coleman (RB)	29.9	Will increase holdings to 100%
Harley Temple Group (Financial Planners)	James Brearley (RB)		James Brearley remains a partnership with Harley Temple & Gray acting as a limited partner
Hawley Group (Diversified)	Fyshe Horton Finney (RB)	29.9	
Lancs & Yorks Investment Co.	Battye Wimpenny & Dawson (RB)	25.0	Will increase holdings to 29.9%
R. Nivison	Nivison Cantrade (SB)	50.01	Balance owned by Bank Cantrade, itself owned 85% by Union Bank of Switzerland
Mercantile House (Financial Conglomerate)	Laing & Cruickshank (TB)	100.0	
	Carr, Workman, Patterson, Topping (RB)	100.0	By Laing & Cruickshank
	Wishart Brodie (RB)	100.0	By Laing & Cruickshank
Robert Fleming Holdings	Robert Flemming Securities (SB)	100.0	
Save & Prosper (Fund Manager)[7]	Montagu Loebl Stanley (MB)	100.0	
Smurfit Paribas[8]	Dook & Co (RB)	20.0	

Table 4.1 *continued*

Buyer	Stockbroker/ stockjobber	Holdings %	Remarks
Union Discount (Discount House)	Aitken Campbell (SJ)	50.1	

TJ	Top Jobber	1 Fomerly Bisgood Bishop.
TB	Top Broker	2 Formerly Henderson Crosthwaite (Far
SJ	Specialist Jobber	East).
SB	Specialist Broker	3 72% owned by Royal Trust of Canada;
MB	Medium Sized Broker	28% owned by NordBanken, (Stockholm).
RB	Regional Broker	4 Result of merger between Vickers da Costa
		and Scrimgeour Kemp-Gee.
		5 Bought stake from NM Rothschild.
		6 40% owned by Elders IXL, Australia.
		7 59.4% owned by Robert Fleming Holdings.
		8 50% owned by Groupe Paribas.

Source: Updated from Baring Brothers, 'Integration in the London Securities Market' quoted in *Euromoney*, August 1986.

them from corporate predators. The capacity entering the retail markets, in terms of deposits, lending, and other services, has been greatly enhanced.

In Japan we have seen steadily greater access to the securities and deposit markets, although it would be a brave man who said that the foreign banks had managed to make a great deal of money in that process. But at least the Japanese heart appears to be in the right place.

In the USA there is steady deregulation. The Glass-Steagall Act now has less support in Congress, and there is the possibility that legislation may be passed which will formally weaken it, although not this session. It is being undermined by a variety of other pressures. The Federal Reserve System is using its authority to widen the capacity of banks, and in this it is supported generally by the courts. Likewise, the weakness of the Savings and Loans associations, and the weakness of banks in certain regions, have led to a welcome being extended to rescuing institutions, and these in turn are breaking down the previous barriers to inter-state banking. The momentum in the USA is towards deregulation and the opening up of the markets, and this should provide opportunities for a wider range of banks around the world.

In Europe we are seeing a very substantial process of deregulation, occuring on a variety of fronts. We have, first, the convergence proposals for capital adequacy, as established at the Bank for International Settlements in Basle. These will be followed by mandatory proposals from the European Commission, for the first time setting out a common capital base for banks within Europe. This will set out the so-called level playing field. It will for the first time also make it easier for banks to 'play away', that is to establish business in other countries. The protection which has been established by central banks over their own banking businesses and markets will inevitably be lessened. It does not matter if the playing field is not even, if you are not allowed to play away anyway. But that protection has now been removed.

Changes are taking places through the second banking coordination directive and the investment services directive, which I will not detail here. These will have the effect of establishing banking and securities licences throughout the Community, based on a bank or securities company being authorised in its home country, and then having the right to operate throughout the Community. It will be subject to certain conduct-of-business rules in the host country, but in principle these will not affect its right to operate there.

The corollary of these changes will be that the banking structure within Europe will reflect much more closely the capital resources and earnings power of the European banks, than has been the case in the past where banks have largely been protected within their national markets, and imbalances of commercial strength in relation to capital and earnings power have occurred.

Securitization

The position of banks has not been made easier by the development of securitization over the last decade. This development has been a consequence of technology, customer pressure, and financial innovation. It has three main effects on the banks. The first is that the margin of return on wholesale business has been reduced very significantly under the competition from securitized products. Indeed, given the convergence capital ratios applied to them, much wholesale business does not provide, in its own right, a sufficient return to cover the capital costs.

Second, the proportion of business done through traditional banking rather than through securitization methods has fallen markedly.

Table 4.2 Borrowing on the international capital markets

Instrument	1985	1986	1987	January–March 1987	1988
				($ billion)	
Bonds	169.1	228.1	177.3	57.7	54.1
Equities	2.7	11.7	18.2	2.8	0.7
Syndicated loans	43.0	52.8	88.8	13.3	32.8
Note Issuance Facilities	34.4	24.8	28.1	5.3	7.5
Other back-up facilities	8.5	4.5	1.8	0.6	0.5
A. Total securities and committed facilities	257.7	321.9	314.2	79.7	95.6
Euro-commercial paper programmes	12.6	59.0	55.3	12.2	17.1
Other non-underwritten facilities	10.6	8.6	14.3	2.4	5.5
B. Total uncommitted borrowing facilities	23.2	67.6	69.6	14.6	22.6
Grand Total (A+B)	280.9	389.5	383.8	94.3	118.2

Table 4.2 sets out the major international financial flows around the world, from which it will be seen that the securitized share has become greater than that from direct bank lending in recent years.

Third, the securitized business is open to, and is done largely by, institutions which are not traditional banks. Thus the banks have seen a sharp fall in the return on bank lending, in the amount of bank lending which can be done, and have not been able to obtain a similar share in the securitized business which has replaced it. This feature has in due course led to major reassessments of banks' internal structures. The main securitized changes are irreversible. While the financial flows may move back and forth between banking and securitized instruments from time to time, and new instruments may be developed, customer pressure will nevertheless demand both the most efficient service and a service at the most competitive price. It will thus be a mistake for banks to plan on the assumption that there may be a return to the level and terms of bank lending which we saw, for example, in the 1970s.

Capital

For the first time bankers are having to adapt to capital as a key feature of their business situation in two marked and separate ways. The first is that bankers have to accept what I believe has for years been common in the insurance industry, namely the concept of a capital cycle. When there is excess capital in the insurance industry then business tends to be written on a large scale and premiums are forced down. In due course this leads to losses and/or weakened profitability, when capital is removed from the business. This then has the effect of making capital relatively scarce, so premium rates increase and in due course profitability becomes substantial. Capital is then attracted into the industry and so the cycle is repeated. The concept of the appropriate scale of capital for the entire banking industry has not so far been regarded as a feature of banking, in business terms. But that is now the case, and I believe that in past years there has been an excess of capital in the banking industry, and indeed there could be in the immediate future. The advent of the Japanese banks, claiming their rightful place in the world market-place, given the commercial strength of their economy, has substantially increased the capital in banking, leading to a marked shift in market shares and to very substantial price effects, notably in the wholesale markets. In some countries clearly there is excess banking capital, and in others there are pockets of deficient banking capital. These anomalies will have to be remedied through the market-place. The rules laid down by the Bank for International Settlements and by the European Commission may have made the amount of capital in banking appropriate to the market-place, but my suspicion is that there may still be a slight excess.

The second feature of capital relates to the regulatory and supervisory process, where we now have the minimum rules introduced through the Bank for International Settlements and through the European Commission, as implemented by national central banks. By far the greatest constraint on banks is Tier One capital, which is essentially equity. Banks will have to maintain a total capital ratio, Tier I and Tier II, of at least 8 per cent, of which Tier I must be at least 4 per cent. In principle, Tier II capital is relatively cheap and relatively easy to obtain, so by far the tightest constraint on banks is their Tier I capital. Banks will thus have to watch carefully their business development and their earnings programme in relation to the capital used and to the return on equity which they wish to achieve.

The cost capital is also very relevant and this in turn relates to the share prices and the price-earnings (P/E) ratios in the various countries. These ratios vary markedly among the European and North American countries, both between individual banks in the same country and between banking systems. Japan is also unique, with extremely high P/E ratios, which in turn imply a relatively cheap cost of capital and therefore the ability to raise capital at a lower price than elsewhere. The cost of capital, its availability, and the return on it, will become far more crucial elements in banks' strategies than they have had to be in past years.

Global Competition

This concern with the total return on total capital becomes more important as one realises that the banking industry has changed its competitive structure recently, to one of global competition. In the past one would consider competing with certain companies in certain markets. But now the major institutions are concerned with the global market-place and with competing with their main competitors in total and in all the market-places which are available. This concept has been relevant to many manufacturing industries, such as the automobile or chemical industries, for some time. One may attack a competitor to weaken him somewhere else. One has to take into account one's available resources, and ensure that in a global sense they are used to the greatest advantage. These concepts are now beginning to enter banking, and will colour the resource deployment of banks in the future. It will be essential to use scarce resources to obtain the globally most effective return, rather than just to obtain a particular position in a particular market.

Developing-Country Debt

The developing-country debt issue has had a series of effects on the banking industry, which have by no means worked themselves out, either for the banks or for the indebted countries.

When the debt situation became apparent in August 1982, the assumption by the OECD countries and by the banks was that it was purely a liquidity problem and that correct policies plus time would do their own healing. That assumption became less credible as time passed, and it has now become the conventional view, both informally among governmental organizations and as shown by the banks' provisioning, that the issue contains both a solvency and a liquidity element. It is not entirely solvency for most countries, nor entirely liquidity, but a mixture of both.

This means that the common front, the sense of community, which originally existed between banks has now weakened, and the banks accept that their relationship to the developing country situation is inevitably part of the competitive relationship between them.

Even if banks did not wish to take this view, the stock market has taken it for them. In most market-based systems, such as the UK, Canada and the USA, the markets have taken a view of a bank's exposure to Third World debt, and have priced its shares according to their view of that exposure and of the bank's general handling of its business affairs. There is thus now a wide range of price–earnings ratios for banks in North America depending on these factors.

A bank's share price and its capital are crucial to a bank's strategic decisions in relation to acquisitions or to being the victim of mergers. Given the restructuring now taking place in the North American banking system, and likely in Europe, these features are keys to the future of management interests, banking interests, and shareholder interests. The banks are now engaged in deciding their best strategy, which in some cases means retaining their developing-country debt because it is so insignificant as not to matter, in some places trading debt, so as to reduce their exposure and increase their level of credibility with stock analysts, and in some cases holding on to debt simply because the bank is too weak to do anything else.

Provisioning levels differ around the world, banks having to take the appropriate level as indicated by their authorities or which they regard as being appropriate under the circumstances. Some Continental banks have very high provisioning levels, made easier in some cases by the appreciation of their currencies against the dollar. The Japanese have very low provisioning levels, determined largely by the authorities' rules and the tax system. North American banks vary. In the UK most banks are within the Bank of England matrix, and my own bank is at the top of that level at about 35 per cent. We regard that as adequate. No one knows the true risk on this exposure. The purpose of provisions is to be one feature in assuring the world of the health and viability of the bank in question. In the case of my bank our total unprovided exposure is only 32 per cent of our equity, and is equivalent to not much more than one year's pre-tax profits. Likewise, our total gross income from the rescheduling countries is about one-sixth of our pre-tax profits. Thus, come what may, the bank is secure and our degree of protection would not be increased significantly by changing the provisioning levels substantially.

Supervision

Central banks have attempted to keep up with changes in the banking scene by tightening their supervision of banks. This has covered a wide variety of fields. In the related securities field, central banks and securities supervisors have calculated very complicated volatility and exposure ratios, and have calculated the capital required in relation to objective statistical risks on the exposure. Black Monday, however, showed that many assumptions about exposure could be inaccurate.

The range of supervision now covers many areas which good bank-management should have had under the close control in the first place. It covers the maximum exposure to individual borrowers, concentrations of exposure, the liquidity position of a bank, its control of total off-balance sheet risk, its capital ratios, and the general quality of its portfolio.

In the UK, the changes stemmed from a transition from an informal to a legal basis of supervision, through the Banking Act of 1987. The effort put in by the authorities in effecting this supervision and in keeping up with market developments has been very substantial indeed. In principle we see no objection to this tightened supervision, and our main problems lie with some detailed features of the controls, and with whether the entire process may not at times be too oppressive. We are also very much concerned with the cost of supervision. If supervision is too tight, then banks simply cannot make money, and they will cease to do business. Two of the strong features of British banking for many years after the war were the relatively low level of supervisory costs, and the extent to which the Bank of England took steps over the years to reduce the implicit taxation inherent in the supervisory process. These led to a profitable and, by and large, healthy banking system, although in more recent years one particular collapse jeopardized that system. We were thus forced down the road towards a legally based and stricter system. If this fell into the hands of officials who became very cautious, then it could become too restrictive. If banks cannot make profits, then

London will decline as a financial centre, and we shall have thrown out the business baby with the supervisory bath-water.

CONCLUSION

What general conclusions emerge from this summary of the risk factors affecting bank managements in recent years? My main conclusion is that banking has moved over the past ten or fifteen years from being in many cases somewhat institutional in character to being totally commercial and businesslike in its structures. Banking is now a totally competitive industry, virtually worldwide, which can be analysed in terms of the same industrial economics as may be applied to the automobile industry or to chemicals. The maximization of benefits from the banks' scarce resources of capital, staff, customers, and knowledge, must be the dominant consideration in the minds of top management. The scope for the luxury of engaging in less commercial activity, which was easier years ago when competition was less, has now virtually been removed.

This will lead to excellent service for the customer and to very commercially minded banks. It has, however, a down-side feature which in due course may become more apparent to the supervisors. If one creates a totally competitive industry, then some companies will not succeed. Some companies will either fail or they will be forced to reduce their activity to the scale of their own resources, their capital. Supervisors may find themselves, whatever their apparent supervisory success, having to deal with institutions which cannot keep up with the competitive rat-race established by the combination of deregulation, technology, and innovation. The coming decade will be an exciting time both for those in the financial services industry and for those in governments and central banks who have policy responsibility for the industry.

5 Competition and Risks in Financial Services: Lessons from Tokyo

Yasuo Kanzaki

SYSTEM OF SPECIALIZED FINANCIAL INSTITUTIONS AND MAINTENANCE OF ORDER IN THE FINANCIAL SYSTEM

The banking and securities businesses in Japan have been separated since 1948. In addition, banks are divided into specialized categories, including regular banks (corresponding roughly to commercial banks overseas), long-term credit banks, trust and banking companies, financial institutions for smaller businesses, and other types of institutions. The objectives of this policy of establishing specialized financial institutions were threefold:

- The first was to restrain long-term interest rates at a relatively low level and to provide an adequate flow of funds to those industries regarded as important for Japan's economic development. To achieve this objective, a number of financial institutions specializing in long-term lending were established, while regular, commercial banks were not permitted to engage in long-term lending.
- The second was to assure the soundness of banks. In line with this objective, commercial banks were not permitted to enter the securities business. At the same time, interest rates were regulated, thus assuring a spread between deposit and lending interest rates.
- The third objective was to prevent conflicts of interest and prevent control of industry by banks through the separation of the securities and banking industries.

Thus, Japan has been able to eliminate excessive competition and maintain order in the financial system through the establishment of specialized financial institutions, with specific regulations governing their activities.

SPECIALIZED FINANCIAL INSTITUTIONS AND THE MANAGEMENT OF RISK

The system of specialized financial institutions was also very effective in controlling risk. Because operations of various types of institutions were organized within an orderly framework, the regulatory authorities were able to set up detailed regulations for management of risk by each type of institution. Also, with interest rates fully regulated, it was possible for banking institutions to earn sufficient profits from their deposit-taking and lending activities. The management and operation of financial institutions was therefore very stable. As a result of this system, Japan has not experienced a single bank failure since the end of the Second World War. But because of the heavy emphasis placed on maintaining a stable and orderly financial system, deposit interest rates have been at a low level for a considerable period and the system has not worked in the interests of individuals.

FINANCIAL DEREGULATION, INTERNATIONALIZATION, AND GROWING COMPETITION

Beginning in the early 1980s, however, this system, which assured the stability and profitability of financial institutions, began to experience pressures for change. First, after the second oil crisis, the financial assets of individuals and corporations began to show significant expansion, as the economy moved into a period of slow economic expansion. Investors began to show increased interest in asset management. Interest-rate-sensitive investors began to diversify their assets from bank deposits to investments with deregulated interest rates and securities. Also, after the first oil crisis, beginning in the mid-1970s, the Japanese government began to issue a large volume of bonds to finance expansion in public works investments. The development and expansion of a large secondary market for government bonds also created pressures for deregulation of interest rates. Table 5.1 details this deregulation from April 1979 to April 1988.

In addition, corporations began to diversify their sources of funds (see Table 5.2 and Figure 5.1). Following the liberalization of foreign exchange controls in 1980, Japanese corporations, which had been heavily dependent on domestic bank borrowings, became much more active in raising funds in the Euromarket and other overseas capital markets. This trend has become even more pronounced since the

Table 5.1 Deregulation of Japan's money and capital markets

Year/Month	Short-term money market	Euroyen market	Expansion of business of securities companies and financial institutions
1979 April	Abolition of quotation system for the call rate		
May	Introduction of CDs (¥500 million, 3–6 months)		Banks: start of CD transactions
1980 January			Securities companies: start of medium-term bond funds
April	Expansion of framework of limits for CD issues (from 25% to 50% of equity capital)		
May	Appearance of CD gensaki transactions (around May)		
December	Deregulation of foreign-currency deposits/impact loans to residents	New Foreign Exchange Law enforced	
1981 April	Enforcement of New Banking Law/Revised Securities and Exchange Law		
May	Start of BOJ sale of finance bills in the market		
June			Banks: start handling maturity-designated time deposits. Trust banks: start to handle BIG accounts

Table 5.1 *continued*

Year/Month	Short-term money market	Euroyen market	Expansion of business of securities companies and financial institutions
October			Long-term credit banks: begin to handle WIDE accounts
1983 February	Expansion of limits for issues of CDs (from 50% to 75% of equity capital)		Banks: start long-term bond sales
April			Securities companies: start public-bond collateral loans
June		Deregulation of short-term Euroyen lending to non-residents	Banks: start government bond-time deposit accounts
August			Banks: start sales of medium-term government bonds/discount bonds
November			
1984 January	Reduction of size of CD issuing unit (from ¥500 million to ¥300 million)	Abolition of principle of actual demand in exchange futures transactions	
April	Staged expansion of limit of for CD issues (from 75% to 100% of equity capital by April 1985)	Relaxation of guidelines for	Securities companies, banks: start actual handling of foreign CP/CDs. Securities companies, shinkin banks:

	Start actual handling of foreign CP/CDs	Euroyen bond issues by residents	beginning of comprehensive fund accounts
May			
June		Japan–US Yen–Dollar Committee Report published. Abolition of regulations on yen conversion. Deregulation of short-term Euroyen lending to residents	Banks: start dealing in public bonds with a remaining period of less than two years. Foreign banks: start sales of medium-term government bond bids
August			Securities companies: start of securities ANSER
October			Three foreign banks: start public bond dealing
December		Relaxation of guidelines for Euroyen bond issues by non-residents. Deregulation of short-term Euroyen CDs. Opening of lead-manager business of Euroyen bond underwriting to foreign underwriters	
1985 March	Establishment of MMCs (¥50 million or above, 1–6 months) Bill market, deregulation of simultaneous purchasing/selling operations	Authorization of establishment of Euroyen investment trusts, realized by Nikko in April	Sogo banks, shinkin banks: start handling MMCs
April	Relaxation of conditions for issuing CDs (from ¥300	Relaxation of bond-issuing criteria for non-resident	City/regional banks, trust banks, long-term credit

(continued)

63

Table 5.1 continued

Year/Month	Short-term money market	Euroyen market	Expansion of business of securities companies and financial institutions
	million to ¥100 million, from 3–6 months to 1–6 months, issuing framework expanded to 100% of equity capital)	Euroyen bonds and yen-denominated foreign bonds. Abolition of withholding tax on the interest of Euroyen bonds issued by residents. Deregulation of medium- and long-term Euroyen loans to non-residents.	banks: start handling MMCs
June	Establishment of yen-denominated BA market (¥100 million, maximum of 6 months)	Diversification of form of non-resident Euroyen bond issues. Zero-coupon bonds, dual-currency bonds, floating interest-rate bonds, deep-discount bonds, currency-conversion bonds	Securities companies: start handling CD distribution. Banks: start handling yen-denominated BAs Banks: start full dealing, increase in number of authorized banks Banks: participation in Japan Bond Trading Company Securities companies: start public bond collateral loans with limitation Banks: establishment of public bond integrated deposit accounts

July	Introduction of uncollaterized call transactions. Creation of 2–3 week call transactions	Nine foreign banks: decision on participation in trust business
August		Securities companies: start handling FFFs
October	Deregulation of interest rates on large-scale time deposits (2 years or less, minimum of ¥1 billion). Expansion of issuing limitation for CDs, MMCs (CDs: to 150% of equity capital, MMCs: from 75% to 150%). Call loan dealers, start of interbank deposit broker business. Creation of bond futures market	Securities companies, banks: start handling securities collateral loans. Securities companies, banks: participation in bond futures market (banks: dealing business only)
December		Trust banks: start handling new money trusts. Two foreign-bank affiliated securities companies: authorized to begin operations. Securities companies: start handling detached warrants.

(continued)

Table 5.1 continued

Year/Month	Short-term money market	Euroyen market	Expansion of business of securities companies and financial institutions
1986 January	Bank of Japan, adoption of gensaki system for FB sales. Issuing of short-term government bonds.		Six foreign securities companies: decision on acquisition of membership on Tokyo Stock Exchange
February	Reduction of size of large-scale time deposits (to ¥500 million)	Prolongation of period of Euroyen CDs (from 6 months to 1 month–1 year)	Securities companies: start handling yen-denominated BA distribution Trust banks: start handling fund trusts for individuals
April	Relaxation of issuing conditions of CDs and MMCs (to 1 month–1 year, expansion of issuing framework to 200% of equity capital)	Diversification of form of resident Euroyen bond issues Relaxation of domestic distribution system of Euroyen bonds	
September	Reduction of size of large-scale time deposits (to ¥300 million).	Creation of Tokyo offshore market	Lifting of ban on handling of foreign CP by overseas subsidiary securities companies of Japanese banks

1987 February		Lifting of ban on handling of foreign CP by foreign offices of Japanese banks
April	Reduction of size of large fixed deposits (to ¥100 million). Reduction of denomination of MMCs (to ¥20 million), prolongation of period (from 1 month to 2 years), setting of interest rates according to period (1 year or less: CDs minus 0.75%, from 1 to 2 years: CDs minus 0.5%), expansion of limit of deposits (to 300%).	
May	Reduction of denomination of BAs (to ¥50 million), prolongation of period (to a maximum of 1 year).	Lifting of ban on dealing on own account by securities companies and financial institutions in foreign financial futures markets
October	Increased flexibility of deposit period for large-scale time deposits (from 3 months–2 years to 1 month–2 years). Reduction of denomination of MMCs (to ¥10 million), abolition of deposit limit. Abolition of CD issuing limit.	

(continued)

Table 5.1 *continued*

Year/Month	Short-term money market	Euroyen market	Expansion of business of securities companies and financial institutions
	Issuing of domestic CP		
November		Lifting of ban on issuing of Euroyen CP by non-residents	Securities companies, banks: start handling domestic CP
1988 January		Lifting of ban on issuing of domestic CP by non-residents	
1988 March			
1988 April	Reduction of size of large-scale time deposits (to ¥50 million) Prolongation of CD issuing period (from 1 month–1 year to 2 weeks–1 year), reduction of issuing unit (from ¥100 million to ¥50 million)		Lifting of ban on dealing by own account by securities companies and financial institutions in foreign financial spot options. Start of government bond counter sales by post offices, life insurance companies, agricultural cooperatives

Notes: BIG   tax-free money trust for individuals.
WIDE   tax-free bonds for individuals.
ANSER   Automatic Answer Network System for Electronic Requests.
text

Source: Prepared by NRC, April 1988. The Nikko Research Center, Tokyo, April 1988

(continued)

Table 5.2   Fund raising by Japanese corporations

(Billion ¥)

		1984	1985	1986	1987	1988 (Jan.-Jun.)	1987 (Jan.-Jun.)
	Bank Borrowings	22 467.6	24 393.3	25 516.4	30 255.4	7 144.0*	8 306.1
Funds Raised	Bonds	2 033.5	2 703.5	3 835.5	6 232.0	2 804.5	3 013.5
	Stocks	966.9	727.9	496.3	1 996.2	758.0	510.6
	Overseas bonds	2 392.1	3 382.5	3 716.9	4 825.4	2 018.1	2 347.0
	CP	–	–	–	1 698.2	3 495.4	–
	Total	27 860.1	31 207.2	33 565.1	45 007.2	16 220.0	14 177.2

Note: *includes estimated figures. Securities include domestic convertible and equity issues of financial institutions.
Source: Bank of Japan; Japan Bond Underwriters Associations.

release of the Japan–US Yen–Dollar Committee report in 1984, the relaxation of restrictions on Euroyen transactions, and the development of swap technology. Also following the liberalization of foreign exchange transactions, more and more new financial products have been imported, including US government bonds and LBO funds. This has also contributed to the range of fund uses available to investors.

GROWING OVERLAP OF BANKING AND SECURITIES BUSINESSES

As deregulation and internationalization have proceeded, competition has become more intense. As regulations have been relaxed, financial institutions have found their traditional activities becoming less profitable and have sought new sources of income. This has led them to move aggressively into new areas and develop new products and services.

As the movement to repeal the Glass–Steagall Act in the USA, the 'Big Bang' in the UK, and the reform of the stock exchange in France all suggest, the barriers separating banking and securities businesses are coming down. In Japan, banking and securities activities are still strictly separated, but because of the recent competition in development of new products, the 'grey area' between the operations of banks and securities companies is growing. Financial institutions now

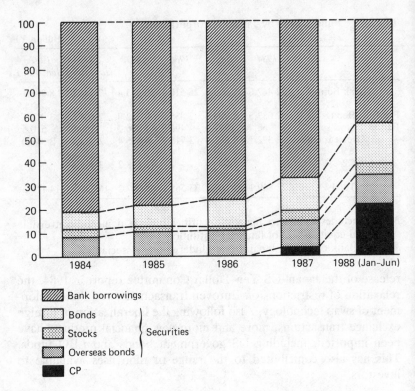

Figure 5.1   Fund-raising by Japanese corporations (percentage composition)

Source: ibid.

have to be concerned with competition, not only from similar institutions, but also from other types of financial institutions and even from other industries. For example, in the past only securities companies were permitted to sell government bonds. But beginning in 1982, banks were allowed to engage in this activity, and, today, banks and insurance companies are permitted to sell these bonds as an individual product or in combination with other financial products. Also, both banks and securities companies have received permission to engage in the yen-denominated bankers acceptance market, beginning in 1985, and the yen commercial paper market, beginning in 1987. This too has led to more intense competition.

Competition is also growing among different types of banking institutions that formerly operated in separate areas. For example, in lending, the principle of having different specialized banks for long-term and short-term lending is breaking down. The short-term and long-term prime rates have become less and less meaningful. Also, as a result of advances in swap technology, the difference between short-term and long-term funding has become less distinct. Another consideration is that corporations are continuing to diversify their sources of funds and are reducing their bank borrowings. As this takes place, large banks, which were formerly the financiers for leading corporations, are turning their attention to smaller business which are in need of bank borrowings and to the individual market. This is leading to greater competition between large banks and banking institutions that have traditionally specialized in servicing the needs of small and medium-sized companies. Competition is also growing more intense between private banks on the one hand and the postal savings system and government-related financial institutions on the other. Insurance companies have also begun to diversify their range of product offerings in recent years from pure insurance-type products to savings-type products, leading in some cases to major shifts of funds away from banks and securities companies.

ENTRY OF FOREIGN FINANCIAL INSTITUTIONS INTO THE JAPANESE MARKET

Along with the growth in Japan's capital exports, a rising number of foreign financial institutions are entering the Tokyo market. At present, eighty-one foreign banks and forty-nine foreign securities companies have branch operations in Japan, and, of these, forty-three have set up operations in the past three years. This entry of so many foreign institutions – most of which are securities companies stimulated by the worldwide trends toward deregulation and inter-nationalization – in such a short period of time, reflects the powerful effects of Japan's own progress toward deregulation and inter-nationalization. The new products and services which these foreign institutions bring to Japan have considerably increased competition in Japan's financial services industry.

INCREASED RISKS FOR FINANCIAL INSTITUTIONS

Growing competition has also brought increased risk for financial institutions. In the case of banks, the deregulation of interest rates

Table 5.3 Entry of Japanese securities companies into foreign markets, and foreign securities companies into Japan

	1969	1970	1971	1972	1973	1974	1975	1976	1977	1978	1979	1980	1981	1982	1983	1984	1985	1986	1987	Total 1987	As of December 1987
Japanese Securities Companies:																					
Overseas branches		4			2		1		2		1	2		1						13	0
Subsidiaries	9	2	1	5	5	3	2		6	5	3	2	4	7	2	3	4	19	11	95	93
Representative offices	4	1	5	5	7	4	4	3		2	4	7	1	3	9	9	22	21	19	132	73
Total	13	7	6	10	14	7	7	3	8	7	8	11	5	11	11	12	26	40	30	240	166
Foreign Securities Companies:																					
Branches in Japan				1		1				2	1		1	1	2	2	11	14	11	47	47
Representative offices	1	4	9	3	23	8	2	2	2	9	11	5	4	9	13	15	30	31	12	193	129
Total	1	4	9	4	23	9	2	2	2	11	12	5	5	10	15	17	41	45	23	240	176

Note: 'Subsidiaries' refers to companies overseas (including subsidiaries of subsidiaries) engaged in the securities business that are 50% owned or more.

Source: Ministry of Finance.

Table 5.4 Entry of Japanese banks into foreign banks and of foreign banks into Japan

	CY 1950–55	1956–65	1966–75	1976	1977	1978	1979	1980	1981	1982	1983	1984	1985	1986	1987	As of December 1987
Japanese Authorized Foreign Exchange Banks:																
Overseas branches	13	34	54	6	11	4	5	12	12	8	9	10	13	16	12	227
Subsidiaries	3	2	37	7	7	10	1	8	7	14	15	16	33	31	14	205
Representative offices	4	14	125	23	12	16	22	24	23	55	42	34	63	36	25	405
Total	21	53	227	38	30	30	28	47	44	80	88	82	109	83	48	837
Foreign Banks:																
(Banks)	14	3	37	4	6	3	2	1	5	5	2	1	4	5	2	81
Branches in Japan	35	4	44	4	6	3	4	1	9	7	4	5	9	6	2	115
Subsidiaries													3	6		9
Representative offices	7	7	95	6	7	9	7	8	8	17	11	9	17	16	10	130
Total	35	11	139	10	13	12	11	9	17	24	15	14	28	28	12	254

Notes: 1. 'Subsidiaries' refers to companies that are 50% owned or more.
2. The row marked '(Banks)' refers to the number of banks with branches.
3. Any discrepancy between the number of offices established and the current number is due to closures or mergers.
4. Numbers indicate offices opened.

Source: Ministry of Finance.

has brought a sharp decline in spreads between deposit and lending interest rates, especially for large transactions. In some instances, funding rates have exceeded lending rates resulting in negative spreads. Banks have also engaged in more period mismatching between deposits and loans. This is because on the lending side, the distinction between long-term and short-term loans has become less clear, but on the funding side the difference between long-term and short-term deposits is still clear, creating an incentive to fund through cheaper, short-term sources. Management of financial institutions now is no longer characterized by absolute safety. If major fluctuations in interest rates occur, banks may incur significant losses.

In the past, banks had to be concerned mainly about credit risk, but more recently they have also had to deal with risks arising from foreign exchange, changes in securities prices in their dealing operations, system risks accompanying the introduction of computers, and legal risks arising from the internationalization of operations.

Along with the increase in and greater diversity of risks for banking operations, the Bank of Japan, one of the principal regulatory authorities, issued a comprehensive list of 200 checkpoint items related to bank risk management at the beginning of 1987 (see Table 5.5). In addition, the Ministry of Finance is supposed to adopt a new system for inspection of banks aimed at improving risk management on an experimental basis in August 1987. Securities companies also are faced with increasing risk (see Tables 5.6 and 5.7). Along with securitization and globalization in recent years, the products handled by securities companies have expanded from stocks and bonds to include options, swaps, foreign securities, mortgage certificates, commercial paper, and bankers acceptances. Also, through overseas banking subsidiaries, securities companies have entered lending and other banking operations and expanded the number of products and services incorporating a range of banking and securities services in cooperation with banking institutions. (In 1984, for example, securities companies introduced comprehensive fund accounts in cooperation with smaller banking institutions.) As financial service activities become more competitive along with deregulation and internationalization, the number of products and services handled by securities companies has increased rapidly and the types and magnitude of risks involved is expanding.

Table 5.5 Major items in banks' risk-management checklist, prepared by the Bank of Japan (implemented in 1987)

I. **Credit risk**

On the books domestically
  Inspection prior to loan, etc.
  Interim supervision
  Maintenance of claims
  Credit discipline
  System support
On the books overseas
  Country risk analysis
  Problem country claim
    management
  Commercial risk inspection
  Commercial risk management
  Global profitability management
Off the books
  Information disclosure
    requirements
  Operational modifications, asset
    sales, and merger limitations
  Collateral, financial ratio
    limitations, material adverse
    change clause
  Default composition items
  Monitoring of numerical
    indicators, credit approval
    limits

II. **Interest risk**
Mismatch positions
  Awareness of directors and
    department heads as to
    interest risk
  The functioning level of the
    ALM committee and the
    interest forecast meeting
  Data base preparation and
    system support for gap
    computations
  Establishment of the gapping
    limits and the decision making
    authority
  Gapping supervision
Dealing in public bonds
  Organization and systems
  System support

  Establishment of the position
    framework and the decision
    making authority
  Management of the limits
    position
  Income management
Security holdings
  Director and department head
    risk awareness
  Portfolio establishment and
    establishment of decision
    making authority in matters
    related to purchase
  Strategies for interest risk and
    currency exchange related to
    investment in foreign currency
    based securities
  Strategies for interest risk
    relating to bond investments
  Securities investments

III. **Liquidity risk**
  Director and department head
    awareness of risk
  Usage strategy related to off
    balance transactions
  Credit crunch strategies
  Funding strategies for the
    securities position

IV. **Exchange risk**
  Director and department head
    awareness of risk
  Organization and systems
  Establishment of position limits
    and decision making authority
  Position limits supervision
  System support

V. **EDP risk**
  Measures against theft and
    disasters
  Backup system

Table 5.5   continued

System development and operational system	VII. **Operational risk**
Supervision of employees	System and structure
EDP audit	Vault supervision and important documents
	Handling of cash
VI. System risk	Customer relations
Director and department head awareness of risk	Handling of unusual transactions, advances, and advance payments
Confirmation of contract clauses	
Organization and system for participating in large scale settlement system	
	VIII. **Management risk**
System support for large movements of capital	Organization
	Internal audit
Supervision of (comprehensive) all purpose accounts	Supervision of affiliate companies
Risk management of on-line cash dispenser systems	

Source: *Kinyuzaisei Jijo* (*Financial Economist*).

ILLIQUIDITY OF NEW FINANCIAL PRODUCTS

An incident in May last year has already shown that forecasting the risks associated with new products is complex and difficult. In May 1987, two large investment banks in the USA incurred major losses in connection with bond option and mortgage securities transaction. Both the products in question were developed using advanced techniques involving complex computer calculations. Many of the assumptions made at the time the products were designed suddenly changed under conditions of sudden interest-rate fluctuations, thus leading to losses. Use of the computer has become essential in developing new financial products in recent years. But because the design of some financial products has become too complex, they lose their liquidity when significant changes in interest rates occur and expose investors to the risk of major losses from their positions in these instruments.

Table 5.6 Securities business expansion and the growing diversity of risks

Basic trends	Areas of business affected	Type of risk (see key)									
		1	2	3	4	5	6	7	8	9	10
Deregulation	Market opening	*	*								
	Development of new types of products	*									
	Loans against securities	*				*					
	Settlement through cards					*	*	*			
	Expansion of stock and CB markets	*	*	*							
Globalization	Expansion of trading in foreign currencies	*	*	*	*						
	24-hour dealing	*	*	*		*	*	*			
	Expansion of the swap market	*	*	*	*	*	*			*	
	Expansion of positions of overseas subsidiaries	*	*	*	*			*			*
	International linkages among futures markets	*	*	*			*				
Securitization	Bought deal type underwriting		*	*							
	Proposal-type underwriting		*								
	Growth of CBs and WBs		*							*	
	Development of various new products										
Computerization	Development of next-generation on-line computer system										*
	Automatic debit/credit of charges on buying and selling of shares						*	*			
	Development of new accumulative types of product						*	*	*		
	Development of information and home-trading services						*	*	*		
	Increases in own-account positions	*	*	*		*	*	*			
	Development of various new products					*	*				

(continued)

Table 5.6 continued

Basic trends	Areas of business affected	Type of risk (see key)									
		1	2	3	4	5	6	7	8	9	10
Institutionalization	Research into fund-management know-how						*	*		*	
	Growing scale of fund movements					*	*	*			
	Sharp expansion of stock and CB markets	*	*	*							

Key:
1. Interest rates
2. Price fluctuations
3. Exchange rates
4. Liquidity
5. Credit
6. Systems
7. EDP
8. Client supervision
9. Securities laws and regulations
10. Operational

Table 5.7 Securities companies major risk-management items

Type of risk	Risk management item	Related risk
General risk management system	State of specialized risk management divisions Enhancement of net worth State of maintenance of computer systems	Operational risk Systems risk EDP risk
Share dealing activities	Positions – setting up, supervising, changing Operating system of Market Outlook Committee Information gathering system Fund management system Systems support Income supervision system (loss-cutting rule)	Interest rate risk Exchange rate risk Liquidity risk Systems risk EDP risk
Bond dealing activities	Positions – setting up, supervising, changing Operating system of Interest Rate Outlook Committee Information gathering system Fund management system Systems support Income supervision system (loss-cutting rule) Ability of systems to cope with 24-hour trading	Price fluctuation risk Interest rate risk Liquidity risk Systems risk EDP risk Credit risk
Stock and bond brokerage business	Systems for gathering and providing information Systems support Business development and management system Client supervision system	Credit risk Systems risk EDP risk Client supervision risk

(continued)

Table 5.7 continued

Type of risk	Risk management item	Related risk
Stock bond and investment sales activities	Business development and management system Client supervision system System for gathering and providing information Systems support	Credit risk Systems risk EDP risk Client supervision risk
Stock and bond underwriting activities (Bought-deal type and proposal type)	New issue system and trading system Financial and capital markets analysis system System for approval of terms Control of underwriting profitability Cooperation with Sales Department Systems support	Interest rate risk Price fluctuation risk Exchange rate risk Liquidity risk Credit risk Systems risk Legal risk
Control of investment securities	Buying and selling approval authority Foreign bond investment and hedging Portfolio policy Systems support	Interest rate risk Price fluctuation risk Exchange rate risk Systems risk
Fund trading system	Positions – setting up, supervising, changing Operating system of Market Outlook Committee Systems support	Interest rate risk Exchange rate risk Liquidity risk Systems risk

Electronic Data Processing (EDP)	Crime and fire prevention strategies Back-up systems Systems development and operation Supervision of required personnel Inspection system Funding plans for capital investment	[Systems risk EDP risk Operational risk]
Branch network supervision	Branch plan deliberation system System for collecting regional information System for control of profitability Branch operations system Systems support	[Systems risk EDP risk Operational risk]

Table 5.8   Japanese securities companies: reserves and regulations on liabilities and positions

---

Reserves under the Securities and Exchange Law

Trading Loss Reserve	(Securities and Exchange Law, Article 56; Ministerial Ordinance on Securities Companies, Article 7, Section 2.) This reserve is set up when negotiable securities' trading losses are greater than negotiable securities trading gains. The size of the reserve amount is calculated according to prescribed rules.
Securities Trading Liability Reserve	(Securities Exchange Law, Article 57, Section 2, Ministerial Ordinance on Securities Companies, Article 8.) Reserve set up, as contingency, based on the volume of trading and other operations related to negotiable securities.
Profit Reserve	(Securities Exchange Law, Article 57.) Reserve of 20% or more of the amount of cash dividends, up to the value of the company's capitalization.

Regulations Relating to Liabilities and Positions

Liability Ratio	(Securities Exchange Law, Article 54, Ministerial Ordinance on Securities Companies, Article 6.) Up to 10% of net assets.
Limit on Holding of Shares	(Specified in a circular by the Head of the Business Section.)
• Trading Account Securities	The lower of (a) 40% of the value of net assets and (b) 1.1% of the average value of stocks traded on a commission basis over the last five business years.
• Investment Securities	30% of net assets.
Gensaki Balance	(Specified in a circular from the Head of the Securities Division of the Ministry of Finance.)
• Gensaki Brokerage	3% of the following: net assets as at the end of the September 1979 term, plus the average value of bonds traded on a commission basis over the

Table 5.8   continued

	five-year period up to and including the September 1979 term.
● Own-account Gensaki	Up to 8× net assets, less total debt.
Limits on Futures Trading Value	(Specified in a circular by the Head of the Business Section.)
● Overseas Financial Futures	Up to the value of net assets.
● Stock Futures	Up to 40% of net assets.
● Investment Securities	50% of the value of total investment securities at the end of the relevant term, or at the end of the immediately preceding term, whichever is higher.
Limits on Short Selling of Bonds	(Specified in a circular by the Head of the Business Section.) 30% of net assets.

RISK MANAGEMENT OF SECURITIES COMPANIES UNDER REVIEW

In recent years, securities companies have worked to expand their operations and the range of products they handle. In the future, they will have to pay increased attention to risk management. In practice, of course, Japanese securities companies are carrying out their own risk management and have imposed internal rules regarding positions in individual products which are even more demanding than those laid down in legal provisions and government guidance (see Table 5.8). In addition, Japanese securities companies are more heavily capitalized than their counterparts overseas and this is a favourable strength in dealing with risks (see Table 5.9). However, as more new products are introduced, securities companies will have to pay especially close attention to the risks of liquidity and price fluctuations.

At the same time, however, one of the main functions of securities companies is risk-taking; they cannot completely avoid risks. Instead, in those areas where they should take risks, the issue for securities companies will be to manage that risk. Important tasks will include attaining accurate risk-appraisals, putting systems in place to deal with it, and training personnel capable of dealing effectively with risk.

Table 5.9   The net worth of securities companies (billions of yen)

Japan		USA		UK	
Nomura Securities	949.0	Salomon Brothers	449.0	Morgan Grenfell	43.0*
Daiwa Securities	624.0	Merrill Lynch	373.9	Klinewort Benson	53.7*
Nikko Securities	583.2	Shearson Lehman	176.5	S.G. Warburg	43.2**
Yamaichi Securities	488.0	First Boston	124.7		
		Morgan Stanley	102.1		

Notes: 1. Japan statistics are from the end of September 1987; US statistics are from
the SIA-Yearbook, end of December 1986; British statistics are as follows:
*1985, **end of March 1986, and *The Economist*, 16 August 1986.
2. In the case of the net worth given above the figures are from financial
statements and in the USA are not considered as net capital. In UK the
figures are not considered as qualifying capital.

MOVEMENT TO ESTABLISH INTERNATIONAL CAPITAL STANDARDS FOR SECURITIES COMPANIES

As the effects of Black Monday, which began in New York, and
spread to Tokyo and London, suggest, world securities markets have
become substantially more international and interdependent. It has
therefore become essential to carry out risk-management from a
global perspective; the domestic perspective alone is no longer sufficient. The bank regulatory authorities in various nations have
recently cooperated in the establishment of uniform capital standards
for banks (see Tables 5.10 and 5.11). Similarly, the International
Organization of Securities Commissions is engaged in discussions of
international capital and risk management standards for securities
companies. Japan's securities companies are cooperating in this
movement and will go on to consider the issue of proper risk management in detail in the coming years (see Table 5.12).

It is impossible to ignore the fact that competition is becoming
more intense and that risk is increasing. In response, we are managing our positions and hedging the risks in a diverse range of financial
products, giving proper attention to the special characteristics of each
of these products. We are also acutely aware of the need to
strengthen our distribution power, which is the best hedge against
risk.

Table 5.10   The Bank for International Settlements capital standards (as agreed on 11 July 1988): definition of capital

Formula (basic rules)	Capital	=	[Tier I] (unlimited inclusion of core capital)	+	[Tier II] (other capital which may be included up to the amount in Tier I)	−	[deductible items]	

> Tier I: Capital and official reserves
> (capital account)
>
> Tier II: Allowance for loan losses (an upper limit of
> 1.25% on a risk asset ratio basis)*
> Hidden profits from negotiable securities (45%
> may be included)
> Non-maturity subordinated debt
> Subordinated debt with maturities (up to 50% of
> the value of Tier I is the limit)
> Obligatory convertible securities

Interim
measures   During the interim period (the five years beginning the end of 1987, and ending with the conclusion of 1992), a portion of the Tier II inclusion will be added to Tier I as described below and this will be considered Tier I.

Up to 25% of the initial amoung considered to be Tier I
(Capital = Tier I × 2.66)

Up to 10% of the amount considered to be Tier I at the end of 1990
(Capital = Tier I × 2.22)

Initially the allowance for doubtful accounts is unlimited.
After the elapse of three years, 1.5% may be included.*

Deductions   ● Goodwill (deducted from Tier I).
● Financing for non-consolidated subsidiaries and affiliates
(deducted from total capital)
● Deduction of capital in cross holdings is up to the discretion
of the authorities in each country.

Note: *With the proviso that agreement is not reached by the end of 1990 concerning the overall method for inclusion of untied reserves and allowances included within capital.

Table 5.11   The BIS capital standards: method of computation of risk assets

On balance sheet assets	Asset value × risk weight by asset categories = risk asset
Off balance sheet asset	Transactions value × risk weight by asset categories × risk asset categories = risk asset

*The four stages of 100% of the assessment rate of collateral (guarantee of obligation), 50% (NIF and RUF), 20% (trade related L/Cs), and 0% (commitments under one year). Additionally, the risk asset amount of interest and foreign exchange transactions (such as swaps) is computed in a different way.

Table 5.12   The BIS capital standards: risk weights

Risk weights		Asset categories
	0%	Cash, deposits and claims in the central bank of the bank's home country, loans to the central government of the bank's country, bonds issued by the central government of the bank's country, loans and other assets maintained by cash and bonds issued by the central government of the bank's country.
	20%	Bonds of domestic banks or foreign banks with a maturity of under one year. Claims on domestic banks with a maturity of one year or more and loans of one year or more guaranteed by domestic banks.
	50%	Private housing loans
	100%	Claims on the private sector; claims on foreign banks with a maturity of one year or over; land, buildings, equipment and other fixed assets used in the bank's business; fund raising instruments of other banks (when not deducted from net worth); all other assets.
Left to the discretion of each country	0 or 20%	Bonds of the World Bank, or regional development banks; public sector bonds and other claims other than those of the domestic central government; loans
	0, or 20, or 60%	guaranteed by public entities other than the central government of the bank's home country.

Table 5.13 Summary of the system of capital regulation in selected countries

	Japan	USA	UK
The regulated aspect of net worth	Balance sheet (B/S) capital + reserve for trading losses + reserve for securities transactions exposure − external outflow of funds + gains from appreciation of securities = Net value of assets	B/S capital + subordinated debt − deductible asset items (fixed assets etc.) − *hair cut* amount = Net capital	B/S capital + subordinated loans + unused limit on guarantees − guarantees outstanding − losses of subsidiaries − asset deduction items + unused position for subordinated loan facilities = eligible capital

Position/
net worth ratios
	Own-account stocks
	Net value of assets* 40%
	Securities investment account
	Net value of assets* 30%
	Gensaki outstanding within the scope of the net value of assets
	Overseas financial futures within the scope of the net value of assets
		hair cut amount
		government securities
		municipal bonds
		CP BA CDs
		convertible bonds
		preferred stocks
		Risk arbitrage and detailed rates for position amounts of each product.
			Necessary amount for total capital =(1)+(2)+(3)
			(1) Position risk requirement
			    Securities
			    Bonds
			    Financial futures, options
			    Swaps
			    NIFs and detailed rates for position amounts of each product

(continued)

Table 5.13   continued

	Japan	USA	UK
The minimum amount of capital required for business operations	Capital Integrated securities cos. ¥3 billion Managing underwriter securities cos. ¥1 billion	Net capital Under basic guidelines $25 000 Not under basic guidelines $100 000	(2) Counter party risk requirement Amount outstanding (unsettled) Margin transactions outstanding, etc. (3) Base Requirement Clearing Companies £250 000 Other companies £ 10 000 and three other types of regulations
Liability limits	10 times the amount of net assets	* 15 times the amount of net capital under basic guidelines * 2% of the asset account balance otherwise (customer transactions)	The condition; eligible capital ⩾(1)+(2)+(3) must be met at all times

Source: Securities Association Deliberative Council, Tokyo, March 1988.

SUMMARY

1. Japan has maintained an orderly financial services industry through the separation of different types of financial service activities and the avoidance of excessive competition. This system of specialized financial institutions has been efficient in managing the risks faced by companies in these various financial service sectors.
2. Beginning in the 1980s, however, the pressures for deregulation and internationalization of Japan's financial system have grown, thus leading to growing competition in the financial services industry. Competition has intensified because of the trend toward introduction of new services and products, the entry of foreign financial institutions into the Japanese market, and the lowering of the barriers between the operations of banks and securities companies. As a result of the growing diversity of products offered by securities companies, as deregulation and internationalization have proceeded, the risks faced by securities companies have increased and become more diverse. Moreover, forecasting the risks which will arise as a result of the introduction of new products is very difficult. Losses, however, in some cases may be very substantial.
3. For banks, the central banks of various nations have recently decided upon uniform capital standards. Consideration of similar standards is underway in the international securities industry. The Japanese monetary authorities and Japanese securities companies are expected to cooperate in giving full consideration to risk management. The capital of Japanese securities companies is large in comparison with foreign companies engaged in the securities business and this works in their favour in management of risk. But, on the other hand, a uniform system for risk management has not been established. Developing and improving such a system will be essential in the years ahead. One of the functions of securities companies is to take risk; they cannot completely avoid all risks. The risk management systems should be able to give an accurate appraisal of the nature and magnitude of risks and to control them.

6 A Universal Bank's Corporate Philosophy: The Challenges and Opportunities Ahead

Walter Seipp

NEW STRATEGIES AND PERSPECTIVES IN BANKING BY THE YEAR 2000

Never before have the banks been subjected to such a transformation as in the past decade. However, there is probably consensus within the banking community that the next decade will also produce major changes. Any remarks on 'New strategies and perspectives in banking by the year 2000' nonetheless seem like an attempt to indulge in crystal-gazing.

This is all the more the case since changes in the business sector and in society as a whole affect banks much more than other enterprises. The banking industry is closely bound up with all the other sectors of the economy through both its lending and its funding activities. Moreover, this is true at the national and the international level.

Not only market conditions but also the overall setting are constantly changing, and these influence the activities of the banks in a highly complex way involving a broad spectrum that includes such concepts as world trade, a world currency, demographic trends and legislation. However, this chapter will be restricted to a few problem complexes which I consider essential and which have a direct bearing on future developments.

GLOBAL BANKING

Let me start with one of the key words of the past decade: 'globalization'. This concept implies more than just the intention to set up a branch, a subsidiary, or a representative office in some part of the world. Rather, it means that the financial markets, with their restrictions removed, are made to work for our customers right around the world and also right around the clock. In addition to the ever stronger trend towards globalization, another phenomenon has emerged over the past few years under the heading 'securitization' – namely, the raising of funds in the form of marketable securities rather than by means of traditional loans.

Since the stock-market crash in October 1987, however, we have experienced a renaissance of traditional lending activity. Our customers are now showing greater interest again in a solid and lasting relationship with their bank. This strengthens so-called relationship banking at the expense of transaction banking, which tends to be typical of the investment banking domain.

I believe that commercial banking can now look forward to a promising future again throughout the world. And it is no contradiction to add that investment banking will retain the significance that it has rapidly gained over the past few years. Quite certainly, we cannot put the clock back here. In the space of just a few years, the character of modern banking has changed more than it had previously in the course of several decades. The driving force behind such a transformation is provided by the underlying economic and financial conditions, which are changing ever more quickly and radically. The movements of interest rates, exchange rates and share prices as the process of deregulation takes effect are the main factors which suggest that commercial and investment banking will have roughly equal weight in future as well.

Naturally, there can easily be fluctuations between credit-based financing, on the one hand, and securities-based financing, on the other. In other words, the globalization of banking, which primarily affected investment banking in the first half of the 1980s, will be maintained in the future, but it will extend to commercial banking as well. Right from the outset, Commerzbank, which – in commercial banking – was fairly quick to establish a presence for itself abroad through individual bases, recognized the significance of globalization. As West Germany's private-sector commercial banks have traditionally pursued a 'universal' – or all-purpose – banking approach, it has not been difficult for them to step up their global banking activities.

Today, my bank has an international organization, which – thanks to its comprehensive and closely-knit network of outlets – is in a position to realize the opportunities offered by the various time zones and the electronic channels of distribution. This represents a *conditio sine qua non* for international business. I personally believe that globalization will continue, though perhaps at a less spectacular tempo as far as innovations and the penetration of new markets are concerned. Yet, if only because of the persistent though somewhat weaker trend towards securitization and the diversification of assets, international securities holdings and trading activities will keep on expanding. While the revenues from the sale of oil are still an important factor, US pension funds and Japanese institutional investors in particular have recently been playing a more prominent role in this respect.

We often hear the complaint that the financial innovations developed in connection with global banking are suitable instruments only for banks and large-scale institutional investors; smaller businesses, above all, are said to have been neglected. Actually, precisely the opposite is true. The instruments and techniques that are available today have been refined to such a degree that they can now be used by smaller firms as well. In view of the uncertainties surrounding interest and exchange-rate trends, and given the large number of companies which have so far been rather wary about using the more recent funding instruments and hedging devices, I expect to see West German firms avail themselves more readily of the opportunities which these instruments offer in the near future.

At all events, foreign-currency options, interest futures, interest-rate caps and, above all, swaps are to be found among the standard products which my bank offers small to medium-sized businesses. Moreover, for some time now, we have registered quite brisk demand for them on the part of such customers.

INTERNATIONAL DEBT

The international debt problems continue to weigh heavily on the world's financial markets. The annual meetings of the World Bank and IMF, held in 1988 in West Berlin, provided no radically new insights in this respect. Quite the contrary, in fact: it became evident that there is no realistic alternative to the course that is already being followed. Nonetheless, some confusion was created before the meetings, and on the sidelines while they were in progress, by renewed demands for either complete, or at least partial, debt forgiveness. This discussion, while unnecessary, of course, did in fact lead to two central points becoming very clear once again – even for the general public.

First, debt forgiveness – either partial or complete – is not a viable option. Second, the West German banks – in a display of solidarity with the international banking community – are adhering to the basic approach that has served them well up to now and is ultimately the only one that is likely to succeed.

We should not overlook the fact that the enormous need for capital on the part of the less developed and newly industrialized countries can only be met in the long run if these states either remain credit-worthy or their creditworthiness can be restored. The prime goal must be to restore the creditworthiness of the rescheduling countries so as to ensure that they can finance their economic future. I am convinced that debt forgiveness would be an admission that these efforts had come to nothing. After realizing their losses, the creditors involved would presumably no longer be willing to take on such risks again. This would prove a fatal strategy for the debtor-country. Not only would the latter lose its creditworthiness, but it would also isolate itself from the world trade system. The country in question would become insolvent and the inflow of capital from abroad would come to an abrupt end. It would be cut off from international flows of funds for years to come. In addition, there would be cause to fear that the negative experience gained with some countries would unfortunately also be projected on to others which are still credit-worthy at the moment and are able to take up credits. The solution of the debt issue today is closely connected, therefore, with lending tomorrow.

Let me add a marginal note here. Often, we as banks are told that we have already forgiven private companies their debts – for example, AEG. Why, then, can we not do the same for the less developed countries? I believe that the answer is clear. In the case of firms which are threatened with bankruptcy yet can be rescued, we are able to exert an influence over who forms the management. In this way, we can infuse the firm with fresh motivation, and generate new ideas and initiative for saving it. It is not possible, therefore, to draw a comparison between the debtor-countries and private companies. Through debt forgiveness, we cannot alter the corruption, misman-agement or simply the wrong choice of economic policy in the countries in question.

All in all, however, I believe that we have no reason to make the debt crisis more dramatic than it really is. We must continue along the stony path of long-term rescheduling, coupled with the – for the time being, involuntary – provision of new loans. In this connection, it would be good to see the menu of options made as broad as possible, so that the largest number of banks will be able to go on participating in the rescheduling process.

One practicable possibility is debt/equity swaps. These represent the transformation of claims on borrowers into equity holdings – for instance, in factories, hotels, plantations, raw material resources or similar objects in Third World countries. This instrument permits rescheduling countries to repay part of their external debt in their own national currency. Up to now, we at Commerzbank have arranged such debt/equity swaps for others. But we now want to use this instrument for the first time in order to take up a direct stake in a bank in Latin America.

Generally speaking, other possibilities within the menu approach can also be explored, on a case-by-case basis. They must be in line with market principles and take into consideration both the specific situation of the countries involved and their economic policy. 'Exit bonds' or debt repurchase agreements can be helpful in this connection. Exit bonds, however, should be used to no more than a limited extent so that not too many banks – and especially the larger ones – shake off the responsibility they bear for the future of the debtor-countries.

The next step must be to find solutions which cover longer periods of time. In this way, we might be able to prevent fresh uncertainties from emerging every year and sometimes even the availability of commercial credit lines from becoming jeopardized. For loan agreements in the future, for instance, it would be worth investigating whether new credits should not be made available over a longer period of time, rather than being granted for immediate use. The funds provided could then be drawn upon if the country found itself acutely in need of financing. It would be difficult to organize a reserve of this kind, yet there should be sufficient good will on the part of debtors and creditors alike to enable us to realize pragmatic solutions here.

At all events the debt crisis should not be dramatized unnecessarily. Since it came to a head in 1982, notable progress has been made. For this reason, the emphasis must generally remain on implementing a strategy of cooperation. The key problem of indebtedness is not primarily the repayment of debts; rather, the crucial point is to ensure that adequate interest is paid. For this to be possible, the problem countries have to become efficiently functioning economies again. Efforts are needed on the part of the countries in question to achieve this goal, for example, through structural adjustment and by reinforcing the confidence of domestic and foreign investors. Equally necessary is action by the industrial nations to make sure that their markets are opened up, or to hold interest rates steady and sustain economic growth in the longer term. We as banks have not abandoned the hope that the debts will be serviced. Moreover, this is underlined by the fact that we have not completely 'written off' the claims we hold; we have merely created loan loss provisions for the time being. In the last analysis, though, we have to bear in mind that the less developed and newly industrialized countries are by definition states that import rather than export capital.

However, despite all the efforts, some especially disadvantaged countries will not in the end find their way back to the market. Instead, they will remain dependent on the charity of the rich nations – in other words, they will require development aid. But we must all work together to prevent a misleading public debate and adoption of the wrong policies – no matter whether on the debtors' or the creditors' side – from pushing into this category countries which do not belong there – the major Latin-American debtors in particular.

EUROPE AFTER 1992

1992 presents the banks with a further challenge. The environment in which we operate within the European Community (EC) will be transformed once capital transactions are liberalized as planned, banks are allowed to set up shop anywhere they choose, and financial services can be offered throughout the entire EC. It is impossible to say in general terms how banks will adapt their strategy to meet these challenges. Here individual strategies, and not least the resources at a bank's disposal, will prove crucial.

Every bank must decide for itself in which markets and in which EC member states it might be worthwhile to increase its presence. Similarly, each bank must establish how it can explore new markets, what organizational form is best suited to 'going European', and to what extent it has the means to pursue this target. However, nobody has yet come up with a definite strategy here. All Western Europe's major banks are involved in working out their own approach to the issue at the moment. For me, the topic of 'Europe after 1992' means first and foremost an enlargement of our home market. Generally speaking, the major West German banks have gained valuable experience through both 'global banking' and the challenge of international competition. This gives them a good basis for successfully participating in the future European market for banking services.

In our planning, we assume that such participation must be smoothly integrated into our worldwide strategy. Otherwise, there would be the danger that, by stepping up our European activities, we would perhaps no longer be in a position to seize the opportunities for expansion in other parts of the world. As an internationally active institution, we certainly do not want to restrict ourselves to the status of being no more than a 'European' bank.

As far as European business is concerned, quite different strategies will have to be adopted for the various segments. We already offer investment banking on a global basis; moreover, we do so rather successfully – and not only in Europe. For wholesale banking, which is the first area in which keener competition can now be expected to develop, the same holds true. Here we already have a solid international position. However, in retail banking we would sooner or later have been confronted with the need to decide how and where we should build up a stronger European presence – which brings me to the real core problem of our future strategy for Europe: are we to buy financial institutions in other countries, or should we seek to cooperate with them? Commerzbank opted for a strategy of cooperation. The decision was prompted, for one thing, by tradition – it can now look back on more than a decade of cooperation within the Europartners Group. But it was, above all, business-policy considerations which persuaded us that this was the right course for us. Through cooperation, after all, we are able to use existing nationwide branch networks in other European countries without having to commit a lot of capital in order to do so.

It is not necessary to establish mutual cross-shareholdings before cooperation is intensified, yet these can prove to be useful. In addition, they serve as a protection against hostile takeover bids. Back in 1984, Commerzbank took a step in this direction by acquiring a 10 per cent interest in the equity capital of the major Spanish bank, Banco Hispano Americano. We believe that the cooperation model which we favour will ensure a more rational employment of the available capital. The joint financial muscle of the partner banks might, therefore, be greater than the sum of the individual parts.

The advantages of such cooperation agreements lie principally in the fact that partners can tap each other's existing know-how and human resources. Differences of emphasis in business activities, or in the banks' regional specialization – or in national mentality, for that matter – can in fact complement each other and therefore prove to be an advantage. As far as the practical results of cooperation are concerned, however, we are probably still in the early stages. We should think very carefully about the products which we could offer on a joint basis in future. Only when such 'European products' have established themselves in the market will the Europe-wide market in banking services have become reality.

ALL-INCLUSIVE FINANCIAL SERVICES ('ALLFINANZ')

In the meantime, the trend towards all-inclusive financial service packages – or 'Allfinanz' as it is called in German – has developed into a topic that can be compared to the debate on the pros and cons of 'universal' banks versus the dual system of commercial and invest-ment banking. Both issues are of great relevance for the future and determine the shape of new business strategies. Although we are still on the verge of any major breakthroughs today, the phase of the outsiders and the experiments is clearly coming to an end. This is inevitable as fresh examples of institutions providing all-round financial services are springing up on all sides. Several banks, in-surance firms and home loan associations have already taken the initiative. In doing so, they have set yardsticks for – and perhaps even brought pressure to bear on – the majority of banks which have up to now adhered to the traditional division of labour in the financial services industry. As a result, we find home loan associations, whose traditional market has been shrinking for some time, moving in the direction of the universal bank by attempting to broaden the palette of financial services which they offer. The life insurance companies are steadily increasing their share of monetary asset-formation. By acquiring interests in banks or through cooperation agreements, they are forming large financial concerns, offering a wide range of services which directly compete with those marketed by the banks.

Today, there is no such thing as a clearly-defined market for bank products and services. Rather, banks are now active in areas which were previously not typical of them. At the same time, non-banks in the financial services sector are offering individual bank products as well. In addition, completely new competition is emerging from the non-financial sector; namely, from department stores, retail chains and mail-order houses.

The public debate on all-inclusive financial services frequently overlooks the fact that the actual root problem is not so much the competition between products as that between sales outlets. Admittedly, the products do still differ to some extent, but not as regards their general targets. In other words, despite certain discrepancies in detail, investment or funding instruments do not differ radically in their overall effect. The variations that occur relate to risks, maturities, interest or repayment terms and tax aspects. Quite frequently, acceptable alternatives are offered to consumers which the latter will select to coincide with their personal preferences and individual situation.

From all this it becomes evident that priority must go to discovering or pinpointing needs rather than presenting customers with a set range of preconceived products and services. The same effort should be put into forging contacts with customers – and non-customers, for that matter – as is invested in the products themselves. These can be shaped, varied or – as we now say in our sector – customized. The distinction, therefore, is to be found less in how well problems are solved, or in the product itself; it is more a question of who is able to pinpoint needs and in what way the latter are met. This is where the systems begin to compete; and this is what the topic of all-round financial services is about. Put in quite concrete terms: is a network of branch offices sufficient for servicing the market, or do we need more mobile sales personnel? This question is by no means restricted to organizational aspects. It also affects the qualifications which a financial institution's personnel should possess and has consequences for the company's internal structure.

Primarily, above-average staff are needed to run a field service of this kind. The negotiations conducted in private with clients tend to call for expert knowledge, the lack of which cannot be offset by greater sales efforts alone. What can, if necessary, be discussed by a number of specialists at a branch or at head office, has to be handled by the sales agent out in the field all by himself, without any help from outside. For this reason, such people have in the past tended to concentrate on a selected range of products. In the meantime, though, they have been constantly obliged to expand the scope of what they offer in order to boost their earnings.

Nevertheless, all-rounders are very rare in the domain of financial services. Consequently, a field service of quality can only be developed through time-consuming training or by poaching qualified personnel from rival companies. From the commercial standpoint, a poor-quality field service fares worse in a cost–benefit analysis than does an immobile sales organization.

If a bank wishes to secure and extend its market position, it cannot simply continue along the traditional paths, offering its products through fixed outlets and doing business within rigid opening hours. After all, its competitors are marketing the same products on a mobile basis. The bank's relationship with its customers should be made more personal. It must be intensified so that the customer prefers to have a steady relationship with only one bank, and remains loyal to it.

Any business strategy geared to individual groups of customers must differentiate more strongly than has been usual in the past. The range of products should be distinctly classified. Modern information and data-processing technology must be employed to make the range stretch from standardized, simple products to customized solutions for individual problems that require considerable counselling and explanation. Service packages will have to replace isolated individual services. Yet even such cross-selling is increasingly becoming insufficient to win new customers. This is because it covers only bank products.

By extending the product range, it is possible to benefit from diversification and achieve synergy effects. In addition, if banks draw upon information from related areas of business, they can efficiently pool human resources and know-how. Undoubtedly, these are all arguments which favour the all-inclusive financial services approach. The question remains, of course, how the latter can be realized. From my bank's point of view, greater variety can be achieved above all by offering home loan and life insurance products. Yet this does not necessarily mean that we must set up or buy companies of our own. A totally independent solution of this type, involving an extension of my bank's product range, would imply confrontation with companies that have previously been our partners.

We have decided here as well to pursue a cooperation course. Under the present circumstances, it is not our aim to adopt the all-inclusive financial services approach – combining insurance, the provision of home loans and traditional banking – since we consider cooperation with established home loan associations and insurance companies to be a more successful way of offering our customers an all-round financial service package. Our experience hitherto with cooperation agreements has been uniformly good, and we shall continue to pursue this course.

Quite independently of such considerations, however, banks will be obliged to change their selling methods in the future. They have operated exclusively from a fixed base up to now, offering their services at set times. It is becoming more and more imperative that they put their sales system to the best possible use. This is especially important as insurance companies have achieved notable successes through hard selling by their services. In some cases, banks have already begun to complement their immobile sales systems by direct phone selling or by writing directly to customers and even non-customers – employing the so-called 'direct mail' method. In the long run, though, this is not enough.

A systematic, sales-oriented organization is becoming increasingly important. In future, it will not be adequate only to serve customers at the bank. Instead, the bank counsellor may have to visit customers and potential customers outside the bank's business premises. Surveys have revealed that most of the more demanding private customers prefer to have advisers visit them at home.

Bank staff will therefore have to become more mobile. Moreover, some will also have to operate out in the field in the future. If the personnel involved have the right qualifications, they can sell certain complex banking services that require additional explanation. Such a network is able to handle standardized products – including home loan savings schemes and insurance products.

Experience has taught us, however, that a bank employee's specialist knowledge is limited in scope. The real problem is still the knowledge which a client counsellor must have at his fingertips. Even today, he must be familiar with the huge number of products and services which his bank provides. This is what actually determines the quality of the advice that is offered customers. On the one hand, we have the specialists who have a detailed knowledge of only one part of the product range, and on the other, all-round advisers, who are familiar with the whole range though not always right down to the last detail. Here, of course, we are confronted with the dilemma of the all-inclusive financial services approach: we are forced to choose between 'specialization' and selling 'odds and ends'. There is no ingenious solution which we can apply to overcome this conflict. Each bank must select the mixture which best suits its own business-policy goals.

TECHNOLOGY

The introduction of electronics into the customer/bank relationship is surely the last major transformation which data processing has inflicted on the banks. We are still at the start of a development whose progress – in terms of velocity and scale – is difficult to predict at the present time. Yet decisive impulses are to be expected that will substantially alter banking services and the business conducted by banks in the future. What trends are currently emerging?

1. The installation of self-service facilities for dispensing cash and providing information (information on rates and prices, investment recommendations and account statement printers), for use during and outside normal hours of business, is in full swing. Such facilities are being used by our customers to an increasing extent.
2. Home banking: up to now, the forecasts as regards the use of West Germany's videotext service, Btx (Bildschirm text), by retail customers have proved to be very wide of the mark indeed. By contrast, corporate customer business is registering mounting demand for integrated solutions in the field of payments transactions and account management. Through the employment of state-of-the-art communication technology, for instance, we are able to offer our corporate customers a sophisticated cash-management system. As required, daily statements on a company's liquidity position at various banks can be provided on both a national and an international basis. The opportunities afforded by direct computer link-up with banks are being drawn upon by a growing number of clients from the business sector. Apart from a more rational handling of their transactions, companies are deriving special advantages in the form of up-to-date information, greater flexibility and the ability to respond more quickly when shifting their assets.
3. Cooperation with the retail trade: in any future point-of-sale schemes, in particular, retailers will take up direct contact with the data-processing service arm of the banking sector. Now that the German banks have reached agreement at long last on the card to be issued, I expect to see this medium gain substantially in popularity at the expense of the cheque over the next few years. Although the so-called 'supercard' may not be a realistic proposition at the moment, Commerzbank will soon be introducing its own card.

Yet probably the most important factor in the employment of data-processing technology in banking services is whether it is accepted by both customers and the staff of the banks. This technology can only be sensibly employed – in relieving personnel of routine work, improving the quality of the advice offered and enhancing the range of services provided – if it is utilized to the full.

In this connection, it is just as important to take the behaviour of regional and supraregional competitors into consideration as it is to consider the overall pattern of customers and, not least, the corporate identity which is established as a strategical concept by the management of a bank. This last factor in particular is crucial in deciding the response of the individual financial institution to the issue of customer self-service. By systematically equipping offices with computer terminals rather than concentrating on self-service devices, we give priority to improving the quality of the advice we provide. We do so in preference to encouraging our customers to make greater use of self-service installations for handling their transactions. Those who bear the responsibility for taking decisions must make sure that, with technology playing an ever greater role in banking services, the human being – no matter whether an employee or a customer – is not overlooked.

Anyone seeking to develop strategies has to have a corporate philosophy, which describes the goals of the enterprise. These must be accepted by the owners of the company, the employees and the customers alike. The owners will have no difficulty in reaching a consensus over the desire to make profits. But this in itself does not amount to a corporate philosophy. For me, corporate philosophy means that in all areas we have to achieve excellence on our customers' behalf. The yardstick for measuring our success here is, and must surely be, the earnings generated. In order to work towards this end, we at Commerzbank have developed a corporate identity. In other words, we are consciously trying to shape our image and our corporate culture in this direction.

In terms of our strategic planning for the bank, this implies that we risk more by not changing than by changing. This applies to our behaviour and to our goals in equal measure. Ambitious goals are necessary but they must be in harmony with the available resources. Our aim to remain a leading universal bank in the financial markets, and even to reinforce our position, should not be misinterpeted as the ambition to outpace our competitors in quantitative terms. Size alone does not put a bank up among the leaders.

7 Towards the Twenty-First Century: New Strategies and Perspectives for Banking

Rainer E. Gut

A LIKELY SCENARIO FOR THE YEAR 2000

What could the world economy and banking be like in the year 2000? By the turn of the century the USA could account for less than a quarter of world GNP, compared with 40 per cent in the 1960s. The economies of the industrialized countries of the Far East will probably be approaching the national income of the European Community. (Table 7.1) The People's Republic of China will have incorporated capitalist Hong Kong and will be moving towards a free market economy. The Eastern bloc should have had its first taste of trying to create a balance between an open market and socialism. The major objectives of the EC's single-market project will probably have been attained, although Europe will still be a long way short of monetary or even political union. Southern Europe will have considerably narrowed the gap between itself and the North. The international debt crisis may have been overcome. (Table 7.2) The industrialized nations in general may well be suffering less from unemployment than from a distinct shortage of skilled manpower. This will stimulate investment aimed at rationalization. New materials, progress in health care and alternative energy sources will also stimulate capital spending. Modern techniques in the fields of organization, communication and automation could boost productivity considerably.

The corporate environment will have changed radically. Competitive pressure will have led to mergers and takeovers, and a good number of firms could have gone to the wall. The 1990s could have proved to be a difficult period in spite of the numerous advances and opportunities; the restructuring process will have claimed a large number of victims. The forces of 'creative destruction', which the economist Schumpeter saw as the underlying principle of free market

Table 7.1   Gross National Product

| | 1965 | | 1988 | | 2000 | |
	US$bn	%	US$bn	%	US$bn	%
Whole world, of which:	1 750	100	16 000	100	38 000	100
USA	702	40	4 850	30	9 500	25
EC	459	26	4 700	29	9 600	25
Far East*	60	9	3 450	22	9 000	24

* Japan, Australia, New Zealand, Hongkong, Singapore, Taiwan, South Korea, Malaysia

Table 7.2   International debt, 1988

| | Total developing countries | | Latin America | |
	US$bn	%	US$bn	%
Total debt of which:	1229		411	
long-term guaranteed	928	100	381	100
Official	481	52	98	26
Banks	375	40	210	55
Other private	72	8	73	19

economics, are likely to have been especially relentless in the 1990s. Many of the companies that survived, on the other hand, should be in much better shape than they are today, The more intensive the search for new methods, the greater the need for highly-skilled staff. In many countries, by the end of this century only one in four, or even five, members of the workforce will be working in industry; the rest will be involved in services industries.

Banking is one of the branches of the dynamic services sector that is powering the world economy. What changes could have been taken place here by the year 2000? The harsh climate which also prevailed in this sector of the economy in the 1990s will have weeded out inefficient firms and reduced the number of banks that can claim a truly global presence. Over-capacity will have been corrected, under-capitalized companies will have found shelter with capital-rich partners or disappeared from the market. Generally speaking, the banking industry will probably have become healthier; investors in equities are likely to acknowledge this fact, which will subsequently be reflected in higher price earnings ratios of bank shares. Increasingly, banks will be 'up all night' as 24-hour trading is extended to new banking operations.

In the USA the Glass–Steagall Act could well have become much less rigid so that the only sectors still closed to financial institutions will be insurance and real-estate development. Japan will have made more progress towards a universal banking system. The EC's single market will also have helped to make full-service banks more attractive. A universal bank licensed in one EC country will be able to offer its full range of services in any member-state – including any EC countries that retain a legal division between commercial and investment banking. Pressure to remove this division worldwide will, therefore, have become intense.

STRUCTURAL CHANGE IN THE BANKING INDUSTRY: THE FULL-SERVICE BANK IS THE SHAPE OF THINGS TO COME

So will European-style full-service banking be the organizational form of the future? 'Universal banking system: going from strength to strength'; 'Is this the age of the universal bank?' These are the kind of comments we often hear. The efforts of legislators and regulatory authorities in the major countries are directed at dismantling the barriers between commercial and investment banking. A number of governments have already dispensed with these divisions either in part or completely. In the UK the equity and bond markets were opened to banks some two years ago. Canada removed most of the barriers between the business carried out by banks, trust companies, insurance companies and securities houses in mid-1987. In Japan the strict partition between commercial and investment banking is already being breached. Japanese commercial banks have set up investment banking subsidiaries abroad which in turn maintain an unofficial presence in Japan. Similarly, the four big Japanese investment companies have banking subsidiaries in London. In the USA, liberalizing measures have the fundamental backing of the Treasury, the Federal Reserve Board and the Federal Deposit Insurance Corporation. The process of securitization was an important catalyst; it deprived commercial banks of a slice of business with their major clients and gave them in turn the urge to move into securities business. There is still a wide spread of opinion in the US Congress. The current thinking in both Chambers is that banking and investment business should be carried out through separate subsidiaries under one holding company. Further legal divisions could be built in. American financial institutions fear that in their country, where there is a long tradition of regulation in the banking and financial systems, a multiplicity of controls could take away some of the muscle they have recently acquired. Nevertheless, the universal banking system is gaining ground the world over.

Why is there this preference for a mode of operation that allows almost all banking services to be carried out under one roof? Banks, governments and regulatory authorities consider that the benefits of this system far outweigh the disadvantages. Let us therefore briefly examine the strengths and weaknesses of the two systems in order to find out which is better suited to the challenges that lie ahead.

THE STRENGTHS AND WEAKNESSES OF FULL-SERVICE BANKING

The first weakness resides in the possible conflict of interests between individual business sections of the same bank. The sale of securities to investors can clash with the bank's deposit business. The interests of the securities underwriting departments may well run counter to those of investment advice and portfolio management. Credit departments will have viewed with suspicion the process of securitization, that is, the move away from bank loans and into tradeable securities. Employees who see their area of operations being eclipsed may become disillusioned. In fact, there is a kind of poetic justice at work here in the long term; lending business has recently become more attractive again, after a long period when stock markets and investment banking boomed.

Second, there is a danger that the standard of services offered by universal banks will slip to mediocre levels and fall short of the performance of specialized companies. This phenomenon has often been referred to as 'supermarket banking'.

Third, it is not easy to reconcile all the demands placed on the overall infrastructure of a universal bank. Commercial banking and, in particular, deposit operations require a wide scattering of bank branches, whereas investment banking generally needs only a presence in important national and international centres. Different mech-anisms are therefore necessary to maintain a network of outlets, and at the same time to limit and monitor risks.

Fourth, the demands made on management – because of the complexity and range of banking activities, the international scale of operations and possible conflicting objectives – are heavier than when the banking system is divided along comparatively simple lines into commercial and investment operations. This may well result in friction.

These disadvantages can be countered through adjustments in business policy and organization. Crédit Suisse has established a divisional structure that provides for – and actually encourages – healthy competition; but senior management is still there to ensure that we do not lose sight of the ultimate purpose, that is, the good of the bank as a whole, its shareholders and customers. The bonus earned by managers is not linked solely to the performance of their section but to individual performance and the results achieved by the bank generally. We accommodate the wish of big clients, especially multinationals, to transact business with various sections of the bank, but at the same time to have a single relationship manager who coordinates their business with the various departments. We counter-act the risk of mediocrity by appointing product officers with a high level of specialized knowledge who lay particular stress on basic training and regular advanced training, and who are able to entrust the *crème de la crème* of our clientele to especially qualified and expert staff. I will be returning to these questions later.

The potential weaknesses, which can be counteracted by the right policy decisions, have to be set against considerable strengths. The full-service bank's involvement in practically all business areas means that all the customer's diverse financial needs can be catered for under one roof. This makes it easier to retain our clients and to build up a lasting relationship with them. This is again emerging as a particularly strong advantage now that the extremes of deal-based banking seem to be going out of favour.

A full-service bank also has a wide range of cross-selling options. These can boost the net value of a customer relationship. Finally – and this is probably the most significant advantage – universal banks enjoy a wider earnings base. A decline in earnings in one sector can be made good to some extent by increased profits in other areas. For example, after the worldwide stock-market crash last October, losses incurred in securities business could be partially offset by improved earnings in loans and foreign-exchange business. The possibility of spreading risks in this way encourages a bold business policy. Greater earnings stability makes universal banks more attractive to investors. A bank's rating also tends to benefit from a more solid earnings structure, a factor that is all the more important since the fight for survival in the years to come will focus mainly on the struggle for profits. The fundamental question a bank's management will have to answer is how to ensure the long-term profitability against a background of changing financial circumstances and fiercer competition.

THE UNIVERSAL BANK AND THE CHALLENGE OF INVESTMENT BANKING

Given that the benefits of a universal banking operation far outweigh the disadvantages and that almost all sections of the financial world accept the advantages of this type of bank, can the big Swiss banks therefore rest on their laurels and watch as rivals from other countries wrestle with a system that is new to them? Are we simply to wait until these competitors have created an organizational structure that matches our own?

We should not jump to this conclusion. Certainly it is my belief that by the turn of the century the full-service bank will be the dominant organizational form in the financial sector. It will differ in character, however, from the traditional universal banks now seen in continental Europe. These were shaped at a time when domestic markets were still largely self-contained and economic measures such as the deregulation of financial markets were not high on the agenda of Western governments.

The organization and philosophy of universal banks were therefore determined by national traditions. Foreign branches were processing offices without any significant powers of their own. The corporate culture was dominated by traditional lending operations, even though the proportion of off-balance-sheet business to total turnover was already high. It was not uncommon for four or five executive directors and also the Chairman of the Board to come from the credit sector. Stable client relationships were a feature of such a culture. Banking was seen as a business that extended over generations. But tradition and established practice also dominated underwriting and investment counselling. Agreements and syndicates of all kinds had the effect of limiting competition. Arranging and processing transactions took up a great deal of time. Investment policy was viewed from a long-term perspective and its primary aim was the conservation of a client's assets. Investment advisers were guided by the principle that money should be left in peace to accumulate. Staff were usually engaged more in administrative and monitoring tasks than in active selling.

By the same token, different cultures have grown up in countries with a legal division between commercial and investment banking. There, investment banking is characterized by intense competition, haggling for the most favourable terms, a looser client relationship, an investment philosophy based on performance and trading, a thirst for experimentation and innovation, and a workforce with an eagle eye for market opportunities, whose remuneration is largely linked to success.

For a long time, these two different corporate cultures existed fairly happily side by side. Then they were brought into opposition by deregulation in the banking industry and the globalization of financial markets. The big American securities houses, in particular, attracted attention because of their active marketing, the aggressive commitment of their staff and the speed of their decision-making. There was a danger that the traditional full-service banker would be steamrollered by the new breed of bankers. Crédit Suisse, which for years has been able to call on a leading operator on the Euroissue market and a prominent securities-trading organization in the form of Crédit Suisse-First Boston (CSFB), was not unfamiliar with this 'new world' of investment banking.

Traditional universal banks must come to terms with this new corporate culture and make any necessary structural changes if they want to avoid seeing their business activity suffer in the 1990s. This would appear to be immediately self-evident. But is it in fact accurate? Did not last October's stock-market crash finally lift the veil from investment banking? Are we perhaps about to return to the old school of conservative banking that has proved itself over many years?

THE DYNAMIC FORCES IN BANKING IN THE 1990s

In my opinion the answer to the questions posed above is, basically 'no'. The worldwide collapse in share prices has certainly provided a welcome rest from the rapid process of structural change in international financial markets. But the wheel of change does not turn backwards. In other words the developments that have characterized the 1980s, and which brought about this collision of the two corporate cultures, will continue to shape the 1990s. This applies to the removal of barriers between banking operations, the convergence of individual financial markets, securitization and the tougher competitive climate in which market participants have to work. Particular stimulus in this direction will come from the EC's 1992 programme, which aims to create an integrated financial market in Europe and which will act as a catalyst in certain areas.

Competition between financial centres to remove barriers and thus create more favourable operating conditions will continue in the years ahead. It is true that the regulatory authorities will probably have to take care to ensure that the reins are not slackened excessively. Besides working towards harmonizing banking controls, their efforts will increasingly be directed at establishing an all-embracing regulatory structure for financial markets. But it is surely going too far to talk of this as a re-regulation of the markets. The authorities in the industrialized countries have recognized, after all, that banking is one of the most highly wealth-creating sectors of the economy and one which is extremely remunerative to the fiscal authorities. We have travelled a long way from the masochistic economic policies of the 1970s, which in many countries penalized commercial success and subsidized failure – in vain – using public money. Most governments will continue to espouse the fundamental economic philosophy of encouraging market forces and free enterprise. In particular, we can expect additional moves to liberalize the still highly regulated Japanese market, the further opening-up of banking in Australia and easier access to the markets of Taiwan and South Korea. But the most significant milestone will be laid in the European Community, where the financial markets of individual member-states will be more closely intermeshed and will become more effective as they shrug off their chains. The EC's financial institutions have already started to flex their muscles so that they will be ready to resist the expected onrush of foreign companies or risk a sally of their own beyond their national frontiers.

The stock-market crash has not reversed the trend towards globalization. Admittedly, a number of banks and securities houses have streamlined their international operations and withdrawn from some areas of international business. They were paying the price of over-hasty expansion and their rush to build up outsized structures. But it would be a mistake to pull back to domestic markets on all fronts. The integration of the world economy and the multinational scale of operations of large companies are contributing to the trend towards the globalization of the banking industry. I believe that the movement towards conglomerates will continue on a worldwide basis. Firms are keen to enlarge their product range in response to stiffer competition, to build up their distribution networks and combat the threatened squeeze on profit margins by stepping up production and thereby lowering unit costs. Cross-border takeovers, mergers and new acquisitions will become more and more common. The EC's single-market project will again be a motivating factor. Many EC firms will be trying to establish a presence throughout the Community. Non-EC companies would also like to gain a footing in order to exploit a market of 325 million potential consumers and to gain access to new outlets. The opening-up of the world trade within the framework of the Uruguay Round of GATT talks will also encourage mergers between companies from different countries and continents.

Internationally active banks will be following the path already taken by the companies they service. Advances in telecommunications mean that the technological facilities are certainly there. The prospects of greater stability on foreign exchange and money markets in the 1990s lend weight to this trend. The banks will be able to offer special services in mergers and acquisition deals. This area of activity will more than ever become one of the mainstays of investment banking.

Another reason why investment banking gained in importance in the 1980s has been securitization (the process which changes bank loans and deposits into tradeable securities), for which the death knell was prematurely tolled after the stock-market crash. It is true that syndicated loans have enjoyed a resurgence in the past two years. Surprisingly, however, 1988 has also seen a swift and definite revival in securities offerings. The volume of new Eurobonds this year (1988) for example, will probably be somewhere near the record of $188bn that was set two years ago. This is all the more astonishing given that interest rates have been rising since the spring and the exchange rate front has been rather jittery. So the popularity of borrowing in the form of securities has not flagged by any means. Despite the hard lesson of 19 October 1987, excesses are to be observed again. This is demonstrated by the latest jumbo leveraged buy-outs and the linked use of junk bonds as a financing tool. The decline in interest levels that we may well experience in the course of next year could give a further boost to the securities sector. I expect this trend to continue in the 1990s.

This leads us to the fourth main aspect of investment banking – the sharp rise in significance of institutional investors, which hold the key to large concentrations of capital. Institutional investors prefer securities instruments because they can be traded and therefore allow market opportunities to be exploited. The growth in importance of institutional investors is largely a result of measures aimed at strengthening work-related provisions and at laying a more solid foundation for retirement schemes. Although there is much talk of calling a halt to the expansion of social insurance schemes, there are no plans to reduce actual benefits. With wages rising and interest revenues on the increase, therefore, pension funds and similar social insurance provisions in virtually all the industrial nations will continue to enjoy vigorous growth in terms of their capital assets. Japanese pension funds are currently among the world's largest investors, with total assets worth around $300bn. By the year 2000 the figure is expected to climb to $3000bn. Investment managers throughout the world compete fiercely for the portfolios of US pension funds, whose combined assets amount to roughly $1600bn; by the turn of the century they are likely to be worth $8000bn. Swiss insurance companies and pension funds currently have assets of around Sfr300bn, a total which is expected to more than double by the year 2000.

This relatively small group of VIP clients is in a position to play off banks from various countries against each other and extract far-reaching concessions on commissions. This means that profits are squeezed even harder. Institutional investors are also under pressure to make sure their investments perform well even in the short term. Hence they need banks which can act swiftly, spot lucrative market openings, offer portfolio-management services at a global level and develop attractive new instruments: exactly those qualities which give investment banking its special character.

THE CONSTANT FACTOR IN A CHANGING ENVIRONMENT: TOUGHER COMPETITION

Institutional investors are among the banks' most demanding clients. At the same time, as custodians of large quantities of savings they have also become the banks' direct rivals. Insurance companies are another powerful source of competition for commercial banks. The dividing line between banking and insurance is becoming more and more blurred. Long-standing business partners are now turning into rivals, at least in some market sectors. For example, this is happening in mortgage lending, underwriting of capital market transactions and, in Switzerland, in the provision of tax-privileged retirement savings schemes. Insurance companies are offering more and more services which are similar in character to bank accounts. They are moving further and further into mutual fund business and investment advice, in connection, for example, with the placement of matured policy funds. And because of their well-developed infrastructures they can offer policies similar to bank accounts also outside normal working hours.

Further competition in the banking sector will come from the quasi-banks. These are bank-like companies providing services which so far fall outside the scope of banking legislation. Unhampered by official controls, reporting regulations and capital adequacy requirements, they can thus concentrate on attractive lines of business, notably investment advice and issuing activities. The net result of such competition scarcely needs explanation: pressure on profit margins.

In one important business area, commercial banks face a relatively new source of competition in the form of the major multinationals. Many big corporations now do their own cash management. They try to protect themselves from currency and interest-rate risks and exploit price movements on the financial markets without engaging a bank's services. During the long stock-market boom, this undoubtedly led to certain excesses. The worst of these have now been rectified, but 'in-house banking' is here to stay. Indeed, the changes in the corporate landscape outlined above may well encourage the 'do-it-yourself' trend.

METICULOUS RISK APPRAISAL: AN ESSENTIAL COMPONENT OF BUSINESS STRATEGY

Strong pressure on profit margins will be a constant feature of banking in the next decade. This will present the executive boards of large financial institutions with fundamental decisions. If the right choices are to be made, there must first be careful analysis of the risks to which the banking industry and the financial markets might be subject.

Many financial institutions will be tempted to respond to fiercer competitive pressures, the growing tendency for customers to shop around for the best terms and tighter profit margins by increasing their business volume. This tendency will exist not only in lending operations but also particularly in off-balance-sheet areas such as securities business, investment advice and foreign-exchange trading. Banks following this course are going to discover that higher volumes will bring at best temporary improvement and are no substitute for a truly adequate level of profitability. Deliberately forcing business volume to expand might even have the opposite effect and hasten the company's extinction. One implication of this is that partners in interbank business will have to be selected more carefully than ever.

Risks are also inherent in a number of new financial instruments. Innovative features such as the options and futures markets certainly have their merits, but in terms of risk they are more exposed than the traditional securities markets. Interest-rate swaps and currency swaps, which can in extreme cases involve up to eight parties from all five continents, frequently entail such a complex web of risk-bearing and contractual relationships that it becomes almost impossible to gauge the risk of counterparties defaulting.

Another factor in the risk equation was highlighted by the stock-market crash: the risk of insufficient secondary market liquidity. The crash showed that issuing securities and listing them on the exchange does not necessarily make those securities marketable. Essentially, only leading capital market products find buyers every time. The smaller the volume and the more distinctive the type of offering, the narrower the market for it will be. After the experiences of October 1987 the extremely wide range of instruments available was pruned back, not least as a result of pressure from investors, but it remains to be seen whether the lesson that was learnt will be remembered for long in such an extremely competitive market.

Finally, risks can arise from changes in the macroeconomic operating environment. Business cycles are still with us. The downturn may be postponed for political reasons and by means of monetary and fiscal measures, but sooner or later the day of reckoning will come. One risk is that, in the event of a recession, over-generous lending might quickly result in cash-flow problems for the banks concerned. Similarly, the financing of leveraged buy-outs through junk bonds can create problems; investors then make a new risk-based assessment of their investments and this high-yield paper can come under heavy pressure. Assets, moreover, suffer qualitative deterioration in times of recession, thus, increasing the need for provisions and write-offs. At the same time, worldwide changes in the corporate landscape will mean the demise of many firms, and this calls for extra foresight and caution on the part of the banks.

STRATEGIES FOR THE 1990s

All that has been said so far shows that the financial markets will be the scene of fierce competition in the 1990s. By no means all existing institutions will be able to withstand such pressures. Risks should not be underestimated. Expansion of business volume is no lasting solution: the sole answer lies in maintaining and reinforcing earning power. Universal banks are likely to be the best-equipped to face the challenges ahead, although they too will have to make adjustments. They will have to widen their existing corporate culture to include the kind of approach already usual in investment banking. Which strategies are to be adopted to achieve these aims? In the following six points I would like to suggest some answers.

1. Management will have its work cut out to wed the two distinct corporate approaches. We cannot afford simply to throw the achievements of full-service banking out of the window. Long-standing customer relationships based on trust are a valuable asset for any bank. On the other hand, sticking rigidly to the system as it stands would result in stagnation or indeed regression. So business philosophy must be framed in such a way as to allow the investment banking approach and that of the universal bank to be of mutual benefit. There are many ways of doing this. Crédit Suisse has chosen its own course and with the recent reorganization of the Crédit Suisse (CS)–Crédit Suisse-First Boston (CSFB)–First Boston Corporation (FBC) constellation which proved so effective in the 1980s, it has laid the foundations for continued success as a leading international investment bank in the next decade. Simplified management structures, a clear delineation of product responsibilities and the regional division of business activities will make it easier to achieve our ambitious goals in investment banking. We expect a high degree of synergy from the partnership between Crédit Suisse – based in Switzerland but globally active and with great placing power at its disposal – and CS First Boston Inc. – a wordwide investment-bank group. This synergy will derive from the fact that each partner can contribute what it is best at doing.

2. As with any company, a bank's success and long-term survival depend on how well the customers' needs are identified and how far its products and services satisfy those needs. The old attitude of 'if you want us, you know where you can find us' has finally had its day. Borrowing requirements can only be recognized and satisfied by approaching clients, showing them what the options are and working with them to find the one that is most effective. Hard selling is the key to success: this tenet of market economics is particularly valued in the hotly disputed financial markets.

Another attitude that is now obsolete is expressed in the old marketing dictum: 'Every client is a king.' The needs of a universal bank's smaller customers can be met properly and adequately by standardized products. 'Standardized' does not, of course, imply settling for less than the best. Quite the reverse, as such products constitute a distillation of all the expertise of an internationally active bank. But major clients require more intensive servicing and more comprehensive advice tailored to their particular circumstances. In return, they are willing to pay the sort of commissions justified by such attention. It is in these areas that full-service banks must be able to hold their own against the more specialized financial institutions. The universal banks' main advantage lies in their ability to mobilize their operations swiftly in any of the major financial centres and, for instance, put together complex financial packages within hours. High-quality research is an important aid to selling and an area in which a bank can distinguish itself from its competitors. Research units operating in the major centres emphasise the specialized skills of a bank with worldwide activities. These units provide deeper insight into the countries and markets in which they operate, while Head Office has to ensure that the bank speaks with one voice on major economic and investment policy issues and that all research products are up to international standards.

3. Imitating our rivals' activities will not help us to find out what the customers' needs are. Nor will continual market surveys, at least not on their own. What we need is employees who like front-line action, who have daily contact with what is going on and a thorough knowledge of the customers' problems. In other words, they must go out to the clients. This requires comprehensive and up-to-date training, especially on the job. The nature of a bank employee's work will

continue to change greatly. In the 1990s career advisers will no longer recommend the civil service and the banks as equivalent career options. Soon, junior management will be sent on placements abroad as a matter of course. Someone who has never been exposed to different cultures runs the risks of becoming blinkered and being forced onto the defensive. Managers will increasingly be judged by their ability to discover and promote their subordinates' talents.

4. To be a full-service bank does not mean trying to have a finger in every pie. It is necessary to place special emphasis on certain business areas. Over the next few years, for example, the Far East will see investment banking expand more strongly than lending operations. The leading Swiss banks are unlikely to establish a network of retail operations abroad in the foreseeable future, but within Switzerland they will probably intensify their efforts to ensure a stable deposit base. The countries in which retail banking would be viable already have a high density of banks. It is difficult to compete in the high street against local banks which already have well-developed branch networks. Likewise, Swiss banks are unlikely to begin setting up branches throughout the world. Instead, they will focus their attention on the leading financial centres in the important nations. In Europe our immediate aim is to consolidate our organization in Germany, the UK and Luxembourg, expand operations in France and establish a presence in Italy, the Netherlands and Spain.

Another question to consider is: how far should universal banks branch out into neighbouring areas? The answer will vary according to individual countries. In Germany, for example, non-bank stock holdings are more traditional than in Switzerland. I think it would be inappropriate to change our policy on this, on account of Swiss capital adequacy requirements and because it would be unwise to spread ourselves too thinly. It is not the Swiss way to have banks with travel agencies tagged on – which is not to say that no new, bank-like services will be made available. Without question, consultancy facilities will be expanded. The banks' range of products is likely to be widened to include management seminars and fiscal and legal advisory services for small and medium-sized companies. A much thornier problem will be future cooperation with insurance companies. Options range from expanding our dealings with insurance companies by means of joint ventures to the possibility of gaining a stake in a strong insurance firm.

5. One considerable challenge of the next decade will be to ensure the systematic early detection and prevention of risks and the establishment of effective cost control. Given the threat to some assets and the extent to which profit margins will be squeezed, these management techniques will be all the more important. Cost-centre accounting methods will be refined and used to help to provide dynamic cost–benefit analyses. This will increase our ability to assess the profitability of clients, client groups and specific services. Such complex calculations are made possible by modern technology, and serve to determine suitable levels for customer charges. Cost accounting in banks will thus become less and less a simple book-keeping aid and more and more a key component of profit-oriented business policy.

Control and prevention of risks will also benefit from advances in electronic information and data processing. Risk-monitoring will cover all the bank's activities worldwide: it must be possible to get a view of global exposures to clients and the composition of those exposures at any given moment. Another factor which will influence risk policy is the possibility of funding loans to foreign borrowers in the country where those borrowers are based. This avoids currency and transfer risks. A constant task for the bank's management will be to ensure that subordinates adhere to risk policies without being prevented from showing professional initiative.

6. Fierce competition means that decisions will have to be taken swiftly and new ideas tested without delay. If this is to be achieved, the decision-making process needs to be streamlined and more authority assigned to units abroad and officers responsible for products. This new, flexible management style and structure goes against traditional notions of bank hierarchy. Among the important tasks that fall to the directors of the leading banks will be that of balancing the organizational constraints of a large company against the need to allow smaller units a suitable degree of freedom.

PROFITABILITY VERSUS SIZE?

The future of banking lies in strong profitability. Profitability comes before size and market share, quality before quantity. The race to achieve the greatest total assets has run itself into the ground. Companies which consistently register unsatisfactory profit levels will have to look for cooperation with stronger partners or else go under. Many will do so in the coming decade. In this context, however, there are two misconceptions which must be cleared up.

The first is that only large, internationally active banks will stand a chance of survival. That is not the case. In the future there will continue to be room for small, flexible financial companies with products that are tailored to clients' needs and that are not always offered by the larger institutions. In fact, demand for specialized services is growing. But the smaller companies must be of a certain minimum size, perhaps achieved through mergers, in order to provide a secure base for banking operations and effective client advice.

The second misconception is that profit growth and volume growth go against each other. This is not true either. Financing operations are on such a vast scale, and will be even more so in the next few years, that any bank wishing to participate at the global level must be of a certain size if it is to take a leading role in attractive and lucrative transactions. Mergers and acquisitions business often involves substantial bridging loans. Undewriting frequently entails taking on board large amounts of paper before it can be placed elsewhere. The key consideration is that expansion of total assets must not take place at the expense of asset quality and a solid deposit base and that gains in market share should not be made to the detriment of suitable profit margins. Strong capitalization is another crucial factor: in this the leading Swiss banks are among the best-placed and thus enjoy a considerable competitive advantage.

CONCLUSION

If we bear in mind the turn-of-the-century scenario depicted at the beginning of this chapter, we see that the banks have to meet a number of challenges during the 1990s in order to move forward into the next century.

1. They have to channel their resources effectively. By this I mean equity capital, deposits, modern technology and, last but by no means least, their skilled, highly-motivated staff. Dynamic allocation of resources should contribute to enhancing the overall stock market capitalization of the banks. In order to achieve this, it must be accompanied by a friendly treatment of shareholders and greater transparency on earning power.
2. They will face a persistently high – and rising – degree of competition, from other banks at home and abroad and from rivals outside the actual banking sector, such as insurance companies. This will lead to a constant need to consolidate profit margins.

3. Linked to this is the trend towards business concentration in industry as a whole and particularly in the financial sector. This means that strong capitalization will be one of the main aims of bank policy. At the same time, flexible organizational structures are necessary to avoid the danger of becoming cumbersome.

4. The continually shifting economic environment will be characterized over the next years by the completion of the EC's single internal market and the growing importance of the Pacific Rim countries. The appropriate responses are to internationalize the bank's management and strengthen operations in the world's top economic and financial centres. At the same time, the internationalization of the corporate landscape will lead not only to great business opportunities for the banking industry but will also increase the potential risks. Detecting these early on and avoiding them should be given high priority.

The 1990s are not going to be simply a carbon copy of the current decade. Fresh changes are under way and, overall, the climate will be harsher than today's. Our task is to make sure we trim our sails accordingly.

8 Banking in Europe after 1992

Jacques Thierry

The European Community's end-1992 deadline has become a much-talked-about political topic in a number of member-states, even if its implications have not always been fully thought through. Far be it from me to criticize this. Experience has shown that the media's focus, well in advance, on some future step forward has enabled Europe to make progress in the past. This will no doubt be the case again today.

Events are often identified simply by the year in which they occurred. For example, merely mentioning the dates 1789 or 1929 is enough to recall the French Revolution or the Great Depression. In the context of European integration at the close of the twentieth century, 1992 seems set to be associated with the major changes that are bound to result from the completion of the EC internal market. There is, of course, the rhetoric and the reality: they do not necessarily coincide. Yes, 1992 will symbolize a great advance. But the rhetoric of 1992 also contains a number of illusions. It is a necessary task to demystify the exaggerations that are kindled by an unbridled enthusiasm if we are to have a clear idea – rather than a simplistic vision – of the changes we will probably see in the years ahead. Let us therefore consider the basic facts, including the original policy document and the key treaty texts.

BASIC FACTS

Fundamental Principles of the Community

The Treaty of Rome has established the European Economic Community on the basis of four fundamental freedoms, unconditional in kind, plus a fifth freedom necessarily associated with them. The four are the following:

- freedom of movement for goods;
- freedom of movement for persons;

121

- freedom to provide services;
- freedom of establishment.

However, because these four forms of freedom, which are of direct application, are meaningless if restrictions on capital movements make it impossible to pay for goods or services or to transfer the capital required for establishment, the free movement of capital, a corollary of the four fundamental freedoms, is likewise needed.

Disputes have often arisen between the authorities of the member-states and their nationals over the implementation of these various forms of freedom. However, the Community has an efficient judicial system for the settlement of such disputes.

Thus the Court of Justice was established under the Treaty of Rome to settle matters arising from the application of the Treaty's provisions. It has been accepted that Community law takes precedence over national law when the two clash. Consequently, all disputes have to be settled in accordance with Community law, and this is now recognized by all member-states. It must be stressed that the jurisprudence established by the Luxembourg Court is remarkably coherent and faithful to the priniciples of the Treaty. Indeed, the Commission has been able to rely on the decisions of the Court not only for founding its interpretation of the Treaty's articles but also for finding fresh justification for pushing forward European integration.

The White Paper on Completing the Internal Market

For over twenty years, the main Community concerns were the free movement of goods, the common agricultural policy and the enlargement of the Community itself. But the climate became more propitious to the intensification of the process of European integration once a solution was found to the problem of Britain's EC budget contribution at the European Council meeting in Fontainebleau in June 1984.

The EC Commission over which Mr Gaston Thorn presided (1981–4) had already started to give serious attention to the challenge of reinforcing the European internal market. Then, in late 1984, M. Jacques Delors, who had recently been appointed to become the next Commission president, was looking for a programme that could give a new impetus to the Community. His tour of the European capitals persuaded him to opt for the goal of completing the internal market. This goal was officially endorsed by the European Council in Brussels in March 1985. Lord Cockfield, one of the new EC Commissioners, was thus assigned the task of drawing up an inventory of the measures to be taken and the principles to be applied for the realization of the large internal market, in conformity with the guiding principles and rules of the Treaty of Rome. His proposals were adopted in the form of the now famous White Paper at the meeting of the European Council in Milan in June 1985, and the commitment to complete the internal market was subsequently embodied in the Single European Act.[1]

What means does the Community now have at its disposal for completing a unified internal market in the sphere of financial services?

Until the beginning of the 1980s, whatever progress had been achieved by the Community had been the result of the process of harmonization of national laws. But the White Paper argued that this method, which had been the preferred method of European integration during the first twenty-five years, no longer permitted satisfactory progress because the difficulties encountered had become more technically complex, the number of member-states had increased, and more sensitive issues from a national point of view were being addressed. Furthermore, unanimous agreement was required for the coordination of most matters related to banking. Besides the difficulty of reaching unanimity, experience had shown that it was not possible to harmonize everything, so it was clear that other methods had to be used.

The fundamental principles of the new approach to the creation of a single large financial market by the end of 1992, as laid down in the White Paper, were as follows:

- minimal harmonizations of regulations;
- mutual recognition by the member-states of what each does to protect the interests of the public;
- home-country control of credit institutions.

These principles warrant some further consideration.

Minimal harmonization does not mean harmonization at the lowest possible level, but rather a harmonization limited to the essential rules. It is complemented by the principle of *liberalization without prior harmonization* applying to both the provision of cross-border financial services and the establishment of banks in other member-states.

The White Paper underlined two major obstacles to progress. The first is restrictions on capital movements. A directive was recently adopted on 24 June 1988, which provides for the full liberalization of capital movements by 1 July 1990, at the latest for most member-states (with four others being granted a delay of two and a half or even more years). The other major obstacle is the existence of national laws and regulations that make for insuperable barriers to truly European competition.

As regards this second obstacle, the removal of discrimination is insufficient. Imposing the same national rules on credit institutions from other member-states as on resident institutions makes the cross-border provision of services from one country to another costly and difficult. However, partly inspired by the well-known *Cassis de Dijon* judgement of the European Court of Justice on 20 February 1979, the Commission maintained in the White Paper that if a product or service is legally produced, provided or marketed in one member-state, it must be allowed to be supplied to customers in other member-states, without the undertaking from which the product or service emanates being obliged to establish itself in these other member-states. Furthermore, the Commission argued that if an undertaking sets up in another member-state, it is not necessary that it complies with all the legislation of the host-country and – notably in the case of the unified financial services market – with the legislation relating to the control of financial institutions.

Here the Commission's approach has been based on the principle of *mutual recognition* by member-states that their various regulations on the licencing and supervision of credit institutions are equivalent in effect. Given the high level of prudential standards in member-states, the latter should consider as adequate the controls exercised by the national authorities of the institution's country of origin, including the controls on activities carried out beyond national frontiers since such supervision is effected on a consolidated basis. *Home-country control* is indeed a development with a wider international background, witness the work achieved by the Cooke Committee which will enable twelve of the world's leading industrial countries to use as from the end of 1992 a common concept of banks' own funds (consisting of defined 'core' and 'supplementary' capital), apply a common solvency ratio and thus, with accounts on a consolidated basis, systematically supervise the operations of large banks across the world.

Mutual recognition does not rule out moving on towards harmonization. Instead of being a *sine qua non* condition and fully comprehensive in nature, harmonization in the logic of mutual recognition should preferably be confined to an indispensable minimum and be carried out, often at a later stage, without being in any way a prerequisite for liberalization (that is, it should be *ex post* harmonization). Only for exceptional matters should liberalization be delayed until harmonization is complete. In principle, liberalization should be seen as a stimulus to *ex post* harmonization or even to the approval of Community regulations designed to replace numerous and diverse national ones.

The Single European Act

The Single European Act, which came into effect on 1 July 1987, is not just the embodiment of a political design; it is an addition to the treaties that laid the foundation of the European Communities. The Single Act adopts the internal market programme contained in the Commission's White Paper and makes provision for its completion as well as for complementary action in a number of areas, notably economic and monetary policy cooperation, social policy, economic and social cohesion, research and technological development, and protection of the environment.

The Single Act defines the internal market as an 'area without internal frontiers in which the free movement of goods, persons, services and capital is ensured'. It specifies that this market will be gradually completed during a period ending on 31 December 1992. It provides the means for accomplishing this. Especially important is qualified majority voting by the Council of Ministers on most matters. The adoption of directives by the Council of Ministers is indeed the privileged legislative means for advancing the internal market. The Single Act also maps out areas for harmonization, approximation or mutual recognition. There is the aim of balanced progress in all the sectors concerned by the 'completing the internal market' programme, and, for those countries whose economies are vulnerable, there is recognition that derogations of a temporary nature may be necessary.

CURRENT OBSTACLES TO THE INTEGRATION OF BANKING SYSTEMS

After the preceding summary of the guiding principles and treaty texts, and prior to a consideration of new legislation drawn up in the framework of the 1992 programme, it is fitting to summarize the present situation as regards obstacles to an integrated European banking system.

Banking Regulations

A recent survey on the differences in regulatory environment from one Community country to another shows that the principle of freedom of establishment for banks from other member-states is accepted everywhere, but formal approval must nonetheless be given by the authorities of the host-country. The latter are moreover responsible for setting the rules governing these banks' activities and for their supervision. The host-country authorities have likewise charge of authorizing the provision of cross-border services by banks established in another member-state. Branches of foreign banks are generally subject to the same capital adequacy requirements as local banks. However, the UK has already adopted the principle of home-country control for solvency. In general, foreign banks tend to be somewhat more restricted than local banks in the range of activities they can undertake. But restrictions on the number of branch outlets exist only in Ireland, Italy and Spain. Countries with major banking centres tend to have generally a regulatory environment that is more liberal and attractive to foreign banks than that elsewhere. This is notably the case of the UK and Luxembourg. National regulations do not generally discriminate between foreign banks; in other words, the regulations are the same, regardless of whether the banks are from other EC member-states or third countries.

Deregulation and modernization of the financial markets has advanced far in the UK, with the result that there are few barriers to banking and other financial service activities. But this transformation has led to no regulatory vacuum. Indeed, there has been reregulation since the 'Big Bang' in late 1986, and new supervisory bodies have been set up.

Restrictions on banking activities are often important in those countries which have foreign exchange controls and/or special legislation for foreign investment. Foreign-exchange controls can prevent banks established in such countries from carrying out certain types of operation and may make it impossible for banks set up in other countries to develop activities affected by these controls.

The countries that joined the European Community in the 1980s have participated in varying degrees in the common effort of financial services liberalization, and they are lagging somewhat behind other member-states. However, since its EC accession on 1 January 1986, Spain has embarked on a course of far-reaching change so as to adjust to Community regulations, with the intention of avoiding discrimination against third countries as much as possible.

There are certainly fewer obstacles to banking activity now than when the OECD drew up its comprehensive inventory of such obstacles in 1984. Yet its survey, which covered all OECD member-countries, showed that the degree of liberalization achieved in international trade in banking services was already relatively high at that time in much of the present EC area, with the important exceptions being the major countries applying foreign exchange controls.

The progress achieved by 1984 was only partly a result of Community legislation. An EC directive on the freedom of establishment and the provision of services had been adopted on 28 June 1973: it constituted a first step but had little or no practical effect. It was followed by the First Banking Coordination Directive of 12 December 1977. Its aim has been to apply the principle that credit institutions are free to expand throughout the Community by setting up branches. But this directive has left three obstacles to such freedom still in place:

1. the setting up of a branch requires the permission of the authorities of the host-country;
2. the branch is subject to supervision by the authorities of the host-country and its range of activities may be constrained by host-country rules;
3. in most member-states, branches have to be provided with earmarked 'endowment capital', as if they were newly incorporated banks or subsidiaries.

It may be mentioned that the First Banking Coordination Directive already enunciates the principle of reciprocity in respect of the establishment of branches by credit institutions whose head office is located in a third country.

Tax Harmonization

The entering into full force of the freedom of establishment and the free cross-border provision of financial services within the Community, combined with the full liberalization of capital movements, implies some degree of tax harmonization between member-states. The reasons are not hard to find.

Whenever a shift of financial resources or activities from one country to another is easy or just simply feasible, disparities in tax systems may encourage transfers of savings or financial service operations, and indeed the relocation of financial intermediaries themselves, to the countries whose tax regimes are perceived as particularly favourable. Thus tax discrepancies between member-states are at present prompting financial intermediaries to adopt a diversified strategy for the location of their activities both inside the Community and in third countries. This means that differing tax regimes may be a crucial consideration in decisions to set up branches and subsidiaries and to provide certain banking services. Luxembourg, for instance, attracts financial service activities through its not applying a withholding tax and Belgium has appeal for banks able to take advantage of its notional foreign tax credit system.

In its communication to the Council of Ministers on the 'Creation of a European Financial Area' in November 1987, the Commission drew attention to certain questions associated with the full liberalization of capital movements. It thus highlighted four issues in the field of taxation: the harmonization or approximation of company taxation, tax evasion, discriminatory provisions in national tax systems that provide an incentive for private individuals to invest in national securities, and restrictions on investments by pension funds in other member-states. According to the Commission, the solution of the problems raised by these issues should not be considered a precondition, chronologically speaking, for the full liberalization of capital movements. The latter is indeed conceived as providing the decisive impulse to the creation of a European financial area, in which tax harmonization will certainly have a full part to play even if it is realized only at a later stage.

It should be mentioned that the Single Act does not empower the Council of Ministers to decide by a qualified majority on tax matters. Unanimous agreement continues to be required (article 18).

Indirect Taxation

The complete harmonization of indirect taxes is not a major priority from the standpoint of credit institutions. Banks should be able to take within their stride certain disparities in VAT rates on fees. As for taxes on stockmarket transactions, they are tending to be done away with.

Direct Taxation

Company taxation Although banks deem it desirable to harmonize general company taxation, applying to all business enterprises, they are also concerned about specific taxation aspects of direct relevance to their sector. Given the nature of their activities, they are effectively subject to a special sort of tax regime. Varying in its details from one country to another, it covers depreciation and provisions, capital gains (on bonds, equities or other assets), interest income from abroad, and so forth. In France, there is even a separate body of tax legislation for the banking sector. The direct taxation of banks must therefore be considered as a whole, in all its diverse aspects.

For a bank to have branches and subsidiaries subject to different tax regimes is not necessarily unworkable. But the differences must be kept within bounds. Otherwise, they will encourage the transfer of activity from one country to another at least if there are no other offsetting considerations or advantages.

Taxation of portfolio income There can be no doubt that the taxation of portfolio income, especially interest income, is one of the most difficult problems to resolve. This tax is indeed of primary concern to banks.

It would be unrealistic to think of tax exemption for portfolio income in Europe: such income is taxed in almost all countries for reasons of fiscal equity; and, if it were not the case, the tax burden on other categories of income or on consumption would have to be correspondingly higher.

This leads to the question of tax exoneration for non-residents, even if they are residents of another EC member-state. The creation of the single European internal market implies that all the economic agents based within it should be put on the same footing and be considered equally as residents, with non-resident status being reserved only for residents of third countries. There would therefore seem to be no room for tax discrimination between Community residents.

Interest income According to the Commission, there are two main options:

1. a generalized withholding tax on interest income, at a relatively low rate, throughout the Community;
2. an obligation on banks to disclose information about interest

income, received by Community residents, to their tax authorities.[2]

A generalized withholding tax would make life more difficult for tax havens within the Community but would not affect those outside. There would therefore be a tendency for funds to be shifted to third countries. But other solutions are also possible, for instance the positive welcoming of 'tax competition' or the introduction of a generalized withholding tax that is exonerative in nature in its application to EC residents (that is, once paid, no further tax is due on the income in question).

Thanks to the liberalization of capital movements, the dismantling of tax frontiers and the choice that would be available between different tax regimes, 'tax competition' would be likely to exert a strong pressure in favour of tax harmonization. Thus savings would be attracted towards countries where taxation is the least onerous, and, in response to this, there would be a widespread concern to achieve a greater degree of harmonization of taxation of interest income. Tax harmonization would accordingly be imposed sooner or later by market forces.

Indeed, as has just been mentioned, another solution could be the introduction of a standard EC withholding tax of an exonerative kind: it would be a tax fixed at a relatively low level in view of the external constraint, that is, the rate of taxation in third countries, notably in the USA and Japan.

Dividends   As for the taxation of dividends, 100 per cent tax credits would offer many advantages. They would lower and could even eliminate double taxation of distributed earnings, allowing shareholders declaring their dividends to benefit from the corporate income tax paid by the company. Furthermore, this system would tend to discourage tax evasion in the case of individual taxpayers who are not subject to very high marginal rates of income tax. Indeed, in the framework of the tax reforms already carried out or envisaged in Europe, of which a common characteristic has been a tendency to fix a maximum rate of very roughly 50 per cent for personal income tax, the introduction of 100 per cent tax credits would have the effect of encouraging most investors to declare their dividends.

Another positive move – abstracting from its effects on 100 per cent tax credit systems – would be the harmonization of the corporate income tax rate at a relatively low level. It would reduce existing adverse discrimination in the tax treatment of companies' risk capital funding (as opposed to their raising finance through borrowing).

The Boiteux Report The preliminary report presented to the French minister of finance, M. Edouard Balladur, in February 1988 by the 'Economic Policy Review Committee on the Preparation for the 1992 Deadline' – called the Boiteux Report after the name of the Committee's chairman – deals mainly with the 'tax dimension of increased competition . . . on the market for financial savings products' as a result of the completion of the financial internal market, given 'the risk that savings will be transferred to other countries because of this competition'. It thus considers that it is of prime importance to adjust French taxation so as to remove the inducement to shift savings out of the country.[3] Besides advocating a modernization of the French tax system, the Boiteux Report argues for lower taxation of savings income in France and for harmonization throughout the Community. It says:

> The increased internationalization of financial markets, the forthcoming liberalization of capital movements and the wider freedoms awaited in the sphere of the provision of financial services make it imperative to remove as soon as possible from our tax system any element that would make for an incentive to transfer national savings abroad.[4]

The report of a working party set up by the Conseil National du Crédit in February 1988 and chaired by M. Daniel Lebègue comes to a similar conclusion.

The Dassesse Report The report on 'Tax Barriers to the Completion of the Internal Market', prepared in October 1987 by Professor Marc Dassesse for the Economic and Monetary Commission of the Belgian section of the European League for Economic Cooperation, argues that exclusive reliance on the jurisprudence of the Community's Court of Justice does not appear the most satisfactory way of eliminating tax measures that are incompatible with the basic freedoms laid down by the Treaty of Rome.

The idea of achieving a fully integrated European financial market through the force of court judgements takes no account of the fact that 'all tax systems form a coherent whole and underpin important elements of economic policy, which can vary form one state to another'. 'Declaring one of the rules of the system to be ineffective on the grounds that it discriminates against the nationals of other EC member states' states Professor Dassesse, 'may have the perverse effect of creating discrimination that is prejudicial to the nationals of the country in question' or else have economically absurd consequences.[5]

For Professor Dassesse, the harmonization of tax legislation provides no workable solution either. This is because the experience of the past twenty years has underlined the difficulties of harmonization, especially in the sphere of direct taxes. And he raises the question of whether, in the field of taxation, it would not be better to adopt the approach of the White Paper based on the aforementioned *Cassis de Dijon* judgement and thus assume *a priori*:

- that national tax regulations merit mutual recognition;
- that the absence of their harmonization cannot therefore justify restricting the free competition of financial institutions originating from other member-states in respect of the provision of services and the freedom of establishment.

According to the Dassesse Report, this approach could be made to work if there were progress on three fronts:

1. extending to the area of direct taxation arrangements between member-states for the recovery of tax (in the area of indirect taxation, there is already cooperation for the recovery of VAT);
2. obtaining recognition that the rule of non-discrimination between Community residents (whatever the taxpayer's nationality or place of residence), which is one of the Treaty's basic principles, is also valid for direct taxes;
3. extending to institutions established in other member-states tax-exemption measures granted to nationally based financial institutions and/or their customers (one example of such measures being the special tax regime for Belgian-franc-denominated savings deposits in Belgium).

Thus, while the Boiteux Report advocates tax harmonization prior to the dismantling of frontiers, the Dassesse Report opts for the liberalization of capital movements in the framework of the application of the principle of mutual recognition of different national tax legislations, that is, without their prior harmonization or even their approximation or *rapprochement*.

In the sphere of taxation, there is the great risk that the way ahead will be beset by difficulties and delays. There are differences in basic approach as well as in the proposed reforms. But, as has already been mentioned, unanimity is the rule for such matters in Community decision-making.

Monetary Integration

The absence of a European currency area, characterized either by perfectly substitutable currencies (with exchange rates that are unadjustable or permanently fixed within the EMS) or else by the emergence of a common currency, is an obstacle to the expansion of banking activity within the Community. It prevents the creation of a large unified money market and thus the centralized management of bank treasury activities. It complicates lending and deposit-taking to the extent that they must pass through foreign-exchange markets. It inhibits the expansion of banking networks into regions situated on other sides of intra-Community borders. Furthermore, the existence of a multiplicity of different currencies constitutes a menace to the freedom of movement of capital, which can never be fully assured as long as there is the possibility of governments' reintroducing exchange controls (through safeguard clauses) to deal with capital flows or exchange-market pressures prejudicial to their economic policy.

Despite these problems, it would be unrealistic to expect that a European central bank or a single European currency could come into being before the end of 1992. However, neither a European central bank nor a single currency is indispensable for the functioning of the internal market. What is indispensable is a greater stability of exchange rates and thus far closer monetary cooperation.

An independent European central banking body, regrouping the functions of the European Monetary Cooperation Fund (EMCF) and the Committee of Governors of the Central Banks, could perhaps be set up before 1993. It would be responsible for coordinating and developing monetary policy. But it would not be a fully-fledged central bank with the power of note issue.

The full liberalization of capital movements will act as a catalyst for European monetary integration. As long as EMS exchange rates have not been fixed once and for all, there will be a need for cooperation because of the dangers associated with capital flows of a speculative or even a long-term structural kind. Significant pressures on European exchange rates or the possibility of such pressures will not be completely eliminated as long as the EMS exchange rate mechanism is one of 'fixed but adjustable exchange rates'. The need for unadjustable exchange rates will become progressively more urgent and will no doubt lead one day to the creation of a single currency, though at a later stage of Europe's integration.

The transition from a system of adjustable exchange rates to one of totally fixed exchange rates or a single currency presents not only technical problems. It also raises a major political issue: this is the issue of sovereignty posed by both the transfer of monetary powers to an independent European central bank and the transfer of increased budgetary powers to other Community bodies, notably the European Parliament.

On a less long-term horizon, it needs scarcely be said that banking structures within the Community will continue to be marked in 1993 by the absence of a single EC currency and by member-states' retaining a large measure of control over monetary and fiscal policies.

Economic Distortions

An inter-country analysis of interest-rate margins and fees for banking and other financial services shows that there are often considerable differences within the Community. The advent of the large integrated financial market, with the full liberalization of capital movements, will lead to reductions in these differences or else to movements of capital, the cross-frontier provision of services or the establishment of new branches or subsidiaries in other member-states.

Although there is relatively little research on the matter, it would seem that there are substantial variations in productivity in the banking sector between Community member-states. It is therefore not surprising that there are differences in the costs of financial-service products and in the overhead costs of running banking networks, and, consequently, in intermediation margins.

BANKING AFTER 1992

We may now turn to the problems posed by the implementation of the White Paper and the Community legislation currently in preparation as well as to the difficulties and resistance to change which will inevitably surface after 31 December 1992.

Problems Posed by the Implementation of the White Paper

The application in parallel of the principles of liberalization without prior harmonization and of mutual recognition with home-country control raise a number of difficulties:

- it risks being viewed in certain EC countries as a *regulatory short-cut imposed from above by the Commission and the Council of Ministers*, which is a perception that could lead to an increased reticence in the future to pursue further progress; indeed the argument that one cannot build up the Community against the wishes of a number of its members is an argument which will tell in determining the speed and manner of the completion of the internal market;
- there is also the fear that financial intermediaries will seek to put to their advantage the *most liberal or most lax national regulations* in force in the Community, though the fear of abuse on this score seems unwarranted in view of the high standard of banking rules and supervision in EC member-states;
- there is the fact that creating an integrated European financial market presupposes that sooner or later a number of national requirements will have to be abandoned, which means that the problem of *reregulation* or the *setting of common rules* at European level will have to be faced.

These difficulties will be experienced above all at retail banking level (in other words, banking conducted with private individuals, the self-employed and small business undertakings), since the wholesale or corporate banking market has long functioned in an international framework, with little interference or constraint from national authorities. However, there is the possibility of recourse to safeguard clauses:

- thus, if the *general interest* or *public order* narrowly defined (in the sense of protection of savers and consumers, protection of parties deemed vulnerable or protection against unfair or improper competition) is prejudiced in one member-state by the activities on its territory of an undertaking established in another member-state, the authorities of the host-country are empowered to eliminate this prejudice and may to this end count on the cooperation of the authorities in the country where the undertaking is incorporated;

- in addition, during the course of the creation of the integrated financial market, there are safeguards to take account of the national authorities' need to maintain sufficient room for manoeuvre for the proper management of *monetary policy*.

The Second Banking Coordination Directive

The legislative implementation of the principles formulated by the White Paper in the area of banking is the purpose of the Second Banking Coordination Directive, whose aim is 'to achieve only the essential harmonization necessary and sufficient to secure mutual recognition of authorization and of supervisory systems, thus enabling the application of the principle of home-country control and the granting of a single licence recognized throughout the Community'.[6]

The proposed directive accordingly privileges the idea of freedom for the expansion of banking activities throughout the Community and is marked by the ambition to create a coherent set of rules and prudential controls so as to ensure the stability and solvency of financial institutions. Thus the proposed directive is planned as the centrepiece legislation for the creation of a more efficient banking system that will be the fruit of greater competition within the Community. And, in addition, it is designed to provide sufficient security for savers and depositors.

Its coverage is wide. As in the case of the First Coordination Directive, it covers not only banks but also savings institutions and other financial intermediaries that fall within the definition of a credit institution.

Authorization of a credit institution will remain the responsibility of the authorities in the country where the credit institution is incorporated – that is to say, its country of origin. The competent authorities in the country of origin will deliver a single licence valid for the whole Community. With this licence, credit institutions will be able to expand at will through setting up branches in other member-states of the Community and providing services across intra-Community borders without being obliged to be authorized anew by the host state(s).

Freedom of establishment is a fundamental principle of the Treaty of Rome. It applies to all legal persons, both individuals and companies. A bank established in one member-state may exercise this freedom by setting up a branch or a subsidiary in another member-state. However, under the Second Coordination Directive, these two types of establishment will be controlled differently. Thus a branch will be controlled by the competent authorities of the home member-state, that is to say by the authorities of the country where the parent institution has its registered head office. A subsidiary set up in another member-state has a separate legal identity. The registered office of a subsidiary will always be in the member-state in which it has been incorporated, as is indeed the standard practice today. The control of a subsidiary will therefore remain the responsibility of the competent authorities of this member-state, which is effectively the subsidiary's 'home country'. A subsidiary will, of course, be free to expand its business through setting up branches in other member-states and these branches will also come under the control of the competent authorities of the state in which the subsidiary's registered office is located.

By way of comparison, it may be mentioned that the exercise of freedom of establishment through setting up branches and subsidiaries at will is not accepted in the USA. This is because of the tendency of the authorities to adopt a negative attitude towards both multiple-branch banking and interstate banking. Consequently, US banks are usually confined to their state, country or town, and are forbidden to build up an extensive branch network (though the experience of the superregionals goes to some extent against this tradition).

Another remark is in order. The free cross-border provision of services as defined in the proposed directive is restricted to credit institutions licenced within the Community: only banks with their head office in a member-state and third-country banks 'naturalized' in the form of a subsidiary authorized by a member-state will be able to avail themselves of this freedom. In other words, the application of the principle of the free provision of services will not be *erga omnes*, since third-country banks will not be authorized to provide services freely from a base outside the Community. However, they will remain free to set up within the Community provided their country of origin accepts the principle of reciprocity.

The prudential supervision of credit institutions on a consolidated basis will be the responsibility of the competent authorities of the home member-state. This sort of supervision will cover not only the activities of branches established in other member-states and the cross-border provision of services but also the activities of subsidiaries established in other member-states (for which otherwise – as just mentioned – the 'home country' will be the member-state in which the subsidiary is incorporated).

As regards the freedom of establishment for branches and the free cross-border provision of services, the following responsibilities will remain by way of exception in the hands of the host member-state:

- the supervision of the *liquidity* of branches established on its territory (until further coordination) (article 12, § 2);
- complete responsibility for measures relating to the implementation of *monetary policy* (ibid.);
- the taking of measures to require credit institutions authorized in other member-states to make sufficient provision against *market risks* in respect of operations on securities markets on their territory (article 12, § 3);
- the prohibition, in the interest of the *public good*, of branches from engaging in certain activities that are not prohibited by the licence delivered by the country of origin yet which are not on the directive's list of recognized banking activities (article 17, § 4);
- the prohibition of activities in the event of non-compliance with the legal provisions in force in the host-country on the grounds of the *public good* or else pursuant to the provisions of the directive itself on the host-country's powers (article 19, § 3).

The proposed Second Coordination Directive contains an extensive list of the activities that are integral to banking and that are to be included within the scope of mutual recognition. Drawn up on a universal banking model, the list includes all forms of transactions in securities. The proposed directive also contains rules for credit institutions' equity participations in the non-financial sector: the rules put forward are relatively liberal in nature and may be described as inspired too by the universal banking model.

The coverage of the single banking licence delivered by the member-state of origin may cover all types of banking business contained in the directive's list but it will not be mandatory for it to include all of them.

If the licence granted by one member-state turns out to be more restrictive than that granted by another, it could prove a handicap for banks originating from the former (at least if obtaining authorization for a less diversified range of ativities is considered to be a disadvantage). However, in view of the likely progressive convergence of national regulations, this sort of handicap will become of increasingly less significance.

Certain activities not figuring on the list will be able to be exercised by Community credit institutions provided they are not prohibited by either the EC single banking licence or the national legislation of the member-states in which the activities are to be exercised. Thus the competent authorities in the home-country may authorize types of business not on the list (for example, insurance broking, commodity trading, travel-agency activities) independently of the EC single licence, but the types of business in question will not be covered by the application of the principle of mutual recognition.

Timetable

The internal market for the banking sector – and indeed for all credit institutions and the financial sector as a whole – as planned in the 1985 White Paper – should be completed, in theory, before 1 January 1993. The proposal for the Second Coordination Directive, which will mark a path-breaking advance in the making of European banking law, was submitted by the Commission to the Council of Ministers in February 1988. The official timetable for its examination and adoption is as follows:

- opinion of the European Parliament   30 June 1988
- opinion of the Economic and Social Committee   30 June 1988
- common position of the Council of Ministers   31 December 1988
- second reading of the European Parliament   31 March 1989
- adoption by the Council of Ministers   30 June 1989

But this timetable is already out of date: the opinion of the Economic and Social Committee will not be delivered before the end of September of this year and the European Parliament still has far to go in its deliberations before it is in a position to deliver its opinion. It is probable that the Council of Ministers will reach their common position only towards the end of 1989 and that the directive will be finally adopted, after the Parliament's second reading, only during the course of 1990.

The implementation of the Second Coordination Directive is

conditional upon the adoption of two other directives harmonizing essential supervisory standards: one of them is to define equity funds, and the other is to set a harmonized solvency ratio. The directive defining equity funds is behind schedule. It must take account of the Cooke Committee's work. The date of its taking effect was left open since the definition of equity funds will assume its intended practical significane in the framework of the application of the Second Coordination Directive and the setting of a harmonized solvency ratio. As regards the latter, considerably less progress has been made towards adopting the directive in question; there is only a Commission proposal as yet. The Second Coordination Directive will be able to take effect only after the adoption of these two directives on the harmonization of the definition of equity funds and the fixing of a common solvency ratio (see article 22, § 1 of the Second Coordination Directive). The foregoing is one of the very few preconditions proposed by the Commission for governing the implementation of the Second Coordination Directive.

Other progress is under way. Thus various related measures are planned or have already been taken in the wider context of creating a 'European financial area'. The Directive of 24 June 1988, provides for the full liberalization of capital movements. In addition, a certain degree of tax harmonization has been urged by the Commission as well as the removal of tax discrimination between EC residents. Finally, there is the desired future reinforcement of the EMS. Even if these measures are closely connected, the Commission has felt that the final stage of the liberalization of capital movements must take place as soon as possible and without preconditions. Thus the logic of capital movement liberalization is that it should provide the necessary impetus for completing the internal market in the financial sector:

> An integrated financial market will not be achieved by simultaneously implementing all the necessary measures. On the contrary, it will be achieved by creating a dynamic movement towards integration and accepting some disequilibrium within an overall programme which is both coherent and binding. The liberalization of capital movements will itself provide the momentum for this process.[7]

Thus, according to the Commission, the liberalizaton of capital movements should lead to the creation of a unified market in financial services, with both credit institutions and their customers being allowed to transact their business in full freedom in the other member-countries (and in the currencies of those countries). The removal of frontiers for capital movements should put pressure on governments to harmonize their tax systems and prepare the way for the application of the Second Coordination Directive and the various ancillary measures that are required for creating a European financial area.

It may be mentioned here that, by virtue of an EC directive adopted on 20 December 1985, all intra-Community barriers to the sales of units or shares issued by 'undertakings for collective investment in transferable securities' (UCITS) were dismantled on 1 October 1989. In other words, there is now a common market on that date for mutual funds, unit trusts, investment trusts and SICAVs.

The full liberalization of capital movements, as ordained by the EC directive of 24 June 1988, will take place only gradually and on a staggered basis. This is partly because of the aforementioned difficulties relating to taxation and partly because of the wider challenge of member-states being sufficiently prepared in terms of the relative strength of their balance of payments and the maturity of their financial systems. Thus the full liberalization of capital movements will become mandatory for Belgium, Denmark, France, West Germany, Italy, Luxembourg, the Netherlands and the UK as from 1 July 1990. What this really means is that France and Italy will have to remove their remaining restrictions on capital movements by that date since the six other countries already allow either total or virtually full freedom of movement for capital. Spain, Ireland, Greece and Portugal are being permitted to maintain certain restrictions until 31 December 1992, that is to say the date fixed for the final completion of the internal market. Furthermore, in the case of Greece and Portugal, there is a provision for a further delay of three years, if necessary, until the end of 1995.

The directive as adopted by the Council of Ministers also contains a timetable for taking whatever measures are deemed necessary in respect of the taxation of savings income. This represents an addition to the directive as compared with the proposal originally put forward by the Commission. A decision on taking such measures must now be made before the provisions for the full liberalization of capital movements start to come into effect. Thus the Commission has been enjoined to submit to the Council of Ministers 'proposals aimed at eliminating or reducing risks of distortion, tax evasion and tax avoidance linked to the diversity of national systems for the taxation of savings and for controlling the application of these systems' before 31 December 1988. The Council of Ministers was to take a position on these proposals by 30 June 1989. However, juridically speaking, the Council's resolution of the issues in question is not a precondition of the full liberalization of capital movements. It is no more than an obligation to give careful consideration to the question of tax harmonization. Even so, it is a potential source of future conflict.

The European Council, which brings together the Community's heads of government or state, met in Hanover on 27–8 June 1988, at the end of the German presidency of the Council of Ministers: at the forefront of the agenda was a review of the major progress achieved under the programme for completing the internal market, including the then very recently adopted directive providing for the full liberalization of capital movements. At this meeting, the European Council agreed that a point of no return had been reached so that there could no longer be any turning back from the progressive implementation of the programme. This, the Council noted, was the general perception of all actively involved in the economic and social life of the Community. More than a third of the 300-odd measures put forward in the White Paper have already been adopted. Such progress has been made possible through full recourse to the system of qualified majority voting. By the end of 1988, the Commission will have presented the main body of its proposals as laid down by the White Paper's timetable. And in the not-too-distant future the Council of Ministers will have to take a number of decisions in respect of proposals for banking and other financial services.

One of what are termed the conclusions of the presidency at the Hanover summit was that 'the European Council recalls that, in adopting the Single Act, the member-states confirmed the objective of progressive realization of economic and monetary union'. The European Council meeting held in Madrid in June 1989 examined the means of achieving this union. To this end, a committee has been set up and entrusted with the task of studying and proposing concrete steps to lead to the realization of this aim. Such steps would eventually include the creation of a European central bank, but this was not mentioned in the conclusions of the presidency, notably because of the opposition of Mrs Thatcher. The committee consists of M. Jacques Delors, the central bank governors of member-states (including the executive head of the Institut Monétaire Luxembourgeois), another member of the Commission (Mr Frans Andriessen) and three experts designated by common accord, namely Messrs Niels Thygesen, Alexandre Lamfalussy and Miguel Boyer.

Difficulties and Resistance to Change

There is little likelihood that the large single European banking market will be fully completed by 1 January 1993. It will no doubt be realized in a discontinuous fashion rather than as the fruit of a gradual and smooth progress.

Resistance will emerge at national level to progress on matters where unanimous agreement is needed. These matters include taxation and institutional changes for advancing monetary integration. It is also to be feared that in certain other areas qualified majority voting will not always ensure the passing of measures that are necessary for the completion of the internal market before the deadline, 1 January 1993. Moreover, it may already be expected that individual member governments would resort to safeguard clauses, to avoid, delay or modify the implementation of general rules.

The Commission's wish that member-states should give priority approval to certain key decisions, without attaching prior conditions to the same, will not necessarily be accepted by national governments. The latter are likely to continue to set preconditions, make *non possumus* declarations or insist upon agreement to packages in which there is a balance of national advantage.

Such resistance arises both from governments' fears of seeing their national sovereignty or decision-making powers eroded (witness, for instance, the British refusal to have sterling join the EMS exchange-rate mechanism) and the real difficulties confronting certain governments (for instance, chronic public finance imbalances leading to a high tax burden and a 'reservation' of national savings for covering the budget deficit).

When account is taken of factors of this kind, it is not unreasonable to think that there may be the trauma of one or more crises before the internal market can be fully realized. But such crises could also lead to a two-tier or multi-tier Europe, with different groups of countries at different stages of advancement.

The implementation of the Second Coordination Directive will probably result in an enormous regulatory tangle. Twelve sets of home-country controls with their corresponding versions of the single banking licence will have to mesh in with the regulatory systems in force in the different host-countries. With home-country control in each case extending in principle to eleven host-countries, this gives a total of 132 sets of bilateral arrangements. The complication does not end there since many banks will be subject to home-country control by more than one authority, with this being a function of the greater or lesser diversification of their activities (that is, they could be subject to the tutelage not only of the banking-control authority but also, for example, to that of the stock-market authorities or the supervisory authority for mortgage-credit institutions). The granting of the single licence and the supervision of branches established in other member-states will mean an administrative shuttle between different authorities, with all the delays this implies. Moreover, the lack of prior harmonization will lead to distortions, but these will tend to disappear as banks and credit institutions adjust to the new situation and measures of harmonization are eventually introduced. This is indeed the strategy of the directive itself: its inner logic is that it should be a catalyst of change.

The Commission's watch on the respect of the EC rules on competition should also be borne in mind. Mergers will be subject to supervision whenever they involve credit institutions with total assets of more than Ecu10bn. Yet the principle of intervention by the Commission, when a merger leads to the abuse of a dominant position (defined as a market share of 20 per cent or more), is unlikely to create problems. It should be added that, for certain banking activities, it is not very meaningful to speak of a dominant position at European level inasmuch as the market in question has become a truly world one.

STRATEGIES AND SCENARIOS FOR BANKING EXPANSION UP TO 1992 (AND AFTERWARDS)

Now that we have considered the principles at the base of the Community, the legislation in force or in preparation and the likely obstacles on the road ahead, what are different scenarios which we can present for the expansion of banking activity up to 1992 and indeed afterwards?

Different scenarios partly reflect the different highlighting of different sorts of banking experience. Each bank's experience depends upon its history, ethos, size, type of activity, specialization in various markets, degree of internationalization and geographical location. Its perception of its own power of market penetration and of the magnitude of the obstacles in its way will be an element entering into its choice of action. However, no bank is entirely free in determining its strategic choice: account has to be taken of the readiness of its customers to accept it. It is virtually impossible to put precise dates on the changes in question in any particular scenario, and what cannot be realized by 1992 may perhaps take place five or ten years later.

Professor Jack Revell produced a report in 1987 on the role of the large private banks that dominate the banking systems of most industrialized countries: these are what he terms the 'core banks'.[8] He shows that the number of core banks and the degree of concentration of the banking system are mainly determined by the size of the country and the competition that these banks face from public sector financial institutions, cooperative financial institutions and foreign banks. He concludes that no country can have more than a fairly lmited number of large efficient banks, the number depending (not surprisingly) on the size of the country. Given the virtual certainty of an increase in competitive pressures between now and 1992 as well as afterwards, there will be even less space for many core banks in various countries and their numbers will tend to drop.

However, the existence in certain countries of an extensive and powerful financial sector in the hands of the state or other public-sector authorities constitutes an obstacle to a *rapprochement* between credit institutions, whether or not of the same nationality.

All this having been said, there is often a too unilateral concern with banking structures and not sufficient attention is paid to the operational data relating to costs, income and profitability, which must be an essential consideration in the strategy of any business undertaking. The considerable differences in this respect from one Community country to another will be a source of increased competition. It will to a large extent be increased competition for existing business since there is already overbanking and the cost of setting up a branch network is very high. At least for those banks which have a widely implanted branch network, the most profitable types of customer today would seem to be the SMEs (small and medium-sized enterprises) and private individuals rather than the large firms.

A bank's choice of the types of both customer and financial service product to which it wishes to give priority in its business development is therefore fundamental. It partly determines the scale of its operation: national (or regional), European (superregional) or truly international (that is, a worldwide presence). Scale cannot anyway be an end in itself, since there must also be the basic aim of profitability.

The current rise of the so-called 'superregional banks' in the USA is instructive in this respect.[9] These are banks or bank holding companies which are generally established outside the large financial centres and whose activities are concentrated on the retail banking market of either two or more states or else one big state, such as California. Their working resources are largely the stable and relatively low-cost deposits provided by their retail banking customers, whereas the 'money centre banks' must 'buy' a large proportion of their working resources on the money market. The superregionals' choice of business has proved highly profitable. As a general rule, these institutions have shied away from both international lending and corporate banking, which has spared them heavy losses on doubtful debts. They have thus been able to build up substantial shareholders' equity and score high price–earnings ratios while, for the future, they enjoy favourable growth prospects. Thanks to this prosperity, the 'superregionals' are now overtaking the 'money centre banks' in terms of stock-market capitalization.

National Bastion Scenario

Under this scenario, 'each must seek to reinforce itself within a national framework so as to be the strongest, in absolute terms, when frontiers are removed'.[10] It excludes the idea of two or more banks of different nationality joining forces to take advantage of the synergies resulting from the completion of the internal market, with establishments straddling intra-Community borders. Instead, a bank will favour a strategy of growth centred on the home market, with the possibility of acquiring other banks of the same nationality or merging with them, in order to become larger, stronger and more profitable, and consequently better able to withstand competition at home without harbouring any ambition to cross national frontiers.

Traditional Policy Continuity Scenario

Under this scenario, nothing very spectacular will happen. There will be no major transformation of banking structures, given that the Community is already criss-crossed by dense branch and automated banking networks and is overbanked in certain regions or for certain types of customer or product. Much has already been achieved by banks to assure their twin-track expansion in multi-purpose domestic 'retail' banking and in 'wholesale' banking activities centred on large firms and financial markets, with resort on the 'wholesale' side to the opening of establishments in other member-states, notably in the larger financial centres (as witness the expansion of 'international banking' in London, Paris, Frankfurt and Luxembourg).

Dampening the ardour for further expansion will be the fact that considerable resources are required to penetrate new markets, especially at a time when capital adequacy requirements are being made more stringent. Also to be borne in mind will be the 'social costs' of mergers or acquisitions, including possible reductions in the number of personnel. Finally, since banking is a 'sensitive' sector, with implications for national sovereignty in the monetary and financial sphere, certain governments will deem it their duty to prevent a too rapid or a too wide opening of their banking system to foreign competition.

Many banks will seek to preserve their independence through a policy of boosting their market share or through a policy of specialization. It will be essentially a policy of 'go it alone', a continuation of what has happened in recent years. Thus the major banks, and especially the leading banks in the larger countries, will base their expansion policies for the greater part on their past practice of acquiring smaller banks or other financial institutions in other member-states. On the other hand, banks of smaller size will pursue their independence by specializing in regional banking, in servicing specific types of customer or in developing certain types of investment service banking.

'Oil-slick' Scenario

Under the 'oil-slick' scenario, the expansion of local branch networks will lead to banks establishing branches on the other side of their intra-Community national frontiers. Its logic will be to exploit fully one's own home-based area of expansion through the spreading outwards of branches and automated bank networks into neighbouring countries. The fact that this development has not yet taken place is because, until now, it has been more worthwhile to provide services to residents of neighbouring countries in bank branches located just within the borders of the national territory. However, this situation will be radically altered, first, when the residents of other member-states are no longer considered as non-residents (as defined in national territorial terms) but instead as Community residents, and then at a much later stage, when a common European currency replaces the different national ones. This scenario is of varying relevance according to a bank's geographical position: it would, for instance, represent a more likely development for a Belgian bank than a Portuguese one.

Radical Change Scenario

Under this scenario of considerable upheaval, there will be a radical restructuring and concentration of power in the banking sector in Europe. This will take place in a variety of ways, some of which may be combined. The upheaval could continue well after 1992.

For such *rapprochement* and integration, banks will be able to choose between quite different courses of action, depending upon how far-reaching the initial steps are intended to be. The wide array of possible arrangements could thus include bilateral or multilateral cooperation agreements or alliances and a variety of forms of participation, ranging from a purely symbolical shareholding through a minority interest to a majority one, with the added option of cross-shareholdings or not. In some cases, the agreement or taking of the shareholding will be experimental and therefore reversible. In other cases, after a period of 'engagement', the point of no return will have been passed and there will be total integration or merger. Such restructuring and concentration will be accompanied by the acquisition of small or medium-sized banks in one or more other countries.

Furthermore, the banks taking part in this upheaval will also seek to increase their participations in non-banking financial intermediaries – for example, savings credit institutions, mortgage credit institutions, insurance companies, and UCITs.

Savings Flight Scenario

This scenario depicts the possible perverse effects of the Commission's strategy, about which the Boiteux Report has given warning. Whatever its probability, it is not a possibility that can be completely ruled out. Thus, under this scenario, the full liberalization of capital movements without prior tax harmonization, implying the continued existence of significant tax disparities, will result in savings being drained towards the countries with the lowest taxation (or even none at all). This will greatly affect the strategy of credit institutions in which tax planning plays an important role, inasmuch as they will feel obliged to establish themselves in the low (or zero)-tax countries for the provision of the services in question. This will be no short-lived development since any Commission plans for the approximation of direct taxation will be implemented only with difficulty. Thus the European financial area will remain a fragmented one.

External Invasion Scenario

Under this scenario, there will be a massive arrival of Japanese financial intermediaries (banks, brokerage firms, investment banks) as predicted last year by Richard Wright and Gunter Pauli in a book which has aroused much comment.[11] They will perhaps be joined by US banks returning to Europe once the present phase of restructuring in the US banking sector is over. Rather than setting up new networks of branches and automated bank equipment, which would require very considerable investment, these foreign banks will seek to buy European ones. However, as regards the plausibility of this scenario, it should be said that any such invasion would be bound to be limited. It would be checked, for instance, by the reciprocity rules contained in the proposed Second Coordination Directive, not to speak of the negative reactions in individual member-states.

Notes

1. In the rest of the text, the term 'White Paper' refers always to the White Paper from the Commission to the European Council on 'Completing the Internal Market', Commission of the European Communities, June 1985.
2. 'Creation of a European Financial Area', Communication from the Commission, 4 November 1987, document COM (87) 550 final.
3. 'Fiscalité et marché unique européen', Preliminary report of the Commission de Réflexion Economique pour la Préparation de l'Echéance de 1992 (the 'Boiteux Report'), Paris, February 1988.
4. Ibid.
5. 'Les obstacles fiscaux au marché intérieur', Commission Economique et Monétaire of the Belgian section of the Ligue Européenne de Coopération Economique, Brussels, October 1987.
6. Proposal for a 'Second Council Directive on the Coordination of Laws, Regulations and Administrative Provisions relating to the Taking-up and Pursuit of the Business of Credit Institutions and amending Directive 77/780/EEC', presented by the Commission to the Council, 23 February 1988, document COM (87) 715 final, and published in the *Official Journal of the European Communities*, no. C 84/1, 31 March 1988.
7. 'Creation of a European Financial Area'.

8. Jack Revell, *Mergers and the Role of Large Banks* (Bangor: Institute of European Finance, University College of North Wales, 1987).
9. Gary Hector, 'How Banking will Shake Out', *Fortune*, 25 April 1988.
10. Emmanuele Gazzo, 'L'Europe de 1992 impose un changement des mentalités', *La Libre Belgique*, 21 March 1988.
11. Richard W. Wright and Gunter A. Pauli, *The Second Wave: Japan's Global Assault on Financial Services* (London: Waterlow, 1987).

9 Strategies and Prospects for Japan's Banking Sector by 2000

Kazuaki Harada

What trends are likely to emerge in the world economy and in international finance as we move toward the year 2000?

Whether the world economy can achieve stable growth depends on a large number of issues. One of the most important of these is how the new US President will deal with the twin deficits – fiscal and trade – in the USA, which are ticking away like a time bomb and threatening the world economy. Another major issue is how to deal with the problem of excessive external debt of developing nations, principally in Central and South America. The integration of the European Community in 1992 and its ramifications are still another important issue that will influence the course of economic events as we approach the twenty-first century.

In retrospect, the Second World War was a part of the historical process that P. Kennedy describes in his book, *The Rise and Fall of the Great Powers*.[1] It was in fact a part of the process of the decline of the USA as a great power. The era of *Pax Americana* has already ended. The USA continues to show a large trade deficit and it has become a net debtor-nation. It has therefore lost one of the basic conditions for maintaining the dollar as the world's key currency. There is a strong possibility that the dollar-based international currency system will shift to one based on a combination of three currencies, namely the dollar, yen, and Deutsche Mark or the dollar, yen, and ECU.

If we can avoid the 'hard landing' in the world economy – the dollar's sharp deterioration – then international finance will move into an era of true globalization.

Under the sustainable growth of the world economy, some trends, such as the growing sophistication of financial service needs and technological progress in areas related to finance, are irreversible. As the trends continue, financial systems around the world will come to be more uniform. Such developments as the review of the Glass–Steagall and MacFadden Acts in the USA, the deregulation of capital

151

flows in the EC, and the Second Council Directive regarding EC integration are all expected to accelerate the worldwide trend toward universal banking and financial restructuring. With these trends in the international financial system in mind, I would like to discuss my views on changes in the banking environment in Japan and focus on developments which I see likely as we move toward the twenty-first century.

GLOBALIZATION OF FINANCIAL MARKETS AND JAPAN'S ROLE AS CREDITOR NATION

Japan Becomes the Leading Creditor Nation

Japan has overcome the effects of the sharp appreciation of the yen which followed the Plaza Agreement in the fall of 1985. Currently Japan is experiencing a boom in private capital investment of proportions that exceed those during the period of rapid growth before the first oil crisis, and economic growth of more than 5 per cent is continuing. Statistically speaking, Japan's GNP per capita exceeded that of the USA in 1987, and Japan has clearly become the second largest economy in the free world. In addition, because of Japan's large current account surplus, its net external assets exceeded those of the UK and West Germany in 1985, thus making Japan in fact the world's principal creditor-nation.

Japan is now expected to take an active position of leadership and to assist in correcting the imbalances in the world economy and in making continued world growth without inflation a reality. With these developments in the background, Japan is being called upon to do something different from what it has in the past. That is, especially in the area of finance, to use its domestic savings and surpluses in the most efficient and constructive manner. These changes in the environment are having a substantial impact on Japan's financial markets and on the management of financial institutions.

Progress toward Globalization of Finance

The world 'globalization' may be somewhat unfamiliar. In finance, when we say globalization, we mean the trend toward unification of the financial and capital markets of different nations. In contrast, the word 'internationalization' is used to describe a condition where national systems and divisions among markets are maintained, but cross-border transactions among financial institutions grow and they enter each other's markets.

When globalization takes place, domestic and foreign funds are free to move without impediment to their most efficient applications. In global markets, participants are able to overcome the constraints of time and space, and the whole world becomes a single financial market. Dealing in foreign currencies and bonds, which is already taking place on a 24-hour round-the-clock basis is a good example of globalization.

Four factors have emerged clearly since the late 1970s to propel us toward global markets. The first has been the decline in investment opportunities in the real economy accompanying the movement toward slower economic growth. This has lead to increased interest-rate sensitivity among borrowers and investors, and has stimulated international capital flows along with the emergence of growing imbalances in the current accounts of various nations. These developments have given rise to the need for financial services that transcend the boundaries of individual nations.

The second factor has been deregulation of financial transactions. Restrictions on capital flows and foreign exchange controls have been eliminated in one country after another. Nations around the world have proceeded with the deregulation of interest rates and their financial systems, according to their own timetables, but still with the same objective of deregulating financial activities. As deregulation has proceeded and international financial transactions have become easier, we are gradually moving into an era of uniformity of systems among nations.

The third factor has been advancement in technology. The rapid development of telecommunications and computer technology has made possible the development of sophisticated systems that combine the functions of information-delivery and funds transfer, including settlement of transactions. These systems are also capable of processing massive volumes of information, making possible substantial reductions in the cost of financial service transactions.

The fourth factor has been the shift toward more securities-based financing, to which I will refer as 'securitization'. The volume of government bond issues in industrialized nations has increased, issues of bonds in the Eurobond market have expanded, and in the USA especially there has been a trend toward securitization of banking assets in order to increase liquidity. These developments have brought a huge increase in the volume of securities outstanding and expansion in market transactions which take place on the basis of price-related information. Growth in these competitive, market transactions has brought an expansion in the number of market participants and a need for standardization of transaction rules. This has been one of the motive forces leading to globalization of financial activities.

The four factors or trends described are, in many respects, irreversible. These trends are interacting with and supporting one another, leading to further 'financial globalization'. Because of the irreversible aspects of these trends, a return to the previous order is now difficult or impossible.

This movement toward globalization is bringing a trend toward uniformity in the financial systems and regulatory frameworks of various nations. One of the first effects of globalization has been the stimulation of international competition with regard to financial systems. Since in a global market, financial institutions and corporations can choose freely from markets and products, transactions will flee from countries that maintain inefficient restrictions on financial transactions. In other words, 'hollowing out' of the market takes place. Consequently, countries have begun to compete with one another, changing their financial systems and relaxing regulations in order to attract financial transactions. The establishment of offshore markets in various financial centres and the Big Bang in London are examples of this trend. Also, the review of the Glass–Steagall Act in the USA and the movement toward integration of financial markets in the EC are also examples in a broad sense of the competition in systems which have been mentioned.

A second effect of globalization has been a number of requests for a 'level playing field' along with intensification of competition among market participants. The objective of this request for a level playing field is to enable financial institutions to use the know-how they have accumulated in their home markets and other expertise by making changes in regulatory frameworks in other countries and thus achieving uniformity of competitive conditions.

Steps taken to achieve a level playing field include the Financial Services Act in the UK and the sections related to finance in the Omnibus Trade Bill in the USA which aims at strengthening American competitiveness. These pieces of legislation aim at achieving a level playing field through the principle of reciprocity in treatment. The introduciton of international standards for bank capital ratios by the Bank for International Settlements and the imposition of new regulations regarding liquidity by the Bank of England are primarily aimed at setting uniform international standards for supervising activities of financial institutions along with the increased risk of global operations. But another objective, which cannot be overlooked, of the introduction of these international regulations is to achieve a level playing field with Japanese financial institutions.

CURRENT STATE OF JAPAN'S FINANCIAL MARKETS

Rapid Expansion of the Tokyo Market and Japanese Banks

Tokyo's financial markets are undergoing very rapid expansion. For example, the average daily volume of transactions in Tokyo's foreign exchange market from January to September 1987 was $87.0bn, seven times the level seven years ago. Tokyo's foreign exchange market has thus become the second largest in the world after London. The total market capitalization of the first section of the Tokyo Stock Exchange at the end of 1987 was the equivalent of $2.76 trillion, three times the value two years ago. In addition, the market capitalization and volume of transactions on the Tokyo Stock Exchange now exceed those of the New York stock exchange. Also, the total volume of transactions on Tokyo's bond market rose to the astronomical sum of $40 trillion, in 1987, double the level for the previous year. Transactions in Tokyo's bond futures market, which began operations in October 1985, have already exceeded those of the Chicago Board of Trade. Next year, plans call for the establishment of a broader financial futures market in Tokyo, which will also contribute to the development of financial markets.

Along with the growth in the Tokyo market, the operations of Japanese banks have shown massive expansion. This growth has been caused by the large volume of domestic savings, the expansion of domestic financial markets, extension of operations to overseas markets, and other factors. Even by international rankings of banks by assets, Japanese banks have achieved a very high standing. According to recent rankings, the largest five banks in the world in terms of assets are Japanese.

Progress toward Liberalization

During most of the period immediately after the Second World War, Japan's financial system was characterized by strict controls on deposit and other interest rates. In addition, the scope of operations of different types of financial institutions was narrowly defined and carefully supervised. Strong controls were maintained on international capital flows.

During the latter half of the 1970s, however, a number of developments began to bring pressures for change. For example, interest-rate sensitivity among corporations and individuals increased. New investment opportunities became available as the volume of government bonds outstanding expanded very rapidly and the size of the secondary bond market ballooned. Also, the need for freer inflows and outflows of capital became stronger as the economy and industries became more international. Because of these three developments, the older, more restrictive system was no longer suited to the changing times. Disintermediation and other contradictions began to occur as funds shifted from deposits and other investments with regulated rates to those with free market rates. Restrictions came to represent an obstacle to the efficient operation of financial markets.

Besides these domestic developments, requests from overseas for the opening and liberalization of Japan's financial markets and their integration into the international financial system grew stronger. In May 1984, a joint Japanese and US working committee published the report commonly known as the Japan–US Yen–Dollar Committee Report. Since then, movement toward financial deregulation has been steady. Progress, for example, has been made in interest-rate deregulation, expansion of short-term financial markets, and the internationalization of the yen.

Rapid Progress toward Internationalization

Japan has also made rapid progress toward internationalization. Using the large volume of domestic funds, investors have substantially increased their acquisition of foreign financial assets. Overseas securities investments by Japanese investors in 1987 amounted to $1.3 trillion, an amazing forty-three times the level of seven years earlier. In fact, Japanese investors have come to account for one-third of US government-bond purchases in tenders of new issues by the US Treasury. Japan is therefore a major source of funding for the USA.

Rapid internationalization is taking place not only in the corporate sector, but also in the financial sector. Japanese banks have become very active in international financial markets. The share of the assets of Japanese banks in total international banking assets rose to 18.3 per cent at the end of 1987. Japanese banks are therefore moving up rapidly toward the level of UK banks, 21.6 per cent, which is still the largest share.

The swift expansion of overseas operations of Japanese banks is also reflected in the rapid growth in their overseas office since the beginning of the 1980s. Acquisitions of and investments in foreign financial institutions by Japanese banks have shown a sharp upward trend in recent years. On the other hand, the number of foreign financial institutions seeking business opportunities in the Tokyo market has also grown. Currently seventy-nine foreign banks have one or more branches in Japan and the total number of foreign bank branches is 115. A growing number of foreign financial institutions have also obtained securities licenses and set up trust banking operations.

These developments have had a major impact on Japan's financial markets. With the growth of international financial transactions of corporations and financial institutions and the entry of Japanese financial institutions into overseas markets and foreign financial institutions into the Japanese market, information and knowledge flows have expanded greatly. For example, new financial products and techniques, such as cash management systems, swaps, and options, have become commonly known in Japan. This has led corporations and large institutional investors to demand increasingly sophisticated services. For residents of Japan, especially corporations and institutional investors, the overseas markets have come closer and closer. Japanese corporations have become very active in raising funds in overseas capital markets through issuance of securities. In fact, about 40 per cent of all securities issues by Japanese companies took place overseas in 1987. The stage is rapidly being set for full-scale globalization.

Acceleration of Securitization

The trend toward securitization is one of the factors bringing about globalization of financial markets. But in Japan's case, our emergence as a leading international creditor nation and the beginning of globalization have also accelerated the trend toward securitization.

Japan's emergence as a leading creditor-nation and the sharp drop in interest rates in Japan following the Plaza Agreement in 1985 are closely linked. The decline in interest rates brought increased activity in Japan's stock and bond markets. This in turn brought increased activity in investment of funds and fund-raising activities. For example, on the corporate fund-raising side, the anticipation of rising stock prices has led corporations to shift to issues of convertible bonds and bonds with warrants as a low-cost means of raising funds. For example, the percentage of total funding accounted for by equity-linked issues rose from 13 per cent in 1983 to 24 per cent in 1987, or about 10 percentage points.

From the point of view of corporate and individual investors, investment fund-type products which allow investors to participate indirectly in the benefits of rising securities prices have become very popular. For example, the outstanding balance of investment trusts, or what are called 'mutual funds' in America, has exceeded $400bn, ten times the level only five years ago. Development of these investment funds has been aided by the major progress in recent years in computer software technology.

DIRECTIONS OF CHANGE UP TO THE YEAR 2000

Japan's financial markets are undergoing rapid expansion, and full-fledged globalization of markets is being called for. As globalization takes place, Japan's financial system will very likely undergo marked changes. Banks must accept as a given the unavoidable changes that are taking place in the environment. The strategic response they make to change will have a major impact on their ability to survive. I would like to outline briefly some of the changes which I see taking place in the operating environment in Japan.

Japan's Creditor-Nation Standing and the Tokyo Market

The Tokyo market has already moved up alongside London and New York in terms of size. But the individual markets that make up the overall market, such as individual securities markets, short-term money markets, and future markets are still in need of further development. In particular, the markets need further depth and steps should be taken to increase the convenience of transactions. The sharp rise in costs of office space is representative of the increase in operating costs in Tokyo, an issue which must be addressed.

Whether the participants are in favour or not, the Tokyo market will continue to evolve to become a market open to participants in Japan and overseas and to become a freer market. To give one example of the movement toward a more open market, beginning in October this year, 40 per cent of the issues of new, 10-year government bonds, which are the principal maturity issued by the Japanese government, have been opened to competitive bidding.

Deregulation of the Financial System to Proceed

There are two important types of deregulation in progress in Japan, deregulation of interest rates and deregulation of the structure of the financial system.

Deregulation of interest rates has proceeded and is now in the final stages. Freeing of interest rates on large time-deposits has almost been completed. By the middle of 1989, we expect that small deposits of ¥10m (approximately $80 000) or less, bearing interest rates linked to market rates and eligible for deposit insurance, will be introduced.

The next step will be accelerated deregulation of the financial system, which has been proceeding at a relatively slower pace. Thus far, four major distinctions among the activities of Japanese financial institutions have been strictly maintained:

1. the operations of banks and securities companies have been separate;
2. regular banks have not been permitted to engage in trust business;
3. operations of long-term credit banks have been separate from those of short-term credit institutions;
4. specialized institutions have been maintained for small and medium-sized companies.

As globalization proceeds, a review of these distinctions among the operations of different financial institutions will be necessary.

In December 1987, the Financial Systems Subcommittee released a report concerning the steps to be taken regarding the system of specialized financial institutions. This report takes the strong position that if Japan's unique system of maintaining separation between the activities of various types of financial institutions is maintained in its current form, this will lead to a hollowing-out of the Tokyo market and decline in the efficiency of financial services. Based on this view, the report goes on to recommend that the current system should be thoroughly reviewed and that a system which is suited to integration within the international financial system should be established. The basic direction suggested is that specialized areas should not be defined legally for specific financial institutions. Instead, through deregulation of operating areas, the principle of competition should be brought into play and financial institutions can choose their own areas of specialization. This should lead to a more natural and efficient evolution of the financial system.

The principle of joint entry into new areas has already been applied in the case of commercial paper. Both banks and securities companies have been given permission to participate in this market which began operation in Japan in late 1987. Thus, for new business areas where there is strong demand, stimulating competition can be used as a means of expanding and increasing the efficiency of the market. From this point of view, requests for the application of this approach to allow the entry of financial institutions into a wide range of areas are growing.

The Trend toward Universal Banking

My belief is that the gradual pace of deregulation of the financial system will move at a faster pace than is generally expected. I also believe that Japan may adopt the universal banking system, which would imply that various types of financial institutions enter the traditional fields of other financial institutions. Universal banking, I believe, is the wave of the future in international financial markets.

In Europe, regulatory authorities have traditionally given approval for financial institutions to engage in banking, securities and trust management. But national markets were kept separate and the scale of operations was small, so that they had little influence on international markets. However, with the integration of the EC in 1992 a huge market will come into being where universal banking will be permitted. In the USA commercial banks are allowed to engage in trust management, but the banking and securities businesses are separated by the Glass–Steagall Act. Despite this, there is a growing movement in favour of relaxing these restrictions on activities of financial institutions to improve the efficiency of financial markets.

For this reason, the Glass–Steagall Act is coming under close scrutiny and review.

In order to maintain the competitiveness of Japan's financial system and to promote the entry of more foreign financial institutions into the Japanese market, Japan must also move in this direction. Within the regulatory organizations of the government there seems to be already what is called an 'investment banking concept'. That is, there is a movement to give approval to universal banking, with the condition that services are provided only to the wholesale market.

STRATEGIES AND PROSPECTS FOR JAPAN'S CITY BANKS

Next, I would like to state my more concrete views of the present and future response of Japan's major city banks to changes in the operating environment.

The Response to Global Markets

In view of the trend toward financial globalization, the major Japanese city banks have rapidly expanded their overseas networks and systems. Geographically, the expansion has been primarily in three regions: North America, Europe, and South-east Asia, principally in the newly industrialized countries (NICs). In the past upgrading of overseas capabilities has been primarily aimed at providing services to Japanese client companies setting up overseas operations, but the goals of recent expansion have become more diverse. These goals now include the establishment of bases for 24-hour currency- and bond-trading and for participation in local financial markets.

A more detailed analysis by region shows that in North America expansion aimed at supporting the local operations of Japanese companies and at creating currency dealing bases is just about complete. Expansion in North America is now focused on two new goals. The first new goal is creating 24-hour trading capabilities in such markets as futures and options and creating global networks for such information-oriented operations as mergers and acquisitions business. The second new goal is to build stronger ties with local markets through expansion of transactions in the middle and retail markets.

Up to now most of the business of city banks in Europe has centred on currency and money-market operations, other business in the

London-based Euromarket, and on bond underwriting. The banks are now taking additional measures to support the operations of the many Japanese companies which are expanding their presence in Europe in preparation for the economic integration of the EC in 1992. The banks are also taking energetic steps to set up new bases and otherwise bolster capabilities with the goal of increasing their participation in the various continental financial markets which are expected to become more dynamic.

Japan's city banks established positions throughout South-east Asia relatively early, in order to engage in a wide range of activities. Of all the world's regions, this region is expected to achieve the fastest economic growth in the years ahead, and the appreciation of the yen has made continuing direct investments by Japanese companies in the region highly likely. Because opportunities for financial transactions and other bank business are also projected to grow rapidly, the city banks are quickly expanding their presence by increasing staff and facilities.

Several plans have been suggested to ease the problems of the developing nations labouring under the burden of accumulated external debt and from inflation due to depreciating currencies. These plans include debt-equity conversion plans and the scheme presented by Japan's Finance Minister Miyazawa at the recent IMF meeting, which calls for the securitization of debt based on guarantees by the IMF and other organizations. These plans offer hope that the economies of these nations might benefit from new loans and a new influx of foreign capital. This situation may well represent yet another business opportunity for Japanese banks.

As a result of this progressive globalization, business strategies of banks can be seen as falling into one of the four categories described by John G. Heimann, Vice Chairman of Merrill Lynch Capital Markets.[2]

Global Financial Institutions

With round-the-clock trading capabilities, these institutions trade all types of financial products in each of the world's major financial centres. They possess a worldwide network of branches and huge project-funding capabilities. Mr Heimann feels that no more than about twenty-four to thirty institutions will be able to survive in this super-multinational form. In fact, most of Japan's leading banks are aiming to grow into this type of institution.

National Financial Institutions

These institutions provide a full range of financial services, but limit their operations to a single country or to a block of nations such as the EC.

Regional Financial Institutions

These institutions contribute to the domestic region of the country in which they operate by providing a limited range of high-quality financial services.

Specialized Financial Institutions

The strategy of these institutions is to concentrate on the low-cost provision of a limited range of financial services.

Creation of Japanese-Style Bank Holding Companies

Japan's leading banks are implementing strategies with the goal of building comprehensive financial capabilities. They are essentially aiming to become universal banks. In addition to traditional operations of accepting deposits and extending loans, Japan's leading city banks are working to meet all their clients' fund procurement and asset-management needs through new services in such areas as securities, insurance, trust management, and factoring.

Because of the ongoing trend toward securitization, the banks have placed special emphasis on expanding securities operations. They have energetically begun over-the-counter sales of, and dealing in, government bonds, but they are not permitted to underwrite or broker corporate bonds and equities in Japan. The banks are presently expanding and strengthening their affiliated securities companies. It is widely believed, however, that within a few years these banks will be allowed to engage in securities business directly.

All the leading banks established affiliated companies to participate in markets for such products and services as leases, credit cards, housing finance, mortgage securities, guarantees, venture capital, and factoring. Because Japanese law prohibits the establishment of holding companies, the banks are meeting client needs through the Japanese-style equivalent of bank holding companies – by building groups of financial companies centred on the parent bank.

Strategies for Strengthening Information Services

In step with the trend to ever more diverse and sophisticated financial services, banks are steadily developing their strategies for increasing the value-added of these services and for providing them through networks. Information capabilities, in combination with product development capabilities, are crucial requirements for competitiveness in global markets. Today, understanding the movements of money without reference to the flow of information is impossible.

The provision of more sophisticated assistance in business development, managerial advice, and economic and other information services is being energetically promoted by banking institutions as a means of adding value to traditional operations and providing comprehensive financial services. For example, such basic intermediary services as linking buyers and sellers and providing real-estate information are increasingly being expanded to include such relatively sophisticated information services as advisory and organizational services for technological cooperation arrangements, mergers and acquisitions (M&A), services, and real-estate development projects. In addition to promoting this type of business vigorously through relationship management services, each of the leading banks has set up a specialized section in the headquarters to concentrate and make readily available information of value to management.

Accurate information and advisory capabilities regarding trends in currency exchange rates and interest rates are increasingly important in all phases of the marketing operations of banks. Leading banks are working to upgrade their marketing staff's understanding of these trends and, headquarters staff are preparing and providing clients with periodic reports of varying frequency. A development related to this stepped-up provision of information is the establishment of bank-associated think tanks. Sanwa Research Institute Corporation is the first of these research companies established by the leading Japanese banks.

The key words in bank information strategies are 'networks' and 'artificial intelligence'. Emphasis is being placed on the speedy creation of networks that link domestic and international branches and allow for the collection, processing, and accumulation of large volumes of client information. This information is then rerouted through the branches to clients. At present, each of the leading banks is investing from $500m to $700m in such networks. Capabilities of these networks have surpassed simple data processing and they are capable of providing real-time marketing information.

It is expected that artificial intelligence software capable of making judgements will become an indispensable tool for credit analysis and new product development. Together with the shift toward emphasizing return on assets and the closely related stress on expansion of income from fee-based businesses, the transformation of banking into an information industry has clearly begun.

Increasing Emphasis on Return on Assets

A recent milestone in the ongoing globalization of finance, was the decision by the Bank of International Settlements in December 1987 to set international standards for the ratio of capital to risk weighted assets. These new standards will have a significant influence on Japan's financial industry and on the management of Japanese banks. The standards call for banks to raise their narrowly defined balance-sheet capital ratios to 4 per cent by the fiscal year 1992, while broadly defined capital ratios that take account of such off balance-sheet assets as unrealized capital gains on securities must be raised to 8 per cent. Both ratios must be maintained subsequently. Japanese banks at present (1988) have narrowly-defined capital ratios around 3 per cent and will have to work hard to conform to the new standards.

In the past, Japanese banks have been volume-oriented. They stressed asset growth, believing that profits will naturally increase together with asset growth. As a result, the rate of growth in their capital often did not match that in overall assets.

Because of the recently announced standards, however, in addition to the amount of profit earned, such ratios of profits to capital resources as the ratio of return on assets will be increasingly important performance indicators. While return on assets is a widely used performance indicator in Europe and the USA, there is still only a vague familiarity with it in Japan. In the future, Japanese bankers will work to increase their higher-yield earning assets and to strengthen their capabilities further in fee businesses, which do not entail asset growth.

Strengthening Risk-Management Systems

The absence of a single bank failure in post-war Japan is illustrative of the extremely stable conditions that have prevailed, and these conditions have been conducive to promoting trust in financial transactions. Behind this stability are several factors including:

1. restrictions on establishment of new banks operations and what is commonly known as the 'national convoy system' which involves providing protection for small and medium-sized banks;
2. frequent inspections and audits and the large volume of information exchanged by financial institutions and the regulatory authorities;
3. adherence to the basic principle of providing collateral for financial transactions and other such special practices that are due to either legislation or customs.

This Japanese-style safety net is already changing in substance, in the direction of requiring more self-reliance on the part of individual private banks, and there is a growing trend in financial legislation toward promoting more competition. The requirement for providing collateral for loans and certain other financial transactions is also likely to be relaxed as Japanese banks move more in the direction of practices in other countries.

At the same time, the ongoing globalization and liberalization of finance is causing the amount and variety of risks accompanying bank operations to increase. The risks include credit risk; such market risks as exchange rate, interest rate, and securities-price risk; liquidity risk; and system risk. The proliferation of risk is presenting quite a challenge to Japanese banks, and they are moving quickly to upgrade their risk-management systems.

The issue of credit risk will become increasingly important as Japanese banks expand such non-collateralized business as overseas transactions with local companies and domestic transactions with small and medium-sized businesses aiming to commercialize new technologies and ideas. As a result, the banks are working to rapidly strengthen their capabilities for gathering and evaluating credit information. Japanese banks' traditional practice of giving their employees who have higher educational backgrounds a combination of training in financial operations and hands-on experience in several bank departments is a strength in that it enables these employees to gain a comprehensive perspective on credit risk.

In addition, along with the completion of the third phase on-line computer systems, it will be possible to check on changes in corporate performance and identify any falsification of financial statements automatically. The new system will thus include an early-warning system for dealing with potential credit problems. In the future, the banks will have to work energetically to further expedite the development of computerized support systems that make use of artificial-intelligence capabilities and accumulated data and know-how.

The development of effective Assets Liabilities Management (ALM) systems will be the key to the response of Japanese banks to rising market risks, such as currency, interest, and securities price risks. The weight of banks' overseas assets and liabilities is increasing in step with globalization. Domestically, the liberalization of interest on small savings accounts will eliminate one of the last methods of fund procurement that is not sensitive to market trends. On the fund-management side of banking operations, securitization and deregulation are likely to cause growth in securities holdings. All these factors dictate the upgrading of market risk evaluation capabilities. All the leading Japanese banks are taking such organizational steps as creating ALM committees, training ALM specialists and other necessary personnel, and upgrading computer systems for position monitoring and management. In addition, there will have to be intensified emphasis on other means of avoiding risk, such as through the accumulation of expertise in futures trading and through the promotion of spread lending.

The ongoing globalization of finance implies the development of a network linking various types of settlement systems. There is concern that, in the case of a system failure, damage to the resultant large-scale international settlement system might have serious worldwide ramifications. There is therefore a growing need for the establishment of international regulations and a safety net by the public sector. In addition, private financial institutions must work to development fail-safe systems and must make efforts to supervise systems on their own responsibility by carrying out inspections of electronic data-processing systems and conducting training to cope with disasters.

One common point which can be made about all these risk-management policies is that awareness of the importance of risk control must be increased throughout the organization as a whole and that personnel must be trained to manage risk. Down-to-earth activities of this kind will be very important.

ISSUES FOR JAPAN'S FINANCIAL SERVICES INDUSTRY

Looking to the twenty-first century, it is hard to imagine that the USA will find an easy solution to its balance-of-payments deficit and its rising external debt. In view of this prospect, the continued use of the US dollar as the only key international currency will be very likely to continue to destabilize the international monetary system as the dollar experiences wide fluctuations in value. Given the present, wavering state of *Pax Americana*, we may soon be seriously considering a transition to a new international monetary system, based on three key currencies, namely the dollar, the yen, and the ECU (or the Deutsche Mark).

An international monetary system with the yen as a key currency may be seen as appropriate in view of Japan's importance as a major creditor-nation. As the deregulation of Japan's financial and capital markets proceeds, emphasis should be placed on the creation of efficient, easy-to-use markets. We should also work to put into place a global settlement system for international financial transactions that links New York, the Euromarket, and Tokyo. We must also endeavour to maintain the stability of the Japanese financial system to retain international trust and confidence.

Simultaneously with the reform of the financial system by the monetary authorities, Japanese banks should work to develop financial services and products that make the yen an attractive currency. We should also devote considerable effort to upgrading and ensuring the reliability of our international on-line computer systems. We must also increase our efforts to attain soundness of our operations on our own initiative and responsibility.

In addition, as the major participants at one of the three poles of the triple-key-currency system, Japan's banks can be expected to contribute greatly to the efficiency and stability of the world's financial system. Up to now, Japan's financial liberalization and the responses of Japanese banks have followed steps taken in Europe and the USA. At present, however, the transformation of the global financial system is proceeding simultaneously in all areas. The basic shape of the future financial system and ideal standards for bank management are still under consideration in Europe and the USA.

Along with Japan's manufacturing industries, Japan's financial system and bank management have entered a period in which the basic manual has yet to be written. In *The Rise and Fall of the Great Powers*, Paul Kennedy writes that the economic decline of the USA began when US manufacturing power was unable to cope with the costs associated with the nation's role as a global superpower. On the other hand, Professor Kennedy notes that Japan is faced with the dilemma of being in the difficult-to-justify position of economically and financially dominating the USA while not paying the military costs usually deemed appropriate for a superpower. As a major group among the world's banks, Japan's banks must be aware of their responsibility to provide a model for the world's financial system and for bank management. This will be one of the principal issues facing Japan's financial community as we move toward the twenty-first century.

Notes

1. Paul Kennedy, *The Rise and Fall of the Great Powers: Economic Change and Military Conflict from 1500 to 2000* (New York: Random House, 1987) 677 pp.
2. John G. Heimann, in *Nihan Keizai Shinbun* (*Japan Economic Journal*), 2 August 1988.

10 Guidelines for Economic Rigour, Financial Health and Monetary Order: The Work of a Minister of Finance

H. Onno Ruding

MACROECONOMIC POLICY

A healthy banking sector can only exist in a healthy economy. Internal and external monetary stability, sound fiscal policies, and flexible markets are prerequisites for the healthy functioning of all sectors of the economy. Looking after, and improving the national macroeconomic framework and enhancing the development of the banking sector, are by far the most important tasks of the Minister of Finance.

In many ways a Finance Minister's role is comparable to that of a physician. In my case, the patient is The Netherlands, and like most physicians, I am concerned with the general well-being of the patient, something which an economist would call the macroeconomic outlook. When I took office in 1982 my patient was not feeling very well. He was seriously overweight. This was illustrated by excessive government spending and a large budget deficit. His 'blood pressure' meaning high inflation and high-interest rates was far too high. And last but not least, the patient was suffering from 'chronic arthritis' – that is: stagnation and unemployment due to vested interests and inefficient markets. Like other doctors it took me quite some time to convince my patient of the benefits of my medicine. Reduction of subsidies and social benefits, general wage restraint, and measures aimed at a better allocation of resources and improvement of the functioning of markets, were imposed – under some protest – in the first period of treatment. This all under the heading of 'more market and less government'.

Initially, recovery came at a slow pace. The medicine we Finance Ministers have on offer is often – alas – no miracle drug! However, helped by stimulating surroundings and some fresh air – that is, buoyant export markets and lower energy prices – the patient started to improve. Now, six years later (1988), the patient is in reasonably good shape; employment has risen by almost 10 per cent, inflation is down to negligible levels, direct investment has recovered strongly, and economic growth is at a stable and reassuring 2.5 per cent.

The 'chronic arthritis' has not disappeared yet however, and the patient is still quite flabby with a budget deficit of 6 per cent of GNP in 1988. But we are working on it! For 1990, a deficit of less than 5 per cent of GNP is foreseen. In general, optimism and willingness to overcome inefficiencies and spending overruns have increased, and these are very good signs. Government policy for the coming period is moving into another phase. We are planning to implement some important structural changes in the economy: simplification and restructuring of the tax system (including lowering all marginal tax rates and reduction of a number of deductions), of the health sector and of the social security system. By 1990, I hope, the Netherlands will be firmly on its feet again.

This short 'case history' illustrates, where, for many of the countries of Europe, the main focus of national economic policy lies in coming years. Now that monetary and fiscal policy are, to a large extent, back on track, we must concentrate on the structural rigidities in our economies, most specifically on the distortions caused by subsidies and price-fixing in the agricultural sector, in the labour market, and also in some of our old industries such as shipbuilding and steel. Elimination of these structural rigidities, which hinder the general efficiency of our economies, should be a preliminary goal on our way to a unified European market in 1992.

THE BANKING SECTOR

As Minister of Finance, but also as chairman of the Interim Committee of the IMF, I cannot fail to see the importance of stable and efficient capital flows, both between industrial countries and in the framework of the debt problem of a number of developing countries. Bank intermediation still plays an important – and again increasing – role in this context.

On a national level, it would seem to me that the banking sector is of exceptional importance to the rest of the economy. Accepting deposits from the public and operating the payment system are such important functions for society that they warrant the special care of the government for the functioning of the banking system. Here the concern of both the Minister of Finance and the Central Bank's is above all the stability of the financial system. This of course does not imply that bank profitability and a sound competitive environment are not important as well.

I think the history of the financial sector has proved time and time again that a certain degree of government regulation is necessary to guarantee the stability of the system. Too often market participants have turned a blind eye on the risks that everybody is taking, which one could call systemic risks. As John Maynard Keynes commented bitingly: 'A "sound" banker, alas!, is not one who foresees danger and avoids it, but one who, when he is ruined, is ruined in a conventional and orthodox way along with his fellows, so that no one can really blame him.'[1] There is some element of truth in this rather cynical remark. The international debt crisis has in recent years shown once again the vulnerability of the banking sector to systemic risks.

In The Netherlands, as in most other countries, the concern for bank stability has led to a comprehensive regulatory framework for the banking system supervised by the Central Bank, and despite the debt crisis Dutch banks have a very sound financial structure. In some other countries the problems have been – and are – greater mainly because of a larger exposure to Third World debt. From a banking system point of view however, the crisis has now been largely contained, which can be seen as a success for the existing national and international regulatory frameworks.

Structural Change in the Banking Environment

There is, however, no reason to sit back and be complacent. The coming years will see major changes in the structure of international banking, especially in the EC countries. Not only because the process of financial innovation will continue, and confront banks and bank regulators with new – and perhaps not yet fully recognized – challenges; but also because of the EC's goal of one internal market by 1992, which will eliminate most national barriers for banking enterprises in the EC countries. These two developments ask for appropriate responses by the monetary authorities of the countries concerned.

It is here, I think, that the task of Finance Ministers with regard to the banking sector, especially in the EC countries, is most urgent. Why do these developments demand our full attention? First, financial innovation and integration of financial markets will still further diminish the national autonomy with regard to monetary policy. Stable internal and external monetary conditions, however, will remain a major concern for any responsible monetary authority. I think it is wrong to believe that these policy objectives depend on an autonomous national monetary policy. For the future, coordination of monetary policy, on a European level, and whenever possible on a wider scale, will be essential. If we believe that freer and more efficient financial markets will benefit us all, we must face up to the necessity of policy coordination. If we hesitate, the market will force it upon us. It is our task as Finance Ministers, and as Governors of Central Banks as well, to anticipate these events, not to be led by them.

Furthermore I believe that good policy coordination demands an adequate institutional framework. I am not denying the usefulness of *ad hoc* consultations between the major countries in times of crisis. But in normal times a forum where all countries, big and small, are represented will much better ensure stability and cooperation between participants. In the European Community, policy coordination and convergence have become household words. The perspective of a European Central Bank has become more realistic again. We in the Netherlands believe that such an institution will be an essential element in a future economic and monetary union. On a world scale the institution for policy coordination – namely the IMF – is already there. I know that in the past fifteen years the IMF has diversified away from this role to some extent. It would seem to me a very positive development if the IMF were once again to become the main forum for consultations on international policy coordination and the improvement of the international monetary system, and if it were to be allowed to exert its influence on industrial and developing countries alike.

Second, financial market integration, especially in the EC countries, calls for standardisation of national regulatory frameworks. Otherwise, the least regulated national banking sectors will outflank the more strictly regulated sectors. I hope, however, that the monetary authorities of the industrial countries can avoid standardizing regulatory systems by way of political barter. By that I mean that the end-result should not be a kind of average – or worse, a cumulation – of the now existing regulatory frameworks. I think it is important to conceive a balanced regulatory framework in which an efficient and stable international banking system can develop. This does not mean that everything should be as free and liberalized as possible. As I have already said, the banking sector needs a sound regulatory framework. What it does not need is overregulation.

The progress in this area, so far, has been encouraging. The report of the Cooke Committee is a major advance in the field of capital requirements, and can only be endorsed. The European framework, on which discussions are now taking place in Brussels, should draw heavily on this report. Other EC directives for regulating the banking sector can win my sympathy, provided they are useful for building an integrated market, free of unnecessary regulations. An integrated European market does not need protection from external competition. In particular the principle of 'reciprocity', which the EC Commission advocates for the establishment of foreign banks on domestic markets, may in practice evolve into a purely protectionist measure against non-EC banks. As for the Netherlands, measures concerning reciprocity should only be contemplated if they are surrounded by safeguards to ensure their purely defensive character and if they are aimed solely at clear cases of unfair discrimination. A 'fortress Europe' is the last thing we need. It would be good for neither economic rigour, financial health, nor monetary order. I am, therefore, opposed to any clause that could lead to a 'fortress Europe'.

Note

1. John Maynard Keynes, *Essays in Persuasion* (London: Macmillan, 1931) p. 176.

11 Public Authorities' Relations to the Banking Sector

E. Gerald Corrigan

Why is it that governments of all kinds and in all places concern themselves with the well-being of banking and financial markets and institutions? Obviously, there are a variety of reasons, some of them at the micro-level, such as protecting individual investors or depositors, trying to provide for a reasonable degree of fairness in the market-place and so on. But, at a macroeconomic level there are three factors that really stand behind public policy concerns with the well-being of financial institutions and markets:

1. It is widely recognized – sometimes implicitly, sometimes explicitly – that one of the central roles of the banking system is to provide for the efficient allocation of savings and capital resources. At times, that aspect of the financial system does not get as much attention as it deserves. Yet, banking and finance do not exist unto themselves or in a vacuum. They exist because they have an essential task, and the reason we care so much is that to the extent the banking and financial system does that job well, it spurs the life-blood of economic growth; capital formation, productivity gains and rising standards of living.

2. Chapter 10 of this volume has pointed out the connection between macroeconomic stability and the stability of the banking and financial system. But the reverse is also true in that if there is no essential stability and continuity in the banking and financial system there will be no economic stability more generally – the two go hand-in-hand. And that, I think, is the second macroeconomic reason why we care.

3. Systemic risk is the third factor. By this is meant the reality that in the banking and financial system it is possible that the disturbances in an individual institution or in an individual segment of the market can quickly transmit themselves to other institutions and other segments of markets, nationally and internationally. In the

process, they can create more generalized problems and at the extreme can undermine financial and economic stability.

These issues are at the heart of the widespread, indeed universal, recognition that there are public policy considerations associated with the operation of the banking and financial system. It is also true that it has never been easy to strike the appropriate balance between the dictates of the market-place on the one hand – the dictates of innovation, change and competition – and those public-policy considerations which take the form of a strong and flexible system of official supervision that tries to ensure that broad objectives of safe and sound banking are realized.

That has never been easy, but I would argue that today it is probably harder than it has been historically. I think one of the reasons why it is harder is that systemic risk today may be greater than it once was. From a public-policy prospective I believe that we should operate on the assumption that it is. I am inclined to believe that systemic risk may be greater for many of reasons: the whole process of globalization, innovation and high-tech banking. In Chapter 3, Dini has made the point that those things, especially innovation, cannot reduce risk to the system as a whole; they move it around and one question that comes to my mind is whether those who end up holding risk always recognize the extent to which they are at risk. If they do not, then it seems to me that that in itself is compatible with the hypothesis that systemic risk has increased.

I also believe that the increased complexity in the market-place may be working in that direction. There are many intricacies involved with the day-to-day workings of the market and the intricacies and complexities associated with contemporary financial instruments; the options market is a case in point, and is one which is a very difficult instrument to understand fully.

The complex linkages between financial institutions on a worldwide basis can also be a source of new elements of risk. In the banking and financing business consideration must be given not only to the ability of one's counterparty to perform, but also to that of the counterparty's counterparty and his counterparty, in turn.

I have a unique perspective on this because I sit at 33 Liberty Street in New York every day and watch something like one trillion five hundred billion dollars in transactions flow through our computers and those of the clearing house banks in New York. That flow of transactions creates linkages of an operational, liquidity and credit nature that bind together all major international financial institutions in ways which I believe are very profound. This is another illustration of why I believe we should operate on the hypothesis that systemic risk is greater.

Finally, in a market context, we must all be mindful of the dangers of illusions of market liquidity. When markets are as large as they are and position-taking is as large as it is, there is a tendency on the part of each market participant to assume that the underlying liquidity of the market will always be there. There are indeed ways in which any given individual participant can quickly unwind his position and, of course, each one assumes that he is a little quicker, a little faster than the next. But as we saw in October 1987, if that market liquidity proves to be illusory it simply may not work that way.

However, there is another side which is that when we look at financial markets on a worldwide basis over the past dozen years or so, we have to be impressed with the resilience that these markets and institutions have demonstrated time and again. Just contemplate world oil price shocks, violent swings in exchange rates and interest rates, the worst recessions since the 1930s, numerous individual shocks to the system, the LDC debt situation, or the stock-market developments of October 1987. Just think about the potential problems and to some extent the actual problems associated with any one, much less all, of those events, and the fact of the matter is that in each case the system as a whole has performed remarkably well.

Indeed, just the fact that the system has performed so well and the fact that most major institutions on a global basis are demonstrably stronger today than they were several years ago can lead to the conclusion that having overcome all of these problems, the system can handle anything.

I for one certainly do not believe such a sense of complacency is justified. On the contrary, I have at least a nagging feeling that all is not quite right, despite all we have survived. And I think that is understandable because any realistic assessment of the situation suggests that there is plenty with which to be concerned: domestic and international economic and financial unbalances are still very real. The LDC debt problem is still there and I believe some very real dangers may still lie in that area. The cost of doing business for financial institutions is very high and rising; indeed, I sometimes wonder whether that cost of doing business in itself does not create something of a vested interest in volatility on the part of financial institutions. That is, the only way you can pay the bills is by a large amount of ticket-writing, whether it serves an ultimate purpose or not.

Certainly, increased leverage in virtually all countries but most graphically illustrated by what is going on in corporate America, is surely a matter of concern. The biggest concern may well lie or should well lie in the fact that we are now entering the seventh year of an economic expansion and the seventh year of essentially bull markets around the world. Neither the interest rate cycle nor the business cycle is dead. One of the questions that it is imperative to ask is how all this is going to look in a less hospitable economic and financial environment than the one we have all enjoyed over the past few years.

That, of course, is another way of saying that there are a lot of challenges ahead. The heart of those challenges lies in the first instance on the macroeconomic side and our chances for success in meeting these challenges are going to be greater to the extent that we can build on what has already been achieved in the arena of international economic policy coordination.

We have a lot more work to do on the LDC front. But we have much more to do in the area of adapting our approaches to supervision of financial institutions on both a pragmatic and a philosophical level. Capital agreement of the BIS is a big step in the right direction but, here too, more needs to be done in adapting both supervisory policy and philosophy:

1. We need supervisory policies and practices that do not punish the strong and the prudent because of the mistakes of the weak and the reckless.
2. We need supervisory policies and practices that are sensitive to commercial needs and commercial realities.
3. On-sight examinations and inspections of institutions must be a continuing central part of any effective system of supervision.
4. We must expand our thinking to more than just capital. An effective system of supervision must focus on other factors, such as cash flow, liquidity, and asset quality.
5. The supervisory process must look at the consolidated entity as a whole. That is not to say that there is not an important role for functional supervision of component parts, but managers run these conglomerates as integrated companies, the market-place looks at them as integrated companies, shareholders look at them as integrated companies, so it seems to me to follow that we must

do the same. That does not mean that we have to apply the same standards at the consolidated level that we might for particular component parts, but I simply do not accept the proposition that when the temperature goes up, the fire-walls and other corporate and legal distinctions between parts of business entities will survive. The experience around the world is powerful if not compelling in that direction.

6. We have a major responsibility to do all we can to upgrade the skills of our examination and supervisory personnel. This is not an easy task. However, speaking for the Federal Reserve Bank of New York at least, these days we do not hesitate, for example, to use people from our securities and foreign exchange trading desks to work with some of our teams of field examiners where we think their skills may be helpful. Nor do we hesitate to take our own computer people to help examiners when we are looking at certain of the payments and clearing systems.

Those are some of the things that I think are important both in the area of philosophy and practice of supervision, but the one with which I would like to close is one that Sir Philip Wilkinson has broached in Chapter 4 when he began to suggest that there may be a partnership of interest between the supervised and the supervisor.

I believe there is indeed a partnership of interests between the supervisor and the supervised and the more we can do on both sides to build that spirit into the process, the better off we will be. When I contemplate events such as those of October 1987, one of the things that sticks in my mind is the powerful partnership of interests, the openness with which institutions around the world, private and public, were willing to work together hand in hand. To the extent that we can succeed in building that spirit of partnership and cooperation into the process we shall all be very much better off.

12 Monetary Policy and Banking Stability

Markus Lusser

THE MONETARY ORDER

A monetary order is a fundamental requirement. It consists of the rules which define the concept and regulate the creation of money both on a national and an international level. What is the situation today? The prevailing monetary framework is very difficult to define. For internal reasons the Swiss National Bank recently made a survey among the central banks of the Group of Ten countries, in order to determine the principal features of their national monetary order. As was to be expected, no clear trend emerged. Either a monetary order is obsolete – based on the gold standard, for example – or it is simply non-existent – as in the case of 'fiat' money. On an international level, *a fortiori*, no monetary order has succeeded in establishing itself since the breakdown of the Bretton Woods System in the early 1970s.

This lack of a formal system, of clearly defined rules, may seem to be proof of the leeway and flexibility granted to monetary authorities. In principle, they are thus free to react optimally to various shocks. As things stand, however, the introduction, in numerous countries, of purely fiduciary monetary systems has opened the door to inflation and budget deficits. Under these circumstances it is understandable that many people are trying to redefine a monetary order that guarantees adequate price stability in the medium and long term. What is therefore more natural than to look back into the past and call for the reintroduction of the gold standard? Even though this approach may strike many as rather odd, it has numerous supporters as becomes clear when one reads the 'Gold Report' published by the US Congress at the beginning of the 1980s.

For, after all, certain aspects of the gold standard are attractive at first sight. The link between a currency and gold limits the money-creating capacity of central banks, thereby preventing the emergence of inflation. Moreover, by virtue of the ratio existing between different national parities and thanks to the gold-points mechanism, this regime provides for fixed exchange rates and ensures the equilibrium of the balance of payments in the medium term. Such a system, however, will only be viable if the gold is used as legal tender or if the bank-notes issued by the central bank are fully or partially backed by gold. If this is not the case, the consistency and anti-inflationary quality of the system will depend entirely on maintaining the parity, which, after all, is purely a legal definition. What value can therefore be attached to such a guarantee, particularly in a big country where external factors are less constraining than in a small economy? For did not the impressive monetary edifice of the nineteenth century collapse in 1914, when governments were forced to accept budget deficits and inflation in order to finance the war?

Under such conditions the reintroduction of a consistent gold standard which would act as a monetary anchor could only be considered if the yellow metal were again used in money circulation. Such a development seems anachronistic, to say the least, given the fact that modern payment instruments are becoming increasingly abstract. There would therefore be no point in trying to re-establish a monetary order based solely on gold. That is why – since gold has lost its importance – some would like to see it replaced as a standard by other raw materials or by a basket of raw materials. At first sight, the idea is rather tempting. Since raw materials are used in numerous manufacturing processes, stabilising their prices would mean the continuous implementation of an anti-inflationary monetary policy. In view of the host of problems which a raw-materials standard would pose in practice – Which primary products are to be selected? How are they to be weighted? – one school of thought aims at giving preference to an index of raw materials prices as a guide to monetary policy. Such an index has, incidentally, just been included in the set of indicators used by the International Monetary Fund during its exercises in international cooperation and – this is no secret – this is regarded in a favourable light by some governors of the Federal Reserves.

How is such a guide to be judged? Is it reliable? Is it useful? For a small country, the information provided by an index of raw materials priced in the domestic currency is very unclear since it is extremely difficult to distinguish between variations due to exchange-rate fluctuations and variations resulting from internal inflationary pressures. A major economy with an international currency can derive greater use from this type of index. In the USA, for example, it is one of several indicators which usually lead the business cycle and consumer price variations. But to go further by adopting it as the only guide for monetary policy is a step which only the boldest would be willing to take. By their very nature, raw materials prices are so volatile that the link between their fluctuations and monetary policy instruments – the money supply or interest rates – is extremely unstable. The monetary authorities could thus only respond in qualitative terms to changes in raw materials prices without actually being able to gauge exactly the policy stance required by the situation.

Aside from these purely technical problems, there is a more fundamental objection to using such an indicator. The central bank's role is to provide a monetary anchor to the entire economy, in other words, to stabilise the general price level and not one particular price or set of prices. However powerful they may be, monetary authorities actually commit a sin of pride when attempting to influence the development of a real variable in the long term. In the short run, such action may frequently appear successful but economic forces and market forces soon gain the upper hand. That is particularly evident and well-known for real exchange rates. The same would apply to raw materials, whose prices fluctuate in relation to the general price level because of shifts in supply and demand such as a poor harvest or a new discovery. Why should a central bank react in such a case?

That the monetary authorities cannot continuously influence the real variables in the economy and must content themselves with ensuring long-term price stability is the underlying principle on which any modern monetary order must be based. In practical terms this implies that central banks control a variable which influences the price level. And which variable exerts a more immediate influence on the price level than the amount of money or liquidity available in an economy? True, it is a perfectly valid option for a small country to stabilise its exchange rate *vis-à-*vis a large inflation-free economy. However, for the big countries and the smaller nations that wish to preserve some degree of monetary independence, the only possible policy, if they want to create a non-inflationary environment for the economic agents, is to control the growth of money.

This general principle, however, is not sufficient in itself to ensure stable prices. In view of the uncertainty afflicting the markets, notably the financial markets, the monetary authorities who wish to apply this principle have to follow a rule by announcing a growth target for a monetary aggregate at regular intervals. Usually this target is based on structural considerations – potential economic growth, changing payment habits of the public – designed to prevent a surge of inflation. Only by following this rule can the central banks dampen inflationary expectations and, consequently, excessive fluctuations in asset prices. Admittedly, the monetary authorities themselves limit their own room for manoeuvre but in so doing they avoid having to react – and, particularly, to overreact – to every item of economic news which, more often than not, turns out to be only a rumble.

However, the application of this general principle is fraught with difficulties. The relation between the monetary target, real income and prices may change with time as a result of financial and technological innovations. Demand for money sometimes tends to shift significantly, as was the case after the stock market crash in October 1987. A central bank must thus be constantly on the alert and implement its monetary target with the required flexibility.

For this, it has to enjoy sufficient credibility both with the public and the financial markets. If such credibility is gained through successes and perseverance, it is easily forfeited when an error is committed. Just as for any other institution, credibility is a scarce commodity for a central bank. One might therefore justly ask whether writing the principle of targeting a monetary aggregate into the law would not facilitate the task of the monetary authorities.

If this idea appears initially attractive, it bears little close examination. For example, the Swiss National Bank has been setting monetary targets for well-nigh fifteen years. On several occasions however, notably in 1978, it has had to deviate from its course for exchange-rate reasons. If the principle of monetary targeting had been legally enforced, would we have violated the law or would we have allowed the Swiss franc to appreciate beyond all reasonable limits? No one can say what we would have done under the circumstances but the present example shows how a strict legal norm may frequently confront central banks with a difficult choice, if not an inescapable dilemma. We may imagine a more flexible law providing for exceptions to the rule. But the more flexible a law is, the less does it enhance the credibility of the monetary authorities. That is why, taking into account the numerous technical difficulties encountered by any monetary policy, I would prefer to make it mandatory for the central bank to maintain price stability even if it means leaving it to that institution to assume responsibility for putting this general principle into practice. It goes without saying that the monetary authorities do not have a free hand to do so as they please. To some extent they are accountable for their actions to the political authorities – both executive and legislative bodies – but particularly so to the public, which will have the final say as to whether a sufficiently stable price level has been attained.

FINANCIAL HEALTH

A central bank, however, does not act all on its own in some kind of a vacuum. Its task would be made considerably easier if it could implement its policy within a sound environment in both public and private finance. On the public side the credibility of the monetary authorities gains by the fact that a country has no sizeable budget deficit, whatever the finer points of economic theory may be on this subject. The examples of fiscal policies that have led to inflation are so numerous and well-known that I shall not dwell on this point. However, since in a large number of countries the politicians are always tempted to be spendthrift, it is of the utmost importance that the independence of the central bank be guaranteed both *de jure* and *de facto*. It is certainly no coincidence that the Federal Reserve has been able to follow a relatively tight policy in the past few years despite the rapid growth of public debt in the USA. That is an important lesson to be learned by the Europeans, who are now dealing with numerous problems raised by the monetary integration on our continent.

On the private side, the credibility and efficiency of the central bank will be improved if a better supervision of the financial system can be ensured. A stable monetary policy and zero inflation, of course, do considerably enhance the smooth functioning of the financial sector of an economy by stabilising expectations and tempering the volatility of asset prices. Nevertheless it is not sufficient to provide a solid framework for financial operations; also needed are actors who will play the game and not incur any ill-considered risks. Otherwise, the monetary authorities will all too often find themselves compelled to assume their role as lenders of last resort in view of the prohibitive costs, to the economy, of bank failures and financial bankruptcies. They then have to deviate from their target, thereby jeopardising price stability. Only an effective supervision of the banks and the stock markets can prevent potential black sheep from causing harm to the entire financial sector by their dangerous and rash behaviour. Such supervision, however, may not be so demanding as to impede normal and natural market activity. Putting supervision into practice is a complicated and tricky problem but recent experience has shown that it needs to be improved in a large number of countries. In Switzerland, for example, banking supervision works satisfactorily while supervision of the financial markets certainly needs to be made more sophisticated and brought up to date.

ECONOMIC RIGOUR

A final word on economic austerity measures. If these measures are taken to mean the authorities' desire to be restrictive for the sake of restrictiveness – for example, by pursuing an extremely stringent income policy – such a policy is almost certainly doomed to failure. Economic failure, on the one hand, since there is a danger of the foundations on which growth rests being distorted; a political failure, on the other hand, since the public will soon tire of a policy without a clearly defined goal. If, however, economic rigour is seen as an overall framework that embraces a monetary order aimed at price stability, sound public finances and adequate financial supervision, such austerity measures do not need to be discussed in detail for they come naturally as a result of the basic conditions just described. If these conditions are met, the play of market forces will provide for maximum growth, taking into consideration the various constraints that affect every economy. Moreover, the authorities will then enjoy sufficient credibility to depart temporarily from their long-term target if they are suddenly forced to counteract major economic shocks. But after having been compelled to take such action, they will have to return to their stability-oriented policies as soon as possible if the latter are not to become meaningless.

CONCLUSION

To sum up, a monetary order in keeping with our modern world cannot be defined in a few words. However, it seems to me indispensable to assign to the monetary authorities the task of stabilising prices if our economies are to function satisfactorily and for the general welfare. But in our democracies this task can only be fulfilled if the public accepts this final goal and does not regard a temporary economic boom as a sign of gratifying and lasting growth. An important task of central bankers is to call to mind from time to time that long-term macroeconomic action is important even if this may appear to some to be less exciting than everyday activity.

13 Future Developments of Japanese International Capital Markets

Shigeru Uemura

BASIC FACTORS AFFECTING DEVELOPMENT OF THE MARKET

The most important factor in gauging the future development of the Tokyo capital market is the state of the capital surplus in Japan. A high rate of savings has caused a surplus of funds over the requirement for industrial equipment investment and has resulted in the infusion of these funds into the capital market, successfully financing the large Japanese fiscal deficit, lowering interest rates in general, and pushing up stock prices despite sizeable new issues of common stock. This phenomenon was first observed in 1980 and has been accelerating since.

The consensus among economists in Japan indicates that this accumulation of investable funds and the surplus of such will continue in years to come, suggesting continuous development of the Japanese capital market to a size that was expected by no one.

The accumulation of surplus capital is considered to reflect basic changes in Japan's industrial structure rather than an increase of cash flow from cyclical industrial activities. A shift of Japan's industrial emphasis from low-margin, capital-intensive sectors to high-margin, high-technology sectors has reduced the need of heavy long-term investment commitments. This shift is by no means considered temporary but is just the beginning of a lasting change.

This basic change of the industrial structure, together with people's high preference for savings, has had several other important consequences, namely, chronic surpluses in the external trade account, low interest rates, improved corporate earnings, a shift of corporate financing from dependence on bank loans to use of the capital market, low inflationary pressure, and others.

The Daiwa Securities Research Institute forecasts that interest rates in Japan will be the lowest among industrialized countries for the next twenty to thirty years.

With these factors in mind, I feel that there is a good basis for the recent proposal of the Japanese government on the occasion of the last IMF General Meeting to internationalize the yen further. We envisage that the yen will gradually rise in importance and be increasingly used for foreign-exchange-reserve purposes, for financing purposes, for investment and for settlement of international trade. The Tokyo capital market, although it requires a lot of improvement, together with further liberalization, will gradually show itself as the real mother market for yen instruments.

Corporate finance is shifting more to direct financing utilizing the capital market and away from its traditional dependence on bank loans. Such new development is supported by a shift in the pattern of saving. Bank deposits and postal savings have been decreasing in relative importance. Bank of Japan statistics show that among the items making up the balance of personal savings, total cash and deposits of all kinds, together with loan trust certificates, accounted for 67.1 per cent of personal savings in 1983, but had decreased to 61.4 per cent at the end of 1987. Personal savings are put directly into the capital market or reach it through such institutions as insurance companies and mutual funds, which are important capital-market players.

This trend is even more obvious today, with the abolition of the system for tax-free savings. This change together with low interest payments on deposits is encouraging savers to turn increasingly to higher-risk, higher-return capital market instruments.

POTENTIAL SUPPLY OF NEW INVESTMENT VEHICLES

Another important factor which will increase the importance of the capital market is the need of commercial banks and other lending and leasing institutions to securitize their loans and other credit instruments. Commercial banks are particularly in need of securitizing their loans for the purpose of risk management and to meet the new equity ratio requirements of the BIS.

The gradual but steady growth of mortgage financing for housing construction is still another factor which supports the growth potential of the capital market in Japan.

While such factors as securitization and the growth of the mortgage market are supporting factors for the development of the Tokyo capital market, one has to take note of the fact that the Securities and

Exchange Law of Japan does not define them as 'securities' which can be marketed broadly by way of public offering. Under current law, securities companies are not permitted to place them even by way of private placement. Such limitation is one of the legal obstacles to be overcome for real development of the capital market in Japan.

NEW DEVELOPMENTS IN THE CAPITAL MARKET

Setting aside negative factors for the moment, let us consider some important positive developments in the capital market in Japan today.

Admittance of New Players

Financial Institutions

Dealing in government bonds and those of its agencies was a line of business that was originally exclusively the province of securities dealers in the post-war period, but the door to this business has been increasingly widely opened to non-securities dealers since 1984. Today almost all kinds of financial institutions including banks, trust banks, insurance companies, credit unions and even the postal savings system participate in the dealing market. This development became possible by a partial amendment of Article 65 of the Securities and Exchange Law and the related issue of several ministerial ordinances.

Foreign Securities Companies

After several rounds of liberalization measures and changes of applicable regulations and administrative guidance, foreign securities companies have been given more and more freedom to operate in Tokyo. They have expanded their operations there, and a good number have become members of the Tokyo Stock Exchange (TSE).

Statistics on foreign-based securities companies' operations in Japan show 128 representative offices, forty-five branch and four sub-branch operations, and twenty-two members of Tokyo Stock Exchange in November 1988. Of the branch operations, all forty-five had obtained full licences to engage in all phases of securities business including the lead-management of securities offerings. The largest branch was reported to employ some 500 to 600 employees, and the total number of employees in all branches was estimated to be over 5300. The great disruption in the world stock markets in 1987 was causing these houses difficulty in varying degrees in November 1988 and interest in expanding Tokyo presences temporarily subsided. Nevertheless, steady expansion continued among those already operating in Tokyo, and the underlying interest among international financial institutions was still felt to be quite great. We may see a further increase of foreign operators, since (except for TSE membership) there are no barriers to expansion into Japan now. As to TSE membership there is no discrimination against foreign houses. Quite the contrary, foreign houses have been the beneficiaries of a rather favourable bias in comparison with domestic securities companies, many of which wish in vain to become members of the Exchange.

Primary Market Activity

I believe that the Japanese primary capital market will grow to much greater size as a consequence of abundant domestic surplus capital or investable funds. I believe that much overseas financing by Japanese borrowers will return to the domestic market, and that a variety of securities which are not recognized as such or are not permitted today will gradually appear in Japan and will help to broaden the scope of the Japanese capital market. The Japanese domestic bond market has shown spectacular development as far as the government sector is concerned. Performance of the private sector, however, has been disappointing, despite dramatic statistical growth. I believe this imbalance will be corrected in the not distant future.[1]

It is my belief that the restoration of balance between the private and public sectors of the bond market will come about only after strenuous efforts on the part of securities companies, government officials and other parties involved in bond issues, because so many changes will have to be made to laws, regulations, rules and customs, and the many conflicting interests of different parties will have to be readjusted.

Current Situation

Reflecting the shift to direct financing by corporate borrowers, the amount of funds raised annually in the domestic capital market has increased by nearly four times in the past five years, while bank loan financing increased only 65 per cent.

What should be noted in recent corporate financing activity is that an amount nearly equal to and sometimes more than domestic funds has been raised in overseas capital markets in the past few years. Such overseas financing has expanded nearly three times in the past five years.

Another aspect of corporate finance activity which merits notice is an increasingly heavy dependence on equity-linked financing. Straight-debt financing accounted for 40 per cent of total domestic capital market financing in fiscal 1983 and 20–40 per cent in the overseas markets during 1983–5, but the ratio has come down to merely 15 per cent both in the domestic market and abroad in 1987, indicating a lack of corporate interest in straight-debt finance and a preference for taking advantage of current high stock prices.

What should be particularly noted is the state of inactivity in the domestic straight-debt market where almost the only group of borrowers in 1987 was that of the electric utility companies.

Problems and Solutions

Among the various reasons for the inactivity in the non-government, domestic straight-debt market, the most important may be high issue costs. Another factor of importance may be the relative complexity of registration procedures. Many borrowers prefer to raise funds in overseas markets like Zurich or Frankfurt when interest rates are low there or in the Eurodollar market when swap arrangements reduce the borrowing cost to, or below, the rates obtainable in Tokyo, partly for the reason of simplicity of procedures and flexibility in timing.

In order to restore healthy growth to the domestic primary market, a number of legislative and regulatory measures will have to be taken, be they either changes in laws and regulations or removal or changes in administrative guidance, or so-called 'voluntary' restrictions.

Among the changes needed for further development of the Japanese primary market for debt issues, the most important and urgent is a set of changes to laws relating to bond issues. The Commercial Code sets limits on the amount of bonds which a corporation can float. Such limits restrict only the amount of bonds (but not the amount of other obligations), thus serving no purpose of protecting investors from excessive borrowing by an issuer. Because of these limits, industrial corporations are obliged to restrict their bond issues and to resort to bank loans to make up any funding deficiency. As already mentioned, equity-linked issues are quite popular because of the high stock prices of many corporations. Equity-linked issues give extremely low-cost funds to issuers because of low coupons (the standard rate is 2.7 per cent) and of consequences of limited dilution thanks to high stock prices. This boom in equity-linked bond issues has taken most large companies near the limits of their ability to issue bonds under the Commercial Code, and many have in fact no room for straight-debt issues at all.

Further, there are two kinds of trustees in Japan, each defined by a different law: one is the Secured Bond Trust Law and the other the Commercial Code. One type of trustee is the trustee in its original significance, having the duty of administering collateral attaches to bonds. The other sort of 'trustee' has the function of an agent in offering bonds, and engages in procedural works on behalf of issuers. The Commercial Code was originally enacted in the days when banks were underwriters and no specialized underwriting profession existed. In the early days of the Samurai bond market, the description 'commissioned company' was invented for this second type of trustee in Japan, in an attempt to convey their true function.

The Commercial Code contains provisions to define the commissioned company and to stipulate its role. Though appointment of a commissioned company is optional in the text of the Code, tradition and some procedural problems connected with issuing bonds without a commissioned company have prevented all attempts at removing the commissioned company from the new issue structure.

The trustee as defined by the Secured Bond Trust Law also contains elements of the commissioned company role, which is not necessary in practice.

The co-existence of the two types of trustee makes documentation work complicated and results in initial and annual costs being far more expensive than for Euromarket or even US issues.

The role of the trustee in its real significance is recognized as essential for most bond issues. The securities industry, therefore, together with business federations, have been advocating that these laws must be revised and such complications straightened out, in order to make the Tokyo capital market less expensive and less complicated, and to attract more borrowers in Japan and from abroad.

A semi-public advisory board to the Minister of Finance on capital market matters came to the conclusion that these laws must be changed, and official recommendations to this effect were made to the Minister in 1986. Although the legislative process has been slow, the necessary changes are in sight.

The SEC-type registration requirements are another obstacle for borrowers raising funds in Tokyo. However, recent changes to the Securities and Exchange Law have greatly rationalized procedures. At the same time, a shelf registration procedure has been introduced, giving much more flexibility to qualified borowers. Such changes are certainly important steps forward for the future growth of the Japanese capital market.

Securitization of loans of various types is a new trend in the world today. Securitized loans are widely distributed among broad classes of investors through the regular securities registration system, particularly in the USA. As noted earlier, in Japan loans cannot be securitized into certificates that are marketable through the regular securities distribution system. By law, securities companies in Japan cannot distribute any instruments not defined as securities in the Securities and Exchange Law. Securitized certificates do not fall under the definitions set out in the Law. For such instruments to obtain legitimacy in the securities industry some kind of legislative measures must be taken. Real estate investment trusts, leveraged buy out funds, equity in venture capital partnerships, mortgage bonds, etc. also are not securities in the eyes of the Securities and Exchange Law. Therefore, the securities industry is not permitted to market them through its distribution networks, either by way of public offering or by way of private placement. Major securities companies have mortgage securities company affiliates and venture capital company affiliates, but they cannot market the products of these affiliates. They may introduce their clients to them, but transactions must be booked at the affiliates. Under these circumstances, the incentive for the sales organizations of securities companies is virtually nil.

This problem has been identified and the necessity of a solution is acknowledged. There are legal technicalities to be resolved, as well as the conflicting and complicated interests of the banking industry and securities industry to be dealt with delicately.

It is obvious that problems will be solved eventually, after they have been identified and isolated, and when the need for their solution is generally acknowledged. For this reason I believe that the Japanese capital market has substantial potential for further development, and that this potential is the reverse side of the problems that remain to be resolved – for example, the proper introduction to the Japanese capital market of new types of securities.

It is perhaps of lesser importance, but some other securities are to be found in other technically advanced markets which are practically or legally not possible to issue in Japan. These are preferred stock, subordinated bonds and common stock of multiple classes.

Work is in progress on making preferred and subordinated securities issues possible, and I consider that these moves will create another dimension of the Japanese capital market contributing to its further development. I have not mentioned Japanese government bonds, as I feel the market has reached maturity, particularly as far as its size is concerned. The government's need of deficit financing is sharply decreasing and I anticipate that refinancing will become the only reason for government bond issues as early as 1990.

One important development in the government bond sector is the gradual change of the distribution method. The 20-year bonds and medium-term bonds are all placed by way of public bidding, in which all qualified financial institutions such as securities companies, commerial banks and life insurance companies, among others, participate. But the most important 10-year bonds, which represent the major part of government financing, have been traditionally distributed through a syndicate, which was most difficult to change.

There has been a major move into Tokyo by foreign securities houses in the past few years. The major underwriters with international reputations and power have all been in Tokyo for several years now. These houses were quite dissatisfied by the traditional syndicate system, which could not provide adequate underwriting positions to them.

A competitive bidding system that would give equal opportunity to these major foreign firms also obtained the wide support of the Japanese domestic securities industry, which had also felt frustration at not getting its fair share of underwriting portions in the traditional, bank-dominated syndicate.

The Japanese government, represented by the Finance Bureau as regards borrowing activity, has expressed great concern about this change as well as doubt whether competitive bidding can provide sufficient funds to the government at a reasonable cost even in the worst market conditions. Such concern still prevails in the Ministry and not all 10-year bonds are offered through competitive bidding. The portion of an issue distributed in this manner represents only 20 per cent of the total today and will be increased to 40 from April 1989.

I believe that in the near future competitive bidding will become the only way for the government to raise funds through bond issues. Distribution of bonds through competitive bidding will be accomplished in a more natural way as bonds find their way to dealers with the most appetite at the time of bidding. This change of distribution system may help to develop a better general environment for bond issues of all kinds. A shelf registration system already introduced to Japan, allows corporate bond issues to be bought by the underwriting syndicate which has the best price for issuers.

For healthy development of the Japanese primary capital market another important regulatory improvement necessary is revision of restrictions on or criteria for qualification to issue non-collateralized straight and equity-linked bonds. Pressure from commercial banks has traditionally worked to restrict the list of high credit bond issuers entitled to non-collateralized bonds. The securities industry has thus been forced to work out voluntary restrictions on issuers, even though it has been successful in obtaining increasingly more flexible conditions in the past few years. The utilization of credit ratings by specialized rating agencies in place of screening of issuers by artificial criteria is growing in importance even in ways of voluntary restriction.

In the past, improvements realized in the capital market clearly contributed to its development, and with further improvement in sight I believe we may look forward to even further development for the capital market.

As the liberalization of the capital market progresses, it is obvious that regulatory measures will have to be reviewed at the same time and improved for the protection of investors. Such measures included better disclosure, adoption of appropriate negative pledge clauses and new functions for trustees, and are being actively discussed. Progress is being observed.

Secondary Market

The secondary market in Japan has shown phenomenal development in the past few years. The volume of transactions of long-term government bonds increased by nearly fourteen times between 1983 and 1987, reaching the level of ¥3688 trillion, or $30 trillion. Turnover of common stocks on the Tokyo Stock Exchange reached ¥238 trillion, or $1.7 trillion, in the fiscal year 1987, more than four times over the figure for five years previously.

The direct or indirect shift of personal savings from deposits to capital markets is clearly observed in the phenomenal increase of activity in the secondary market as well as in the primary market. Financial institutions other than securities companies have been increasingly entering the government-bond dealing market. Such new participation, particularly of powerful commercial banks, has accelerated the increase of volume in the secondary market.

What must be added to the domestic supply of new securities to the secondary market through public offerings is the potential new supply of common stock issued as a result of conversion of convertible bonds floated in Tokyo and abroad and exercise of the vast amount of equity warrants floated abroad.

Foreign Stocks in Tokyo

The foreign section of the Tokyo Stock Exchange is another area which must not be neglected. Over 100 different international companies have listed their common shares on the TSE in the past few years. The rise of the yen against foreign currencies, particularly against the US dollar, and the after effects of the crash of 19 October 1987 are still having an adverse impact on Japanese investor psychology, and the appetite for portfolio accumulation of foreign stocks does not appear to be great at this moment.

The Ministry of Finance's national statistics show impressive increases in the volume of both purchases and sales of foreign stocks, while showing disappointing figures for net purchases since the crash of October 1987.

Increases in volume reflect very active trading by Japanese insurance companies, which are buying and selling the same stocks, mainly of high-yielding utility companies, on the same day. These trades are simply for the purpose of securing dividend income and do not represent regular investment by the insurance companies.

Monthly trade figures on the foreign section of the TSE still showed quite sluggish trading a year after the crash. Average monthly turnover remained at 30–50 per cent of that in an average month before the crash.

Although foreign equity investment by Japanese investors is currently (November 1988) quite sluggish, there is no pessimism in investment circles about the future. The basic reason for this is the observation that the Japanese domestic capital market itself may not be able to absorb all the increasing surplus capital flowing into the hands of institutions. Japanese investors realize the attractions of the low-price multiples, higher yields, and sound balance sheets of foreign stocks and companies. Still, the unstable foreign exchange situation and inactive condition of foreign stock exchanges have not encouraged investors to take major action to date (November 1988).

Today there is no direct regulatory inconvenience connected with investment abroad in stocks and bonds by Japanese investors, except for some inconvenience in dealing with tax problems. Institutions are comfortably within their investment limits for foreign investment, particularly in the equity area.

Of course, there are a number of auxiliary problems which must be resolved in future. These problems are mostly those of reconciliation of needed actions for improvement in the manner of transaction with the requirements of existing domestic laws, rules and regulations. Some of these problems even require revision of major laws such as the Foreign Exchange and Control Law. It may take time for these auxiliary problems to be resolved, but they have not presented a serious barrier to foreign investment.

Japanese Common Stock – Some Problems

Very often we hear the comment that Japanese common stock is too expensive to invest in, and trade journals report net sales of common stock by foreign investors. It is true that foreign investors have been net sellers since 1984, but what should be noted is the trend of increasing volume in purchases and sales during these years.

The appraisal of value of common stock changes from year to year, reflecting investors views on economic conditions, foreign exchange and the variety of investments available in world stock exchanges. A sustained high level of activity looks favourable for the revival of foreign investors' interest in Japanese equities.

The recent growth of the Japanese capital market has been accompanied by some undesirable developments. Greenmailer activity has been observed in many stocks of small to medium-sized companies, causing unexpected losses to these companies and to innocent investors. Regulatory authorities have done their best to prevent such activities, but have found deficiencies in the applicable rules and regulations. The problem is being studied seriously and solutions are being discussed.

In the Tokyo capital market, take-over activities have been rare, except for similar-looking activities by greenmailers. In this environment 'insider information' has much less important implications than in other stock markets in advanced countries. Nevertheless, there had been growing suspicion that price formation in Japan is very much dependent on pieces of information not available to the public but only to major securities companies. While the issue of insider trading was very much talked about abroad relative to takeovers and the huge profits gained by insiders, the Japanese authorities and the securities industry had come to the conclusion that legislative measures should be taken and securities companies should be reorganized so that whatever insider information there is could be kept behind a 'Chinese wall' and insider trading be strictly controlled. The Ministry of Finance quickly responded to the conclusion and the Securities and Exchange Law was revised recently to include pertinent provisions therein. Work is in progress to make auxiliary rules and regulations.

Control of insider information and insider trading will be strictly implemented in future, and I believe this development is a sound one for the healthy growth of the equity market in Japan.

Securities companies, on the other hand, were quick to reorganize themselves to establish 'Chinese walls' in their organization. Securities companies are also busy working out new internal procedures and rules applicable to their business activity to avoid careless infringement of the new insider rules and to guide sales forces to observe them.

Registration of bonds – a problem

One perhaps minor problem, but still quite important, is the custody system through which institutional investors hold hundreds of millions of yen bonds without bond certificates issued to them by just registering them with a registar. This system greatly decreases liquidity in the bond market as registered bonds cannot be easily marketed.

Large institutions which do not trade their portfolios do not feel any inconvenience from this system. In fact, it provides them with much convenience and even added profits, as interest is paid without withholding tax. But it is widely acknowledged that increased liquidity helps to bring long-term benefits to both borrowers and investors, and work is progressing in the revision of applicable laws and regulations and working out improved procedures.

Short-term money market

The short-term money market in Japan may be the sector that needs greatest improvement. The biggest problem is the shortage of treasury bills issued by the government. The total balance of bills outstanding seldom reaches a level much above ¥2 trillion or $16bn. Very short-term bills issued by the government, with maturities of 60 days, which are called financing bills, are outstanding in the amount over ¥20 trillion or $160bn, but these bills are burdened by a yield below the official discount rate, which is far below the rate required by the market. All the financing bills are therefore totally underwritten by the Bank of Japan and appear on the market with market rates only in selling in their open-market operations.

There are a number of voices emphasizing the need for various improvements in the current structure of the short-term money market. One opinion is that the financing bills should be offered to the public like treasury bills, instead of being bought up by the Bank of Japan.

Another opinion strongly emphasizes the need for increasing issues of treasury bills. The Bank of Japan has been quite vocal in this regard and has expressed its recommendation often in its publications and public statements. It has been pointing out that a step of foremost importance for the internationalization of the yen is to create an active short-term money market where foreign central banks, investors, and business organizations can manage their yen funds without any inconvenience.

While the need for expansion of the short-term money market is very much talked about, not much action has been seen yet, perhaps because of the lack of an acute and immediate need of such a market.

There is another important deterrent to the expansion of the short-term market. It is the tax problem. All fixed-interest income is charged withholding tax whether such interest is paid against surrender of coupons or by way of discount of issue prices.

Much effort has been exerted by the securities industry and other parties who recognize the importance of the development of the short-term money market to identify the tax problem as a subject to be immediately solved. But these efforts have not borne fruit so far. In today's environment (November 1988), with the tax reform plan proposed by the government encountering great political difficulty, there is no immediate prospect for elimination of the withholding tax on any short-term securities.

As liberalization moves forward, control of the money supply will eventually become the only way of monetary control open to the Bank of Japan. An increase in the amount of issues and outstanding balance of treasury bills would certainly help to make open-market operations by the Bank of Japan far more efficient.

Securities Industry

The securities industry in Japan consists of securities companies licensed under the Securities and Exchange Law, and of forty-five branches of foreign securities companies licensed under the Foreign Securities Company Law. Of these forty-five securities companies all hold full licenses with paid-up capital of ¥3000m or more and are licensed to engage in all aspects of securities business including lead-management of public offerings of the securities.

Supervision and control of securities industry is the role of the Securities Bureau of the Ministry of Finance. The Securities Bureau polices the activities of securities companies, guides them to engage in their businesses in a lawful manner and in accordance with written and unwritten rules and regulations, and protects their interests in cases of conflicts of interest with other groups of financial institutions or in cases of unwarranted criticism from outsiders. The Bank of Japan reviews and supervises the financial health of securities companies which have accounts with the Bank and advises them on risk control and on other management aspects relating to financial health.

Despite the spectacular growth of security market activity in recent years in Japan, the industry has not expanded too radically. The total number of securities companies today is virtually the same as in 1983. The total number of business offices and branches of these companies increased to the total of 2715 in November 1988 from 2188 at the end of 1983. The total number of employees increased to around 143 130 in November 1988 from 102 042 at the end of 1983. These increases were realized over five years of great expansion in the market scale. In the five-year period between 1983 and 1987, for which full statistics are available, daily turnover on the stock exchange had grown 2.5 times, government bond issues increased nearly 50 per cent, the amount of domestic convertible bond issues increased nearly six times with gross trading volume in the secondary market also increasing six times while secondary market trading volume of government bonds increased nine times (new participants like banks and other financial institutions accounted for a great part of the increase) and mutual funds annual sales increased by three times.

The securities industry, having a strong memory of the 1965

depression, is very cautious about expansion and has devoted great effort to rationalization of operations and to raising productivity. Securities companies have always been very conscious of risk-exposure and have devoted much effort to minimizing position risks. The expanding scale of business has required increasingly larger capital, however. Reflecting such a need, the total paid-up capital of all securities companies increased to ¥790bn, or $6bn, at the end of September 1988 from ¥411bn, or a little over $3bn. Since the cash flow of securities companies in the last few years has been impressively high, it is believed that their financial health was greatly fortified by the infusion of a great amount of profits after tax and distributions. Public offerings of convertible bonds and bonds with equity warrants have often been made by major securities companies. Conversion of these bonds and execution of warrants have been factors contributing to the increase of paid-up capital. At the same time the conversion and the execution brought a huge amount of capital surplus which cannot be included in the paid-up capital account. A lot of these equity-linked bonds are still outstanding and a lot of warrants are not yet executed – these are potentially elements to strengthen the equity base of Japanese securities companies still further.

It may be worth noting that the Ministry of Finance has constantly taken a conservative stance in its administrative guidance relating to the expansion of networks and of business operations.

With this background I believe that the members of the securities industry in Japan, particularly the major securities companies, are building up sufficient financial strength to satisfy the increasingly heavier responsibilities imposed on them to feed sufficient funds to the growing economy of Japan.

Japanese commercial and other types of banks are devoting strenuous efforts to the expansion of their own businesses into the securities industry, even while the Securities and Exchange Law prevents such entry in principle. Their efforts have been partly rewarded by being allowed to have investment banking subsidiaries abroad, by being allowed to deal in public bonds and in dealing in commercial paper. They are also permitted to have minority shares in some medium- and small-size domestic securities companies. Although banks' direct holdings are limited to 5 per cent, the control is in their hands through holdings by subsidiaries and affiliated companies. These securities companies are receiving board members, key personnel for business promotion and support in the area of funds-supply from controlling commercial banks.

Should the problem of conflict of interests be resolved, banking institutions could be a factor serving further expansion of the securities industry. Whether this would mean the sacrifice of some members of the present securities industry or not is at present unknown.

The conflict-of-interest problem is a rather serious one in all aspects, some of them having serious social considerations, and it may take some years for bankers' plans to be realized.

CONCLUSION

The capital market is a highly regulated market-place anywhere in the world. The Tokyo capital market may be the one more regulated than any other capital market elsewhere. Having developed in a unique social environment, the way it is regulated presents many unique features causing a number of difficulties for its further development domestically and even more so internationally.

I have tried to describe some of present and future development features of the Japanese capital market and to point out major problems related to the Japanese regulatory frameworks. I have not touched upon the international capital market partly because I do not feel that I have sufficient knowledge and partly because I cannot devote much time for gathering data and information base on which to form a realistic view.

Note

1. The shift to greater dependency on direct financing has resulted in a large flow of funds into the capital market. The bulk of primary market financing is through issues of equity-linked debt issues which are in essence equity financing rather than debt financing. The straight debt issue market has been rather quiet, and its lack of growth is indicative of some problems in this sector.

14 A Banker's Approach to Risks

Georges Blum

From the observation and decision-making post he occupies, the senior executive of a major corporation has been privileged in recent years to witness some exciting new developments in the world of banking and finance. While the principles of sound financial management are as immutable as ever, the parameters, the methods and the means have all been radically transformed. Client-needs are continuously evolving, and to match them satisfactorily, banking services, too, have had to be adapted and refined. Financial dealings are now characterized by a high degree of professionalism – not just on the part of the banker but also among borrowers and investors.

Bankers, borrowers and investors alike have, moreover, been confronted with new – and unexpected – forms of risk. Identifying and mastering them is a learning process. To cope successfully, they have to be vigilant, they have to be constantly alert to new developments and they have to have up-to-date knowledge of all the latest products.

With the globalization of the financial markets, customer requirements have grown increasingly sophisticated. This has led to a wave of innovative financial techniques born of the versatility and inventive genius of the investment banker allied to the imperatives of the market-place. This evolution would have been impossible without the aid of electronics which has enabled decision-making aids to be thoroughly computerized. Thanks to technological progress we now have the tools to compare, to plan and to extrapolate.

This in turn has paved the way for futures, options and swaps, transactions which rely essentially on future projections. And these instruments have now become indispensable for any senior bank executive anxious to optimize asset and liability management and his return on assets.

Among the services offered by the banks to their customers – particularly the international ones – traditional forms of direct lending are demonstrably on the decline. Their role is increasingly being usurped by the securitized products of investment banking which enable large corporate borrowers to raise finance on more favourable terms than those available from the banks which are thus losing their traditional role as financial intermediaries. The effect of this disintermediation, however, has been to alter the business of risk assessment profoundly, quite apart from the pressure it has created on margins.

Before granting a credit facility, it is standard practice among banks to evaluate rigorously the credit risk posed by the prospective borrower. For the majority of products associated with financial engineering and investment banking, however, the overriding criterion is the market risk, that is, how readily the paper can be placed. Not only this, but few new products actually provide real added value. Most of them tend to favour the borrower and offer the investor inadequate rewards in return for the risks he runs. The glamour and novelty of a new product – be it a note issuance facility (NIF), revolving underwriting facilities (RUF) or a 'perpetual' – soon wear off when it becomes difficult to place let alone syndicate among the banks. Hence the appearance of a veritable surfeit of substitute financial instruments.

The ultimate private investor for his part frequently has too little information at his fingertips to assess – and monitor – a borrower's credit rating. The banks, it is true, will sometimes step in and underwrite the credit risk. More often though, they are called upon to act in a back-up role in the event of the borrower being unable to fund himself directly in the market.

This assistance can take a variety of forms depending on the circumstances, with stand-by, back-up or support lines being the most commonly used. For the banks, these are contingent liabilities. But they can present a real risk which has to be taken into account. This is also the case with liability, interest rate and currency swaps which are rapidly growing in volume. This type of deal carries a potential risk for the banks when they act as guarantor and have to stand in if one of the parties to the transaction defaults. Various models have been developed here with a view to monitoring and managing the hypothetical risk involved.

On top of this, the full ramifications of these innovative financial techniques have yet to be tested in a critical economic context. The background conditions, the mood of the money and capital markets, the negotiability of the securities concerned and the business performance of the borrowing corporation are all sources of potential risk.

Certain large scale commercial or financial deals could never get off the ground without a major commitment on the part of the banks, which play a pivotal role. Because of their mega-nature, the sudden-ness with which they burst on the scene and the ripples they create in the market they invariably make the headlines. So far they have primarily been a transatlantic phenomenon – more recently they have spread to Europe, too. These deals go by the name of leveraged or management buy-outs and more often than not are merger- or acquisition-driven.

Such operations – and others like them – are more accurately financial innovations than new instruments as such. When financing them, the bank – or rather the banks – are exposed to sizeable direct risks. The credit facility is in effect only secured on the equity or near-equity of the target corporation. The payment of inflated ac-quisition premiums frequently leaves a substantial amount of good-will on the balance sheet. In other words, to recover its investment the bank has to rely on projected cash-flow streams or the proceeds of subsequent divestments.

Before committing itself, a bank will be careful to conduct the necessary sensitivity analyses. It will run through all the various permutations using different parameters and hypotheses and take into consideration any subordinated loans outstanding. Based on this analysis, it will be in a position to assess the repayment profile of the borrower. Errors of judgement here can be costly ones. There are enough painful legacies around to prove it.

In prudential terms, the banks in general treat their off-balance sheet exposure as rigorously – or nearly so – as their on-balance sheet commitments. All the relevant factors are carefully weighed and to rule out unpleasant surprises the bank will envisage even worst-case scenarios. Before taking on a risk, it will endeavour to anticipate potential developments and will closely scrutinize the borrower's present and future solvency. Consistent with sound business practice, it will seek to limit its own exposure by syndicating the risk. It will keep an eye on the bottom line and will avoid deals where margins are inadequate even though the risks may be acceptable.

To manage contingent risks, the banks establish global lending ceilings, with separate subceilings for individual countries, business sectors and types of transaction. They are careful to ensure that this type of exposure does not exceed certain tolerances in terms of their balance sheet and equity resources. In doing so, they are only conforming to sound risk-management procedures and, at the same time, satisfying the requirements of the credit-rating agencies. Where risks are particularly high, they will set aside prudential reserves.

Contingent liabilities will normally become a factor in a bank's liquidity calculations and kept in a strict ratio to its current assets.

The banks are afforded additional protection by their prescribed capital adequacy ratios, though these also act as constraints on their expansion. Switzerland's capital standards are even stricter than those proposed by the Cooke Committee, under the aegis of the Bank for International Settlements, which are designed to avert the risk of a chain reaction precipitating a crisis within the international banking community.

The self-imposed prudential standards adopted by the banking community in response to the irresistible progress of securitization are all the more vital as the potential repercussions of a default or liquidity crunch on the international financial system are hard to gauge with any accuracy. A system of fire-breaks is essential to contain the potential spill-over effects of global financial operations. The countless hedging techniques that have been developed to offset risks and prevent them from getting out of hand are factors operating in favour of stability. So far they have fortunately not had an opportunity to demonstrate their effectiveness in full.

Be that as it may, the fragility of the stock-market system last autumn served as a warning to us that investment banking instruments need to be treated with particular caution. The internationalization of the markets and the sheer size of certain operations like the huge leveraged buy-outs we have been witnessing of late are compelling reasons for subjecting all the parameters to rigorous scrutiny.

One fact remains, however: no matter how well they perform, the electronic resources that back up the new financial instruments are a long way from reducing the investor/borrower relationship to a mere bookkeeping mechanism. Financing is not an exact science. And that is what still makes the profession such a rewarding one.

15 Responsibilities of a Bank's Board of Directors – with Special Reference to Financial Innovations

Robert Holzach

The subject of innovation continues to occupy centre stage in the media and in business practice. The term has already proved to be unusually and surprisingly long-lived.

The reasons for industrial innovations and the effects they have are largely concrete and understandable, although rapid and often radical technical changes call for an equally rapid adjustment in training and expertise.

Financial innovations, on the other hand, may not be so readily understood, since the financial markets and the transactions that can be carried out in them are mainly abstract. Financial claims, shares in property, future options and rights to shares in enterprises or to interest rate and currency agreements find concrete expression in transferable securities at the very most. Although securities-trading calls for a highly developed ability to perceive the substance and prospects of the securities in question, even greater powers of imagination are needed in the case of contracts that are not securitized and the rights embodied in them. In some cases these rights have only unilateral validity, they often take effect only at a later point in time and in any case are conditional. Financial innovations lead almost invariably to what can be termed a 'right to a right'. The maturity date and conditions determine whether contracted rights are exercised.

In view of the obvious complexity of the problems arising from the continuous stream of new facilities, it is therefore not only useful but necessary to keep the subject of financial innovations permanently on the agenda for training, everyday practice and regulatory bodies. It would be fatal to believe that initial experiences, supposedly proven validity or unquestioning faith in mathematical models enabled us to dispense with further study or analysis.

SUPERVISORY OBLIGATIONS OF THE BOARD OF DIRECTORS

In tackling the question of the responsibility of the board of directors with regard to banking innovations we must set out from the premise that *the responsibility of the banking supervisory bodies as such is immutable*. The supervisory and managerial tasks described in Swiss banking law remain the same, with or without innovations. The same obviously applies to the boards of directors of industrial or commercial firms that use new financial instruments as customers of the banks or become active in new markets. It continues to be the case that 'the persons entrusted with the management, the superintendence, the supervision and the control of a bank are liable . . . for the damage caused by the . . . violation of their duties' (Article 41 of the Banking Law).

The board of directors must use exactly the same instruments as before in exercising its supervisory mandate. In other words, it must examine and assess the periodic reports on the company's business policy, performance and situation. Independent enquiries by the internal inspectorate and by statutory auditors required under banking and company law complete the institutionalised system of reporting. In accordance with the need for transparency, the supervisory body will not only require reporting to be complete but also to include an account of the considerations on which decisions were based. Hence individual transactions and decisions of principle are to be reported to the supervisory body, together with a frank exposé of the inherent opportunities and risks. A loan submission that fails to mention the borrower's weaknesses – in other words, the risks – suppresses essential information. Efficient supervision cannot tolerate such an omission.

Since the board's duties with regard to the increasingly prevalent financial innovations remain the same and the supervisory instruments at its disposal are unchanged, its continuing duty to exercise due care calls first and foremost for a high degree of adaptability in the conduct of supervision. In other words, the dynamic changes triggered by innovation call for dynamic supervisory practices. This means constantly ensuring that the available information is complete and unquestionably true. Moreover, the question of opportunities and risks, which is central to banking, calls for a fundamentally sceptical approach, aimed at tirelessly seeking explanations for inconsistencies and contradictions. Such intellectual curiosity must be applied not only to the situation prevailing at any given moment but also to past and prospective developments.

DYNAMIC SUPERVISION OF FINANCIAL INNOVATIONS

Those responsible for supervision must not be satisfied with half-answers, which are often half-truths. Insistent questioning is the one element in control functions that can also bring about improvements. A further element is scepticism towards reports that rely too heavily on the 'incontrovertible', on generalisations, predictions and the judgements of others. 'Management by questioning' and sceptical optimism are perfectly legitimate procedures. Persistent asking of the question 'Why?' can be irksome, but perhaps for that very reason it is an unavoidable part of supervision.

Calls for a return to greater transparency of information could not fail to be heard immediately after the stock-market crash of October 1987, but this demand seems to have been forgotten again already. The high degree of automation of most financial innovations is not exactly conducive to transparency. In many cases dealers and their support staff are not able to reconstruct the origin of the information fed to them on their screens; this deficiency is even more serious for managerial and supervisory bodies.

Handling banking opportunities and risks successfully requires independence of mind. Supervisors must adopt a sceptical approach, that is to say, they must think coolly and test evidence rigorously. They must not remain shackled by preconceived opinions or accept other people's judgements unquestioningly. Many large loan losses can be attributed to excessive respect for big names and big figures, coefficients and expert opinions.

Independent analysis and personal judgement can be achieved only by discarding set patterns and breaking with routine. Membership of the 'brotherhood of the least mental effort' produces no insight, only a distorted perception. The independent and perceptive investigation of problems is indispensable for those in a supervisory role. '*Sans réflexion, rien ne fonctionne.*'

The board of directors is obliged to achieve the optimum for its enterprise at all times. To operate wisely and optimally means first and foremost regularly coping with contradictions. Expressed in rather more modern terms, the economic agent, and more particularly the business manager, seeks to resolve or overcome conflicts between objectives. This means deciding between alternatives, often opting for compromise, or breaking completely new ground. Thesis and antithesis produce the synthesis, which is both different from and greater than the original elements.

Faced with the lure of opportunity on the one hand and the threat inherent in the risk on the other, the banker aims at long-term optimisation. This will sometimes mean opting unilaterally for one or the other, either seizing the opportunity and ignoring the risk or surrendering to the risk and renouncing the opportunity and potential business. More frequently, the conflict and its resolution are made tolerable by compromise and the search for an individual arrangement.

The board's responsibility for the optimum is the same, whether it involves conventional or innovative aspects of banking activities. No board of directors can exonerate itself by stating that:

- it was insufficiently aware of the nature of the transaction involved;
- the risk was not apparent to the layman;
- it was not reasonable to expect the board to have the necessary knowledge.

INNOVATIONS IN BANKING

As far as banking is concerned, the causes and catalysts of innovation are primarily the structural and cyclical trends in the world economy. In addition to the debt crisis and balance-of-payments relationships, they are chiefly:

- *advances in electronics* for information management, communications and processing;
- the relaxation of national regulations, generally termed *deregulation*;
- *globalization* in the sense of the extension of both geographic and operational fields of activity.

At first sight it would appear that (criminal activity apart) developments in electronics are neutral as far as risk is concerned, but that deregulation and globalization tend to increase the risks. This assertion must be further elaborated from the point of view of the statutory responsibility for supervision, although it is to be feared that general shifts in risks are recognizable only with hindsight and that, as so often, a timely adjustment of supervision is not achieved, nor can it be.

As well as technical innovations in the fields of information, communications, the execution of transactions and price determination and the greater freedom resulting from the reduction in regulation and from an expansion in both geographic and operational scope, new and rediscovered creeds are among the strongest motivations behind genuinely or allegedly new developments on the economic scene or in the financial markets. The fixation with daily, weekly or monthly economic indices and the automatism to which this gives rise are only the first step in a continuing chain reaction. The 'products' of such creeds include sophisticated mathematical models for forecasting economic and interest rate developments, the use of ratios to 'calculate' the riskiness of commercial loans and the 'dead-cert' recipes for foreign exchange and securities speculators. *Mankind never tires of trying to eliminate the vagaries of chance.*

Creeds that have been created and propagated without the slightest critical appraisal are undoubtedly a risk factor in a category of their own. A board of directors aiming to assess the appropriateness of the risks their company bears must therefore tackle this phenomenon.

The effects of the flood of innovations manifest themselves in the form of new instruments and new markets. It is sometimes difficult to ascertain what is the cause and what the effect. This is true, for example, of 'securitization', the growing practice of converting credit positions into transferable securities. The aim of making what was initially a bilateral debt into a negotiable instrument also applies to the placement of deposits. Securitization illustrates the tendency for the banks to move away from direct debtor–creditor relationships towards activities as pure dealers and intermediaries. The banks are being 'forced out of their traditional role as transformers of amounts, maturities and risks into the role of a broker' (Dempfle, 1988). It remains to be seen, however, whether such a shift is largely or wholly a manifestation of favourable economic conditions.

The causes and effects of 'disintermediaton' have also not been fully clarified so far. The term is used to describe the weakening of the conventional relationship between a bank and its customer. In concrete terms it leads to a devaluation of the concept of 'principal banker'. However, it also means the intrusion of other types of economic agent into banking activities in that:

- the banks' role as intermediary is 'short-circuited' by direct access to the market;
- banking business is being developed and offered professionally by insurance companies, supermarkets and postal administrations.

Large firms are increasingly dispensing with the intermediary function of the banks when operating in the capital or foreign exchange markets. For example, non-banking companies are engaging in personal lending and savings business on an increasing scale.

Action to meet the market needs that arise in such circumstances gives rise to innovations. By this I mean new products, in other words new services or new market transactions. On the other hand, I do not count new methods of providing or marketing existing services as innovations. If we abide strictly by this definition of innovations as new services and instruments, they fall essentially into four categories:

1. New variants of bonds, such as warrants, zero coupon bonds and dual-currency bonds.
2. New variants of note transactions, such as floating rate notes, Euro-commercial paper (ECP) and note issuance facilities (NIFs).
3. New variants of swap transactions, such as interest rate, currency and asset swaps.
4. New variants of *forward transactions*, such as options (on currencies, shares, indices), forwards and futures.

Even these new types of transaction are not entirely new, in that existing elements of conventional financial instruments are transformed into new transaction variants in their own right by means of elimination, separation and combination and are then traded in specialised markets. Such dissection and recombination is made possible by modern computers, integrated information technology and faster communications. The components of conventional transactions either become separate tradable products or reappear as an element in a different form of transaction. It is now possible for the first time to entrust intermediation, price determination and administrative processing to electronic systems, which can also perform mathematical analysis and supervision.

Quantitative or qualitative shifts between and within particular categories of banking services obviously have no right to be called innovations. The spread of credit cards and the increasing use of direct debiting are not new. The extension of trading hours for particular categories of shares obviously has nothing to do with innovation, nor can I see securitization as anything other than a shift, possibly a temporary one, from the classical commercial loan to negotiable securities representing a claim in respect of a debt.

EXAMPLES OF OPTIONS AND SWAP TRANSACTIONS

There is no doubt in my mind that the risks associated with most financial innovations are insufficiently well-known or documented. The trial period has been too short for definite conclusions to be drawn, at least as far as the European markets are concerned. It has also told us little about the new instruments and markets, in that few exceptional economic or political events have occurred at world or national level during the period. The new products have not so far had to endure crises or disasters. The fact that the literature available so far is primarily descriptive or contains wildly optimistic recommendations suggests that some of the risks have not yet been experienced or researched.

The Institute of Banking at the University of St Gallen considers the question of 'risk management with respect to financial innovations' to be important enough to be made the subject of a publication. However, one's ears also prick up when the not entirely unknown Diebold Organisation, writing on the subject of 'structural change in the market in financial services', states that in general 'higher individual risks' are to be expected (in relation to liquidity, exchange rate and interest rate fluctuations, securities prices, etc.) and finds 'a concentration of credit, interest rate and currency risks in institutions lacking adequate controls and management tools' (*Diebold Management Journal*, 3/88).

Even the professionals acknowledge that options, despite their many merits as hedging instruments, undoubtedly constitute a danger for the insatiable in view of the higher profits in relation to the capital invested. These insatiable investors close their minds to appropriate considerations of risk and uncompromisingly pursue the goal of quick riches. I shall deal with the question of speculation separately in due course.

Theoreticians attribute 'some accelerating effect to derived financial instruments and procedures' (Kilgus)[1] and concede that once panic has broken out even electronics cannot quell it. The widespread *unease* felt by national and international banking supervisory bodies at the level of risk inherent in financial innovations is finding expression mainly in speeches, articles and guidelines at present.

The more complex problems are, the greater the lack of comprehension. The dwindling understanding of the issue is then swiftly and unhesitatingly replaced by new creeds. In the case of financial innovations, these primarily mean placing one's faith in risk evaluation exclusively by mathematical means and in the omniscience of the electronic computer. However, the behaviour of the markets and of the economy are determined to a large extent by forces that defy logic and mathematics. The idea that 'the complex problem can be reduced to a mathematical formula' (Müller-Möhl *et al.*, 1988) is a deceptive and hence dangerous notion!

Options give rise to new risks, partly by multiplying the number of market participants, without there being any parallel change in the commodity that is the object of such transactions. The investor in 1000 shares of an industrial company was previously one partner in relation to the enterprise he had chosen as a long-term investment. A covered issue can involve a maximum of 1000 option writers as new market participants, who are primarily or exclusively interested in the price performance of the underlying security. It remains an open question what proportion of such operations should be regarded as pure speculation and what specific repercussions they may have.

The apparent absence of risk associated with transactions involving the exchange of assets, in other words swap transactions, disappears immediately if the element of simultaneity is not present or if the simultaneity of the exchange is postponed to the future.

In exceptional cases even cash transactions can become a total risk if the 'break' comes at a time when payment has been made but the counter-consideration is still outstanding. In other words, the time factor is always a risk element *sui generis*. Limiting the term of a swap transaction is therefore equivalent to reducing the risk or improving risk management.

There is a large measure of agreement among state supervisory authorities that open swap agreements are a risk-bearing asset for a bank. The so-called 'credit equivalent' can be calculated by means of procedures that use mathematical formulae in an attempt to give appropriate weights to the creditworthiness of the contracting party, the kind of swap (interest-rate swap, currency swap) and the maturity.[2]

Swaps, options, futures and premium transactions relate to *underlying instruments* worth *several times* the amounts that have to be paid to acquire the right to buy or sell them. The theoretical maximum risks on interest rate swaps, for example, can be up to 100 times greater than the margin required. The contracting party must therefore be 'good' for more than the margin, since in most cases he has a contingent liability for a capital sum several times greater. Inferences such as these can still provoke incredulous shaking of heads on certain management floors. However, even the mathematical considerations behind the 10 per cent margin generally required for swap transactions (5 per cent to allow for market changes and 5 per cent for the risk of insolvency on the part of the contracting party) have not passed the test in practice. Exchange rates, interest rates and stock market indices can show significant percentage changes in a relatively short space of time, thus giving rise to a risk that is not covered by a 10 per cent margin.

In options trading and swap transactions, parties who provide surety solely in the form of margin must replenish the margin account if the market moves outside the limits on which the original margin requirement was based. Credit professionals will confirm that it is always difficult and often impossible to collect additional margin if the original surety decreases in value. At this year's Bürgenstock meeting of the Swiss Commodities Futures and Options Association (SCFOA), Professor F. R. Edwards estimated that $3bn in additional margin should have been called in the USA on both 19 and 20 October 1987.

No allowance is made for disaster in the form of excessive price movements, political impediments to performance of the contract or physical changes in the contracting party or in the object of the contract. However, neither the dead nor the bankrupt can be expected to meet their obligation to provide additional margin. It is obvious that share purchases financed on credit entail specific risks that are accentuated or precipitated if forced liquidation is threatened or carried out when share prices are falling. The credit risks attaching to forward and swap transactions are different and at first sight less obvious, but they are absolutely comparable.

The Swiss Options and Financial Futures Exchange (Soffex) makes the reassuring claim that it 'guarantees . . . the performance of all contracts'. With fully paid-up share capital of Sfr. 5m, however, it is not possible to guarantee the proper execution of around 7000 contracts a day (in September 1988) with an average option value of around Sfr. 3m on *underlying instruments* worth approximately forty times as much, in other words around Sfr. 120m. At best, that can be done only by the shareholders of Soffex and the authorised market makers, clearers and brokers, who are legally bound by the Rules and Regulations. It is true that there are built-in warning mechanisms to guard against the accumulation of risks in individual instruments or with individual market participants, but it has not yet been tested whether a large-scale speculator using tactics of avoidance and concealment can be barred from the market in general or prevented from dealing with a newly opened stock exchange. Nor has the viability of the assurances portrayed as a 'guarantee' yet been put to the test by losses of the order of those sustained in the Hunt, VW or Klöckner cases.[3]

In the first five months of its existence, Soffex has proved itself, to the extent that it functions. That is meant as serious praise for the technical founders of the system. Monthly turnover still fluctuates sharply, however. The number of contracts traded daily has exceeded the 10 000 mark only occasionally (regularly in November 1988). As a rule, the daily turnover of transactions falls if share prices decline. However, Soffex needs to average more than 20 000 if it is to be self-supporting; hence a positive cost-benefit ratio has yet to be achieved. Moreover, the performance of the market in share and index options cannot have indicative value unless the absolute size of the market and the market shares of genuine 'customers' are greater.

Once again, the main model comes from the USA, where the Chicago Board Options Exchange should clearly serve as a prime example. However, the market capitalization of domestic shares traded in New York reached US\$2132bn on 31 December 1987, whereas the corresponding value on the Zurich stock exchange was only US\$129.7bn. This indicates the importance of volume when it is a question of establishing an additional 'derived' market as an off-shoot of an existing market.

As regards the American market, one cannot avoid asking where the crash of 19 October 1987 originated. The New York financial market, which was the epicentre of the shock waves, is merely a proxy for those markets in which the variants of share trading lauded as 'hedging instruments' are most prevalent.

SPECULATION

It is an obvious and generally accepted fact that types of transaction that offer the possibility of large profits for a small outlay, such as options and, in the past, premium transactions, are likely to attract speculation. By this I mean the conscious running of risks in the expectation of above-average profits as a result of price movements. The financial speculator's objective is usually not to make an investment but to carry out a pure arbitrage transaction. Whether one likes it or not, the question of financial speculation is therefore an aspect of the subject of financial innovations, their supervision and thorough investigation. What is euphemistically described as a 'concentration on ultra-short-term performance' (Frehner)[4] means in plain language a pronounced predilection for speculation. If a substantial proportion of transactions are carried out solely or primarily for speculative reasons, a differentiated interpretation of market behaviour is required.

The phenomenon of speculation is a subject that must be tackled by external and internal supervisory bodies as well. The board of directors of a bank cannot simply turn a blind eye to the risks created by speculative transactions, and the same applies to management, the internal inspectorate, the statutory auditors and the state supervisory authorities.

If it is true that the growth in the volume of trading in derived financial innovations is greater because of the proportion of purely speculative transactions, the attendant risks must also tend to increase. The board of directors will therefore pay particularly close attention to speculative positions built up by large investing customers, but it will also subject speculative trading behaviour by its own institution and speculative transactions by members of staff to additional scrutiny. These problems are well known in both securities and foreign-exchange trading. The safeguards applied differ from one institution to another, but without exception they are designed to minimise risks for the bank both internally and in relation to its large customers. It cannot be denied that people in many walks of life, including bankers, apply double standards where speculation is concerned if it is a question of exploiting additional business opportunities for their own account or on behalf of customers.

It would be conceivable to carry out an in-depth study of the specific effects of speculation in addition to normal supervision. It would not be enough to define speculation as a necessary, even desirable component of a free market and to accept it as such. Both quantitative and qualitative distinctions must be made. What proportion of speculative transactions broadens the market base and at what percentage or absolute volume do distortions appear? What level of speculation can be proved to be responsible for unusual movements or even crises?

The qualitative effects of speculation are also too numerous for the matter to be dealt with in general terms. What different effects result from speculation in finite, non-renewable assets such as land or company shares? By contrast, how does speculation behave with regard to assets that are constantly being produced and are substitutable, such as agricultural or mining products or, in a more limited context, national currencies?

It seems to me that a timely challenge has been issued to academics to provide more differentiated analyses of speculation rather than slogans and generalised judgements. Apart from the regulatory mechanisms that might be set up as a result, such an exercise might also lead to an extension of supervisory responsibilities within individual banks and in the banking sector as a whole. The very fact that none of the many attempts to explain the events around 19 October 1987 mentions the absolute or relative scale of speculation in share markets should be reason enough to look into this and comparable phenomena.

NO END TO DEREGULATION?

The euphoria about deregulation, which has broken out in almost all sectors of the economy, must be contained, particularly where the financial markets are concerned. Controls are indispensable. Even the most ardent advocates of privatization and deregulation acknowledge the need for an orderly and controlled development of financial transactions. In any case, it would be wiser not to let matters ride until a dangerous situation develops; the return to an appropriate level of regulation would be many times more difficult if it came as the result of a collapse.

The desire to increase the competitiveness of a country's financial markets, which seems to be behind many expansion plans at present, conflicts with the need for every financial market to ensure maximum reliability for transactions, market participants and price mechanisms. Taking adherence to so-called principles to the extreme always leads simply to the downfall of the principle itself.

The absence of excesses and disasters is of prime importance to the successful conduct of banking activities. The lasting damage inflicted by scandal is felt nowhere more strongly than here. Hormone additives in meat, problems with baby food and building offences are quickly forgotten, but the Herstatt and Kreuger scandals,[5] the massive foreign exchange losses sustained by banks and industrial companies, the German inflation of the early 1920s and the stock exchange crises of 1929 and 1987 are imprinted for all time not only on the minds of those directly involved but also on the memories of entire generations.

When speaking about financial innovations on a previous occasion I raised the question whether the universal bank in the central European mould had a future if the present changes in banking continued. The question remained open, since the optimum structure for the universal bank must be modified continuously in the light of further analysis and the adaptability of the institutions in question. Some doubts still remain on account of:

- increasing conflicts of interests within banks,
- specialisation taken to the extreme and made technically independent,
- growing divergence between traditional bank/customer relations and a bank's relations with customers in its capacity as a dealer.

An extreme opinion has now been published in the USA (*McKinsey Quarterly*, Summer 1988) advocating that traditional lending operations be completely divorced from deposit-taking, though note that deposits would continue to be guaranteed by the state! In my view this would sound the death-knell for the classical banker, who would have to make way for financial companies of specialised dealers. Such a notion may possibly appeal to the American mentality, but let us hope that European bankers committed to their profession could not reconcile themselves to it. For me, the model of the future banker as an extrovert, persistent salesman remains unthinkable.

The discernible competition between the many different directions in which banks may develop will intensify. Generalists *versus* specialists, investment banks *versus* commercial banks, battling for a share of the profits and to demonstrate that they can legitimately meet genuine market needs over the long term. Structural changes in the banking system and in the organisation of individual banks are therefore to be expected.

SUMMARY AND CONCLUSIONS

Every supervisory body has a constant duty to keep up to date with changes in business activities. This process of ongoing education in specific fields therefore places an unrenounceable obligation on the board of directors of a bank. It can also mean changing the frequency of *reporting or even holding* induction and training courses. For more than a decade the Union Bank of Switzerland (UBS) has held regular further training courses for members of its board of directors.

Innovative changes also call for a change in mentality in order to exercise supervisory duties efficiently. Scepticism, intellectual curiosity and an unerring desire to get at the facts by means of questioning should be the tools for investigating the nature and effects of financial innovations. It is always dangerous to make blanket judgements about new phenomena. Ill-considered acceptance would be just as absurd as rejection out of hand.

Financial innovations are a fact and will develop further. It remains to be seen whether they are merely a passing vogue that represents a 'degeneration of the sector in advance of a foreseeable setback' and can be dismissed as a 'seven-day wonder' (Caytas and Mahari, 1988). What is certain is that inflated expectations are out of place. If this applies to active market participants and passive observers, then the need for a sense of perspective in place of euphoria is all the more important for those in supervisory capacities in financial institutions.

If the term 'to scrutinize' is applied in any meaningful way, then it is in describing the manner in which supervisory bodies in the banking sector should tackle the many variants of existing and future financial innovations. Blind faith in so-called experts and in apparent past successes is as inappropriate as the uncritical reading of literature on the stock market crash, bulletins from insiders or the pronouncements of an opinionated business press. *Doubt, scepticism* and occasionally *disbelief* produce more interesting results for supervisors than an unquestioning participation in the incantations of blinkered believers.

Notes

1. See Ernst Kilgers, *Bank-Management in Theorie und* Praxis, 2nd edn (Berlin: Verlag Haupt, 1985).
2. See Ulf G. Baxmann, 'Bankenaufsichtsrechtliche Ueberlegungen zur Reglementierung von Swapgeschäften', *Zeitschrift für das Gesamte Kreditwesen*, no. 22/88.
3. Herbert W. Hunt, Nelson Bunker Hunt (Dallas, USA): silver, 1979–80.
   VW Volkswagen (Wolfsburg, FRG); foreign exchange speculation (losses of about 500 million DM), March 1987.
   Klockner – Humboldt – Deutz Ltd (Köln, FRG): restructuring (losses of about 285 million DM), 1987.
4. W.G. Frehner, President of the Executive Board, Swiss Bank Corporation, Basle, Switzerland.
5. Herstatt Bank, Köln, FRG, bankruptcy in 1970.

Bibliography

Bank for International Settlements (1988) 58th Annual Report, Basle.
Bofinger, Peter, 'Die Finanzmärkte – ein teilweise gerechtfertigter Sonderfall der Regulierung', in Gerhard Schwarz (ed.) *Wo Regeln Bremsen* (Zurich: Neue Zürcher Zeitung, 1988).
Caytas, Ivo G. and Mahari, Julian I. *Im Banne des Investment Banking* (Zurich: Neue Zürcher Zeitung, 1988).
Dempfle, Eugen, 'Finanzinnovationen an den internationalen Geld- und Kapitalmärkten', *Beiträge zur Bankbetriebslehre*, no. 16 (Münsingen: Bancomedia, 1988).
Müller-Möhl, Ernst *et al.* (1988) *Optionen* (Zurich).

16 Macroeconomic Concerns of Central Bankers

Pierre Languetin

The theme of risk management which the Ecole des HEC selected for its banking symposium in 1988 had been envisaged in the first few months of 1987. The stock-exchange crisis which erupted on 19 October of the same year unfortunately confirmed the pertinence of this choice. Managing banking and financial risks was very topical even if, one year after the crisis, euphoria had succeeded the great fright of Black Monday.

Contrary to the fears so frequently expressed, the economic situation did not seem to have suffered from the sudden collapse of share prices. Prices stabilized fairly quickly and then made up some of the lost ground. Economic growth, slowed down for a while, picked up again.

Whether the euphoria of 1988 was justified or not, it is important to examine carefully the developments which led up to the price collapse, together with the measures taken to cope with the effects or to prevent its repetition.

CHARACTERISTICS OF THE ECONOMY IN 1970s AND 1980s

1. Instability This has been seen in many different fields: in the monetary system since suspension of convertibility of the dollar, in the energy sector with the two oil shocks of 1973 and 1979, in the chronic fluctuations in exchange rates, especially with reference to the dollar, and in the considerable variations in interest rates, reflecting both the inflationary expectations of the economic agents and the shifts in monetary policies.

2. The breakdown of the major balances Current account surpluses or deficits, the accumulation of the debts of the developing countries and budgetary deficits, particularly in the USA.

3. The increase in risks This has been generated by instability and economic imbalances and has led to a proliferation of financial innovations which are supposed to ensure cover but at best can only modify the spread.

The deregulation which has occured in a large number of countries and the apparently unlimited possibilities of informatics and telematics have also contributed towards the explosion in the volume of financial transactions and their extension to global level, together with the worldwide integration of the financial markets.

The absence of systematic international cooperation until the middle of the present decade, indeed, the determination on the part of the national authorities to rely, both at home and at international level, on market forces alone, and the replacement of the myth of omniscient and omnipotent public power by the myth of efficient markets governed by rational expectations, gave full scope to a disproportionate development of the financial sector compared with the real economy.

Moreover, financial transactions have appeared to become an end in themselves, with profits and margins alone justifying transactions. The constant rise in share prices, based on the longest period of economic growth since the Second World War, speculative gains and profits drawn from restructuring operations or financial predation have resulted in the links between transactions on the one hand and the profitability of companies and their economic value on the other becoming overstretched. The abundant liquid assets placed on the market through the policies of the central banks or through credits from the commercial banks have had more marked effects on the financial economy than on production and trade. When the Federal Reserve Bank precipitated money-creation in 1986 in order to support the economic situation, it was in fact the surge in share prices that it generated in spite of itself.

DEEPER CAUSES OF THE 1987 CRASH

That was the background against which the events of 19 October 1987 were acted out. The immediate causes of the crisis were seen to lie on the one hand in the tightening of American policy in 1987 – in contrast to the expansion of 1986 – a process which increased the yield from bonds, and on the other hand in the statements of the Treasury Secretary casting doubts on the will of the US administration to maintain the stability of the dollar. But the deepest causes must be sought elsewhere even though, in spite of the numerous and voluminous studies which have been carried out in the USA and UK, for example, opinions are far from unanimous.

In its annual report for 1988, the Bank for International Settlement (BIS) identifies three causes: The first is the uncertainties which exist as to resolving the international payments problem. These worries led to fears of a recession which would undoubtedly have brought down company profits.

The second is the bursting of a speculative bubble which formed in the period preceding the crisis. Share prices climbed to levels way above those justified by the basic economic data. The strong expansion of US monetary policy in 1986 and the rapid development of monetary instruments, transactions on credit and portfolio cover mechanisms were certainly at the root of the speculative bubble. Paradoxically, cover mechanisms, by offering guarantees against a fall in prices – guarantees which proved worthless during the crisis – encouraged investors to act with temerity and thus help to inflate the bubble.

The third cause can be attributed to a momentary failure of certain market mechanisms when prices began to fall, and this failure might also have contributed to starting the crisis. Subsequently, the fall in prices was exacerbated and accelerated by different factors, such as:

- sales by 'programmed operations';
- different reactions by runners, especially those in New York and those in Chicago;
- the disparities in the rules governing the operation of spot markets and forward markets.

Two aspects of the crisis must be underlined in particular. First, the immediate communication to all stock markets of the fall in prices that had occured in the USA, to such a point that we can talk of a simultaneous collapse of share prices on all the world's stock markets. Instructions to sell besieged all the markets, regardless of the quality of the companies concerned or the state of the economies of the different countries. What was striking about this development was the fact that it was automatic and simultaneous, which underlines the globalization and extreme interdependence of the markets.

The second aspect is the extent and above all the speed of the fall in prices, which demonstrate both the weaknesses of the financial markets and the decisive influence of the automatic computer systems.

THE ROLE AND RESPONSIBILITIES OF THE CENTRAL BANKS

The Lessons to be Drawn from the Point of View of Central Banks from the Crisis of 19 October 1987

Opinion is unanimous in recognizing the decisive part played by the central banks to contain the effects of the stock market crisis. Falling into step with the American Federal Reserve Bank, they immediately showed themselves to be prepared to provide the economy with the liquid assets needed to prevent the financial institutions and the system as a whole from coming to a standstill. The generous creation of money, and especially the certainty of being able to count on the backing of the issuing institution, allowed panic to be averted and – after a substantial fall – prices were stabilized.

This intervention by the central banks is diametrically opposed to what happened after the 1929 crash. It proved to be an undeniable success and as such should be regarded as a major lesson for the central banks. However, the lessons should not be limited to curative action. The lessons of prevention seem to me to be even more important. In my opinion, these must be extended to all the different fields of competence of the central banks and governments, and must meet their basic preoccupations:

- ensuring that the economic situation develops in a stable manner;
- keeping the financial markets effective in the service of the real economy;
- preventing excessive and violent movements on the financial markets;
- avoiding unhealthy propagations on an integrated world market.

These objectives call for resolute action on the part of the central banks and governments at several levels, which I shall simply enumerate here.

At macroeconomic level, international cooperation must be intensified with a view to solving progressively and credibly the problem of the major imbalances. The clarity of the objectives of macroeconomic policy and their continuity are essential if one is to re-establish stability, a prerequisite for the development and rational behaviour of the financial markets.

The organization of the financial markets must be revised in the light of this experience. Their efficiency must be safeguarded and improved, which presupposes that these markets are also protected, especially by means of fire-breaks, from excessively violent movements, both upwards and downwards. Avoiding a collapse of the financial system, which might have occurred in October 1987, is a major objective.

International coordination of supervision of banks is essential. In this connection, the action taken by the Basle Committee,[1] with regard to equity capital, is certainly a step in the right direction.

Since many institutions other than banks play a part in financial operations, it is highly desirable for the countries in which the main financial markets are situated to undertake a joint revision of the operation of markets and exchanges and to establish whatever forms of cooperation may be necessary.

These lessons must not be forgotten or disregarded. Curative actions may be insufficient or hazardous. As we saw in autumn 1987 they mean resorting to monetary policy, which alone is capable of having a real and a psychological effect in a short space of time. Their cost must not be underestimated. The clear signs of overheating which can be seen in several major economies and the fear of a return of inflation no doubt reflect, to an appreciable extent, the strong tendency among the central banks to resort to money-creation after the crisis of 19 October 1987. And the slowdown observed in reducing international imbalances is perhaps not unconnected with the abundant liquid assets thrown onto the market by way of a curative action.

There is a great temptation to forget the tremors experienced at the end of 1987 and to let oneself be carried away by the current euphoria with regard to the economic and financial situation. 'Out of sight, out of mind' is a trap that we must avoid.

Note

1. The Basle Committee on Banking Regulations and Supervisory Practices, *International Convergence of Capital Measurement and Capital Standards*, Bank for International Settlements (BIS), Basle-Switzerland, July 1988, 32pp. – typescript; the Basle Committee's agreement is also referred to as the BIS agreement (Tables 5.10 and 5.11).

17 The Swiss Supervisory Approach towards International Banking

Kurt Hauri

GENERAL TRENDS

The Swiss banking supervisory authority when it first originated more than fifty years ago was mainly interested in obtaining information through figures. The documents with which it used to work almost exclusively were balance sheets, profit-and-loss accounts and auditors' reports. Tables, percentages, relationships between figures and minimum and maximum rates were the basis on which a bank could confirm that it was doing business in a serious way.

Over the years, but more particularly during the past ten years, banking activities have developed in all fields, at an ever-increasing pace and sometimes even hastily and jerkily. Their activities, local to begin with, have gradually extended to international level. The traditional image of the sole manager and his one apprentice has been replaced by a complex with thousands of employees. Work-around-the-clock has replaced the old six-hour day. The savings-and-mortgage activity has given way to a whole range of complicated loans with new and ingenuous financial instruments.

EQUITY CAPITAL

Faced with these developments, new barriers have had to be erected. It has become essential to minimize the unintentional distortions of competition which have been appearing and to control new risks. The field of activity of the big banks now calls for international collaboration.

The 'Committee on Banking Regulations and Supervisory Practices of the Bank for International Settlements', a committee with no formal organizational structure, yet no less effective for all that, which brings together the supervisory authorities of the twelve major countries in the financial world, is a significant element in this respect. In a short period of time, thanks to an enormous amount of work, it has prepared an important document entitled 'International Convergence of Capital Measurement and Capital Standards'. This document aims to ensure that within five years the capital of all banks with an international activity will be equal. It provides for the fixing of a minimum basic capital, first to reinforce the stability and solidity of the international banking system and second to reduce the competitive inequalities which exist between the international banks.

INTEREST-RATE RISKS, INVESTMENT RISKS AND COUNTRY RISKS

The fact that a bank has adequate capital and reserves is an important factor which gives it strength. However, there are many others. Capital is mainly related to credit risk. It constitutes protection in the event of the other party failing to be able to meet its obligations. Other significant risks have to be taken into consideration.

In Switzerland, the interest-rate risk does not at present receive the attention that it should. In a world of financial interrelationship, interest on assets and liabilities does not change in the same proportions or at the same time. A single bank alone cannot have any influence on this process. Such a situation has hidden dangers, the mere detection of which creates major difficulties within the context of the changes in course. Despite the research undertaken, no satisfactory method has yet been devised to evaluate these dangers, because they are concealed in the bank's overall activity within and outside the balance sheet.

The stock exchange crash of October 1987 demonstrated with brutal clarity the growing importance of investment risks in securities. In any case, investment risk is not sufficiently controlled and guaranteed by the cover of capital and reserves alone. Additional solutions must be found. Nor is it any easier to measure and define country risk and the risk linked with it, that is, the exchange risk. A simple differentiation between internal creditors and debtors and those abroad disregards the global integration of the capital markets. A quick glance at a bank's equity capital can lead to inaccurate and false conclusions as to its ability to cope with difficulties. Multiple provisions gain considerably in importance when taking suitable account of exchange risks, investment risks and country risk. The establishment of such provisions, apart from the general provisions stipulated by the supervisory authorities for commitments in countries in difficulty, is today left largely to banks and their auditors discretion. That should no longer be regarded as sufficient in the future. In-depth research is already being conducted at international level to establish more appropriate standards.

SUPERVISION OF BANKING GROUPS

One sees less and less the image of a single bank acting on its own. Subsidiaries and financial companies are created and taken over in Switzerland and abroad. This allows the enlargement of the clientele, helps an institute in difficulties, reduces taxation and even avoids intensive banking supervision. Complex groups have thus been formed and the real interrelationships can only be established with great difficulty.

Supervision should grow with and adapt to the increasing interrelation of groups. At present, only a few fields are taken into account in consolidated supervision. Sooner or later complete supervision of groups must be achieved. Consolidated profit-and-loss accounts can therefore no longer remain a vain hope.

The complexity of the problem is exacerbated by the fact that banking groups are not just firmly rooted in the financial fields but are dominated by foreign holding companies or natural persons. In addition, participations are no longer unilateral but take the form of a network of relations intercrossing several times. Sometimes, these holdings constitute an impenetrable and even inextricable labyrinth. Consequently, consolidated supervision cannot be introduced little by little. It should be established in one fell swoop.

ENLARGING THE SCOPE OF SUPERVISION

By virtue of both their number and their activity, bank-like finance companies have been considerably expanding in Switzerland over the past ten years. They are companies which are mainly active in the financial sector and which finance, on their own account primarily, an indeterminate number of enterprises with which they do not form an economic entity. There are 140 of them at the moment, 111 in foreign hands. These establishments are not subject to the provisions of the banking law.

Over the years, the aim of the banking law has developed towards a modern interpretation going beyond the simple protection of creditors. It is no longer a matter of simply safeguarding the confidence of the customer in his bank. In the public interest, it should guarantee in general that all the participants active in the financial market and in credit arranging are trustworthy. This is why protecting the functioning of the financial market as an independent objective of banking supervision has gained in importance. Coincidental with moving on from close protection of the creditor to wider protection of the investor, protection of the person acquiring securities through issuing houses has also increased. Insufficient publicity, especially in the field of notes, and the responsibility of those issuing the prospectuses, which has proved to be insufficient in practice, calls for research into better protection possibilities.

With the growth of large bank-like finance companies and of issuing houses, it is not possible to delimit definitively the scope of supervision. Most professional fund managers not subject today to Swiss banking law carry out activities which – with the exception of public solicitation for the acceptance of deposits – are at least very close to banking activities. The aims and objectives of the banking law are such that one must keep a watchful eye on their activities. Greater intention will have to be paid to them.

SUPERVISION OF THE FINANCIAL MARKETS

Through this enlargement of supervision, it is not planned to set up or implement in a roundabout way any extended supervision of the financial markets. First, one must make up for lost time and adapt oneself to the changing nature of these markets.

The calls for legislation on and institutionalized supervision of the Swiss capital market will not be silenced. Quite rightly, the Swiss stock exchanges are now being resolutely analyzed. Protection of the investor, fiscal, federalist and international aspects, are to be taken into consideration.

As long as the conditions are not sufficiently defined, it is impossible to predict the final goal for which one must aim. Self-regulation must however remain possible and open. The Agreement on the Swiss banks' code of conduct and due diligence and Soffex – the development of which we must await a little longer – have helped self-regulation to acquire a good reputation. The Convention of the

Swiss Bankers' Association on the protection of savers has enabled the Federal Council to decide – at least for the time being – against a revision of the banking law. The State may postpone any threats of repression provided that an independent and responsible regulation, containing numerous possibilities and advantages in itself, ensures an efficient application and real sanctions in the event of violations.

PROSPECTS

A lot has been said on the subject of legislation, case history, the practices of the supervisory authority, international harmonization and self-regulation. One must not deduce from this a rush towards increased regulation. The development of banks and financial markets must go hand in hand with appropriate supervision, and the latter must not allow itself to be overtaken and find itself far behind with no hope of catching up. Fortunately, there is a conviction today that a prosperous banking sector requires suitable supervision capable of carrying out the task. Though restrained it forms a nevertheless effective part of the infrastructure of a bank as do the general staff, the inspectorate and the logistical departments. Banks will find the supervisory authority to be a constructive and critical partner in which they can place their trust.

18 Transnationalization and Global Financial Equilibrium

Gaston Gaudard

The global economy in 1988 – one year after the stock market crash on Wall Street which precipitated a drastic slump in equity prices around the world – was showing some, albeit still inadequate, signs of progress in terms of external adjustment.[1] Nonetheless, uncertainties were still rife and the economy remained acutely sensitive primarily because economic agents still did not have sufficient confidence in the determination of the authorities to resist pressure on the dollar and were not convinced that adequate policies had been put in place to guarantee regular progress in restoring international financial equilibrium of trading partners.

Faced with the undeniable reality of their close interdependence, countries opted in favour of reasonable cooperation as a means of avoiding the worst errors: however, their concerted action was directed solely at reducing the risk of a break in the system triggering a chain reaction which might ultimately precipitate the collapse of the entire edifice. There was agreement with regard to solving conflicts of interest, but this strategy of non-cooperative equilibrium is unlikely for the time being to achieve the desired degree of harmony owing to the continuing strong insistence on national autonomy.[2]

Nevertheless, superimposed on this *international* context, it is important not to overlook the powerful interaction emanating from the *transnational* sector. The latter, by radically restructuring external investment, exerts an acknowledged influence on the variables that determine international financial equilibrium. It is no longer possible to think solely in terms of countries; other – self-contained – dimensions of the economy have to be taken into consideration – those of the transnational corporations.[3] All in all, including the transnationals, there is really a new structure to the global financial market, whose operating parameters have been modified.

233

TRANSNATIONALIZATION AND STRUCTURE OF THE GLOBAL FINANCIAL MARKET

In principle, the global distribution of capital – generated by countries where domestic savings formation exceeds domestic investment and channelled to countries where the reverse situation exists – operates simultaneously through individuals and corporations in response to yield differentials and security considerations, and through the State in response to political and economic considerations in the collective interest. In recent years, however, foreign investment was undergoing rapid change in terms of composition, time and space.

In the nineteenth and early twentieth centuries, a feature of the *composition* of foreign investment was the predominant share accounted for by private portfolio investment. By contrast, between 1940 and 1965 there was a substantial increase in public capital flows. Thereafter, private capital regained its preeminence. A particular phenomenon, visible since the 1960s, has been the rapid increase in direct investment thanks initially to transnational industrial corporations and then to transnational service enterprises. Controversial a quarter of a century ago, direct investment has since become current practice, vigorous new sources have opened up (Japan, South Korea)[4] and a large number of countries that were formerly hostile to it (developing countries, People's Republic of China, East Bloc) no longer reject it.[5] Since 1986, it is true, portfolio investment has taken the lead again, not as a result of any decline in direct investment but because of even more rapid growth in portfolio flows. Indeed the latter – despite a definite slowdown in flows to indebted Third World countries – have surged strongly in global terms. International bond issues – especially Eurobonds – grew at a rapid rate between 1983 and 1986 (dropping back slightly in 1987) and between 1983 and 1987, as new financial markets evolved, the volume of Euro-equity issues alone shot up from $0.2bn to $17.6bn. Thus, for three decades, transnationalization has been a major factor in the structure of foreign investment.

The *spatial dimension* of foreign investment has also changed decisively. The financial centres of yore had relatively specific 'reservoirs' of capital. It was logical in the nineteenth century for London and Paris to channel their national savings surpluses to their colonial empires and to friendly countries in the throes of expansion (the USA and Czarist Russia respectively). The expertise of British and French bankers moreover exerted a centralizing influence on foreign depositors. Today, in all the major financial centres, of which the West no longer enjoys a monopoly, the capital markets have become global as deregulation – more so even than decolonization before it – has led to the dismantling of national and institutional barriers. In our own epoch – the 1980s – the rise of the underwriting syndicate is a typical product of the new spatial context. The spectacular increase in the velocity of circulation of information and the speed of communication, allied to screen-based trading systems, has resulted in a new global simultaneity and sharply reduced communication costs. As the ramifications and interpenetration of the financial markets have grown and participants have a much wider range of choice, the interplay between them has become infinitely more complex. What is more, as a result of the new financial instruments, there has been a marked rise in the off-balance-sheet activities of the banks as well as in participations in international conglomerates, the elements of which are subject to different sovereign jurisdictions and to differing prudential standards. The late 1980s have seen a wave of transnational tender offers: they have contributed incontestably to broadening operating ambits still further so as frequently to constitute bidirectional, intra-industry, oligopolistic markets purveying differentiated products at increasing returns of scale.[6]

The *temporal dimension* of foreign investment has also been transformed. Rising uncertainty has apparently had contradictory consequences. On the one hand, it has encouraged the search for more flexible instruments like bonds whose maturity can be extended or shortened at the discretion of the issuer (call option) or of the investor (put option). Adjustable securities are designed to respond to the same need. A secondary market like that for financial futures permits better management of the exchange risk (which is old) or the interest risk (which is new) by buying or selling a futures contract at any moment between its date of issue and the date on which the foreign currency or financial asset is delivered. In another sense, however, in the industrial countries and in response to changing individual and corporate behaviour patterns and the rise of the institutional investor, securities in general have gained ground, extending average maturities in the process. Since the early 1980s, a growing trend towards disintermediation has been visible in the developed economies and, in a general way, continued on the internal markets after 19 October 1987 even if, in terms of international capital flows, banks' loans were for a time preferred to debt-financing. The reason is that, thanks to the innovative financing techniques available, it is demonstrably more convenient and advantageous for prime borrowers – and this includes many transnationals – to issue securitized debt on internal markets rather than to resort to bank credit. This tendency is reinforced by the fact that major global corporations themselves handle the financing problems of their subsidiaries. Thus – and in opposite directions depending on the case – the durations of commitments are rearranged, even if widespread concern remains because of the prevailing uncertainty and doubts about the capacity to react to disruptive shocks to the system. Under the pressure of global imbalances, the readjustment of economic structures and financial innovation, the entire temporal 'environment' is undergoing change, split between the search for formulas to provide greater stability in terms of duration on the one hand, and on the other, greater flexibility to cope better with a much more unstable evolution than hitherto.

TRANSNATIONALIZATION AND GLOBAL FINANCIAL EQUILIBRIUM

The dual *international* and *transnational* network stemming from the outward development of companies has now progressed to such an extent that the cross-border distribution of tasks by the companies prevails over the international division of labour among states. In other words, we are no longer confronted solely with countries that endeavour to manage their economic affairs in optimum fashion so as to sell their domestic production on external markets. We are also dealing with companies that are streamlining themselves by distributing throughout different national territories the activities in which they are engaged. These companies are in pursuit of three main advantages: the oligopoly (grouping of companies), internalization (concentration of production stages) and localization (benefits of a particular environment).[7] They can thereby acquire, over vast areas, functional dimensions commensurate with the explosion of technological progress and with global competition.

Transnational enterprises and global financial equilibrium are closely linked. By, for instance, their emancipation from national constrictions and regulations, the two phenomena exhibit a similar tendency to globalization, the former in the production sector, the latter in finance. Establishment of subsidiaries abroad implies international mobility of capital and strong growth in the volume of direct investment. Since the early 1980s, indeed, the economy has seen 'the evolution of long-term relations between partners or associates at global level.[8] Besides the well-known big groups, small and medium-sized companies ('baby multinationals') are setting themselves up abroad in specialized market niches, and, under the aegis of 600m consumers in the three main markets, networks of firms with flexible but durable relations are being established so that the specific character of the products is maintained even though the constituent parts are to some extent standardized.[9] Thus transnationalization represents a functional modification of global financial equilibrium.

Transnational enterprises endeavour to optimize their financial environment. The problem arises because various distorting factors (differences in taxation rates, obstacles to capital movements, exchange-rate fluctuations, etc.) exist between countries.[10] Consequently, the choices offered are unequal, in particular when it comes to financing, which can be effected on the capital market or internally within the transnational enterprise. But in either case different variants are possible, depending on interest-rate differentials on the different markets, or on the particular combinations at hand (simple or multilateral, even cross-related) between the parent company and one or several of its affiliates.

On average, a transnational company has several dozen affiliates, thereby allowing a rich choice of combination based on key criteria such as cost of funds and tax burden. For all that, the changeable character of the imbalances can obviously lead to investment solutions which may change in a far-from-negligible fashion in the course of time. Other delicate forms of arbitrage, on the other hand, concern profits for instance, and are therefore apt to weigh heavily on the relationship existing between the constituent parts of the transnational. Partial or complete deduction of interest payable on debts in a particular country is likely to concentrate long-term borrowing there, and the form of taxation imposed on dividends makes their appearance preferable at one rather than at another affiliate or the parent company. The system of more or less realistic transfer prices between the different companies allows more or less effective internal distribution of profits, though due account has also to be taken of possible repatriation barriers. The financial hurdles created by commercial policy are themselves surmountable,[11] as is testified by the well-known formula of the tariff factories. As can be seen, global financial equilibrium in 1988 has to take account of a highly complex system of facts which are regularly challenged by the rapid – and even transient – nature of change (that of currency rates being a pertinent example).

Optimizing of financial environments by the transnationals has important implications for global financial equilibrium. These can be divided into two major categories:

1. Global capital movements are modified. The crucial element for direct investment is no longer the transfer of the savings surplus of one country in order to compensate for a shortfall in investment in another. Rather, it is a question of maximizing the profits of transnationals, regardless of the geographical areas involved. Logically enough, this transformation of the determining criterion changes the direction of capital movements as well as having other economic implications for the country in question. It is, however, impossible to generalize *a priori* on the overall benefits or drawbacks of this change for global financial equilibrium. The increased clout of the transnationals is also reflected in portfolio movements because these firms intervene directly on this market and they do so differently from private individuals or national enterprises. Even short-term capital movements are affected by the precautionary behaviour of the transnationals, which are required by the dictates of sound treasury management to practise hedging and use a system of 'leads and lags' in their corporate financial policy.

2. Not all transnationalizations are reflected to the same extent in external flows. In 1988, the merger of a firm from one country with an already existing enterprise in another country – an enterprise that used to be its client or even its competitor – is common enough.[12] This form of joint venture is achieved by acquisition of a majority holding,[13] thereby conferring both a firm foothold on an external market and the security of being able to make profitable use of local know-how. Strictly speaking, however, recourse to partial acquisition or even to simple service contracts (licensing, engineering, etc.) does not mean that a new affiliate has been set up but that a foreign enterprise has lost some or all of its autonomy. Such forms of cooperation can also be created by the establishment of an affiliate jointly owned by several parent companies of different nationalities. In all these scenarios, the capital transfers

involved are either lighter in comparison with the traditional affiliate set-up or closer to portfolio investment than to direct investment if, for instance, different parent companies of different nationality confine themselves to buying up shares in the same foreign firm simultaneously with a view to developing it jointly. More so than with major direct investments, we are eventually confronted, as a repercussion in such cases, with flows deriving from the current account balance (various charges and dividends, for example), in so far as these are repatriated. If need be, reinvestment in the country of the affiliate can constitute a direct investment without there explicitly being any corresponding international transfer of capital.

In 1988, global financial equilibrium was far from being assured. The latest current-account figures (those of 1987) reveal a deficit of $161bn for the USA and a surplus of $87bn and $45bn for Japan and West Germany respectively.[14] The readjustments initiated in the last few months will have only a very slight corrective effect on these substantial sums. Since the mid-1970s, there has been an upsurge of capital movements on the financial markets (two and a half times the rate of increase in the nominal revenue of the big industrialized countries), and the new look acquired by the financial environment (thanks in particular to the new financial instruments) has left its mark on the conduct and effectiveness of national monetary policies. Instability and speculation have increased, partly as a result of hostile takeover bids. The transnationals have undoubtedly played a part in this transformation and are therefore not entirely free of responsibility for the present state of global financial equilibrium. However, they are not the only force active in this sector. What is more, it would be short-sighted to conclude that the influence of the globally active enterprises is either always deleterious or always beneficial. The true situation is more subtle, calling for in-depth study in a highly complex systemic environment. Besides, the effects of the transnationals probably vary in their significance and weight, depending on time and circumstances. There is, however, no doubt that the existence of the second network they constitute is an added complication compounding the substantial progress of innovation and deregulation that has itself left its mark on financial systems. At all events, the new financial techniques practised by the transnationals have contributed to creating problems in terms of monetary policy and even in terms of overall economic management of sovereign states, thereby making it all the more imperative to improve global coordination.

THE CHALLENGE OF THE COOPERATIVE GAME

The global financial system is affected by the structural changes convulsing the world economy and in this connection the growing role of transnational corporations is a major element. The internalization of operations peculiar to these enterprises favours direct investment, and the growth of large cross-border conglomerates suggests their portfolio issues are likely to expand. The transnationals, through the specific financial flows they generate, bear a share of responsibility for the orderly functioning of global equilibrium. However, precisely because of the cross-border nature of these enterprises, the scope of influence of individual states is limited when it comes to promoting a more satisfactory global order.

It is consequently eminently desirable that there should be cooperation at global level, which implies both the political order (territorial) and the economic order (transterritorial). It is in this direction that work on a 'code of conduct for transnational corporations' is seeking to progress. However, a global consensus between countries and corporations is not easy to obtain for a mixture which has to be simultaneously well-dosed with productive liberties and impediments to unacceptable abuse.[17] Be that as it may, with reference to game theory, the time is definitely ripe to seek a genuinely cooperative solution.[18]

Notes

1. Alexandre Lamfallussy, '58th Annual Report of the Bank for International Settlements' (Basle: June 1983).
2. Thierry de Montbrial, 'Mondes en mouvement' (Paris: Economica, 1987).
3. Gaston Gaudard, 'Régions et nations face à la transformation de l'espace économique', in Mauro Baranzini and Alvaro Cencini, *Contributi di analisi economica* (Bellinzone: Causagrande, 1987).
4. Philippe Gugler, 'Les transnationales japonaises en Europe' (Fribourg: CRESUF 1986).

5. Thierry de Montbrial, *Competitions et affrontements* (Paris: Economica, 1986).
6. Pierre Caille, 'La théorie de l'échange international de produits defférenciés' (Fribourg: Ed. Universitaires, 1986).
7. Peter Hertner and Geoffrey Jones (eds), *Multinationals: Theory and History* (Aldershot: Gower, 1986).
8. Patrick Joffre, 'De la vente au partenariat mondial', in *Chroniques d'actualité* de la SEDEIS, Paris, March 1985.
9. A. Basile, 'Les nouvelles formes d'investissement', in the *Revue d'économie politique* (Paris: Sirey, May–June 1985).
10. Bharat R. Hazari, *The Pure Theory of International Trade and Distortions* (London: Croom Helm, 1978).
11. Gaston Gaudard, 'Théorie de la protection et transnationalisation de l'économie', in O. de la Grandville, *Relations internationales, politique économique et méthodologie* (Geneva: Georg, 1987).
12. Joffre, 'De la vente au partenariat mondial'.
13. From 1977 onwards, half of new US direct investment abroad has been in the form of joint ventures.
14. Bank for International Settlements, *58th Annual Report* (Basle, 1988).
15. G. Russell Kincaid, 'Conséquences sur les politiques de la mutation structurelle des marchés financiers' in *Finances et développements* (Washington: 1988).
16. Christine Lagoutte, 'Innovations financières et contrôle monétaire', *Eurépargne* (Strasbourg, May 1988).
17. Jean-Pierre Béguin, *Vers une réglementation internationale des activités des sociétés transnationales* (Geneva: IU HEI, 1976).
18. Raymond Barre, Arthur Dunkel, Gaston Gaudard, Alexandre Lamfallussy, Jacques L'Huillier, Henri Mercillon, Bernard Schmitt and Robert Triffin, *Les déséquilibres monétaires et financiers internationaux* (Fribourg: Ed. Universitaires, 1987).

19 Bankers' and Regulators' Management of Risks

Zuhayr Mikdashi

In a modern economy, the banking system is crucial for transferring resources; mobilizing savings and allocating credit; clearing payments; facilitating the flow of goods and services; and meeting the diverse financial requirements of banks' customers. International banking has been subject to considerable changes in the last two decades. These have affected notably the different kinds of risks faced by banks; the size and structure of financial markets; the scope of functional diversification and the range of financial products; the geographical extension or globalization of banking networks; and the competitive behaviour of financial and non-financial institutions, including the methods of transacting business.

The central theme of this chapter is to analyze briefly key issues of strategic significance to the principal parties of the banking sector. In particular, it seeks to present an appreciation of major banking risks and reflects on some of the measures marshalled to cope with these challenges. The thrust of this chapter reflects on highlights of the Colloquium's informal exchanges. The author is solely responsible for the analysis.

RISKS AND BANKERS' STRATEGIES

Risks encountered by banks are the product of multiple factors. Some of these factors fall largely outside the influence of bank management, others are within the realm of their internal control. In the former category, one would include unforeseeable, often substantial and abrupt changes in key macroeconomic factors. These could cover interest rates, exchange rates, growth rates, inflation, budgetary and balance-of-payments imbalances, trade–financial regulations, technological mutations, sociopolitical conditions, etc. Factors which fall under the purview of a bank's management can cover those of an insurable nature, and those non-insurable or partly

242

insurable. Commercially insurable risks are those which can be actuarially calculated. They cover incidents such as burglary, employee infidelity, forgery, extortion, computer crime, etc. Certain types of a bank's financial assets – such as consumer loans – are readily commercially insured. By comparison, a bank's liabilities – notably its deposits – have not been able to obtain commercial insurance at reasonable conditions.

Despite certain possibilities of insurance, senior management has the responsibility of setting judicious directives. This should cover *inter alia* exclusions of, or limitations to, certain types or risks; capital allocation and diversification of exposure portfolios; hedging against interest or exchange risks; continuous monitoring of the observance of prudential ratios along with the immediate application of corrective actions when appropriate. All areas subject to risk have to be continuously observed, viz. credit lending, open positions, foreign exchange dealing, swaps, securities trading, contingent liabilities, investments, etc.

In making good use of business opportunities and in coping with risks, up to date, reliable and pertinent information has become very crucial to banks. Banking institutions have thus sought to enhance their productivity and competitiveness by the further development of their expertise. This has been mostly realized through the recruitment of talented executives, the continuous training and upgrading of staff, and the proper motivation of personnel to keep predators at bay. Furthermore, think-tanks with high quality intelligence-gathering and research have been established to serve management, staff, and customers.

Significant investments have been made recently and will continue to be made in information technology: computers' hardware and software; telecommunications; electronic data-processing equipment, etc. The objectives of such investments are multiple: accuracy, safety, speed, efficient global response to varied needs, low-cost processing of banking transactions thereby permitting expanded markets, etc. Significant achievements in monitoring and analyzing risks, with early-warning systems to detect weaknesses and abuses are continually being made, thanks to technological advances. Bankers have also had to respond with initiative and imagination to changing needs of their clientele. These needs have become more demanding in the increasingly liberalized and globalised financial markets and resulting higher volatility in key variables such as interest rates, exchange rates, inflation, etc.

Innovation has served institutional clientele through gain in efficiency and flexibility. Indeed, new financial instruments have offered borrowers financial resources at cheaper terms (for example, debt swaps) compared with conventional bank credits; provided them with instruments to hedge risks (for example, options such as multiple currency option facility, and forward rate agreements) and also to transform maturities (for example, note issuance facilities [NIFs] or the revolving underwriting facilities [RUFs]); and finally widened the scope of fund providers beyond the circle of banks (notably through securitization).

Reflecting on the risks attributed to the new financial instruments mentioned above, a banker of a 'full-service' institution considered that, on the basis of recent experience, new products 'favour the borrower and offer the investor inadequate rewards in return for the risks he runs' (George Blum).[1] Indeed, a bank providing credit has the capacity to obtain more reliable information and to monitor more effectively a borrower's creditworthiness – as compared with an investor limited to published information, including that of rating agencies.

With the opening-up of new markets and the creation of vast integrated markets (for example, the European Community, the USA and Canada, and Japan) several banks have found it profitable to expand sales outlets beyond their home markets. In the financial services industries, activities most sought after in that drive for geographical expansion are wholesale and investment banking. In the expansion of the spectrum of their services, some banks have been guided by the model of 'full-service' banking – also called 'universal', 'generalist' banking, or 'all-inclusive financial services'. The 'all-inclusive financial services' approach has been deemed an attractive strategy for the larger financial institutions. Such a strategy can be brought to fruition in markets which present no legal or administrative impediments. Other banks have chosen to cultivate their comparative advantage and expertise in one or a few niches, thereby providing customers with quality financial products at attractive terms.

The 'all-inclusive financial services' institutions have moved beyond traditional commercial banking (short or long-term), trust management, or investment banking. They have sought to establish or win over potential mutual funds, pension funds and insurance companies, thereby enlarging their range of products and resources, reaping attractive fees, reaching additional segments of customers and tailoring products the better to meet varied needs.

Beyond inter-bank competition in markets where barriers are dismantled or overcome by innovative approaches to clients, bankers are increasingly concerned about non-bank competition, insurance companies, commercial or manufacturing enterprises. Indeed, industrial corporations are developing their own in-house banking operations. These cover *inter alia* raising funds for their own needs directly from financial markets at better terms than can be obtained from banks. They also cover the extension of credit to buyers of their goods or services, and even to their suppliers. As Sir Philip Wilkinson put it, 'Many erstwhile customers are now indeed banks in their own right, such as the treasury departments of multinational oil companies, while many other treasury departments have full banking knowledge, if not yet the same legal structure.' Banks can no more depend on the unconditional loyalty of their customers, be they big or small. They have to provide them with 'the most up-to-date service in price, quality, and indeed fashion'.

The strategy of expansion in all directions – whether geographical, functional or over the 24-hour time zones – has been advocated by its proponents in banks' senior management on various grounds notably: risk diversification; economies of scale; rational use of expertise and resources; exploitation of business opportunities by tapping resources at the lowest cost and by obtaining the highest yields on assets whose risks are deemed reasonable by bank management; ready response to changing or complex requirements of customers, etc.

Several approaches have been tried in the realization of expansion: creation of affiliates or agencies to expand distribution channels for products/services in new markets; cooperation amongst banks, notably through the creation of joint banking vehicles for certain financial products or to customers; tie-in or reciprocity arrangements with partners; equity participation in other financial institutions or the outright take-over of foreign affiliates.

The choice of the optimal strategy for expansion by any financial institution will naturally have to take into consideration multiple key variables such as identification of customers' needs and size of market; available expertise; availability of capital by the expanding bank; profitability prospects of the institutions or projects acquired in relation to the acquisition cost; the compatibility of corporate

philosophies or cultures of merged institutions; the synergy of partner groups; the intensity of competition; the relative attractiveness of
the macroeconomic environment – including fiscal – in certain geographical areas. Banks have often contained their drive for expansion
– whether functional or geographical – to avoid unduly stretching
managerial capabilities.

Banks have had to adapt their activities to new competitive forces.
Barring legal or regulatory barriers, the conventional separation
between (a) investment banks with the thrust of their activities on
arranging outside financing for their clientèle notably through securities and (b) deposit-taking commercial banks focusing on direct
lending, is increasingly being blurred. Indeed, the current trend for
commercial banks is to move away from their sole dependence on
taking deposits to recycle funds to borrowers. 'Credit power' is giving
way to 'placing power' as banks are becoming increasingly more
involved in underwriting, securities trading, and the arrangement of
novel financial packages for their corporate and other customers –
such as leveraged buy-outs. This approach is known as 'disintermediation' by commercial bankers, that is, moving towards off-balance-
sheet activities.

Many of the new financial products initiated by banks – and
notably investment or merchant banks – are not reflected in their
balance sheets, in so far as they do not involve the bank in actual
financing. The investment often assumes a back-up role in providing
funds, should the borrower be unable to raise funds in the market in
NIFs, RUFs and similar activities. In this, the bank becomes exposed
to liquidity risks. The bank also assumes commitments entered into
by its guaranteed customers, should the latter fail to honour their
obligations.

The Stock Exchange crash of October 1987 has not affected enterprises' ability to raise funds, but the composition of their funds has
changed. They have found borrowing from commercial banks attractive again, compared to raising funds by way of new issues in the
capital markets – generally with the assistance of investment bankers.
In some markets, securities issuers have to respond to a new risk
premium required by investors who have become more sensitive to
market risks since the 1987 crash, thereby raising the cost of new
capital funded by the marketing of paper.

The transformation of a financial institution into a 'full-service'
institution is not without pitfalls. Indeed, there is the possibility of
acute rivalry setting in amongst the divisions or sections of the same

institution, in order to obtain the business of a given customer. This was acknowledged by a leading Swiss banker who said:

> The first weakness resides in the possible conflict of interests between individual business sections of the same bank. The sale of securities to investors can clash with the bank's deposit business. The interests of the securities underwriting departments may well run counter to those of investment advice and portfolio management. Credit departments will have viewed with suspicion the process of securitization, i.e. the move away from bank loans and into tradeable securities (Rainer E. Gut).

Relatively few banks now believe they can aspire to be truly global in coverage and range of services/products.

The best of performance in a privately held institution – financial or non-financial – is neither size nor span of operations. The yardstick of performance is unquestionably the capacity of management to generate profits – while at the same time limiting risk exposure, respecting the laws and regulations of markets within which it operates. Inept management is at the basis of problems, such as attracting funds at excessive interest rates, aggressive lending to speculative sectors, deficient controls leading to fraud and other abuses. As eloquently put by a Swiss banker, '*Doubt, scepticism* and occasionally *disbelief* produce more interesting results for supervisors than an unquestioning participation in the incantations of blinkered believers' (Robert Holzach, his italics).

INTERNATIONAL DEBT

The responsibilities for the enduring international debt crisis are complex and are shared by several parties which have generally exercised poor judgement. In the second half of the 1970s bankers rushed to extend mostly balance-of-payments loans to certain borrowers, notably less developed countries (LDCs), without, however, carefully scrutinizing and adequately controlling the ultimate use of these funds. Many Western banks would maintain that their governments actively encouraged them to engage in foreign lending of the kind described, as part of the recycling of the large petro-currency deposits. Several of the LDC borrowers often borrowed excessively from international banks and financial markets at commercial rates.

Some of these funds were used for grandiose unviable projects or to palliate socio-political problems. The public authorities of the creditor countries often lagged in alerting their financial institutions to the adverse systemic and environmental changes occurring in developing or developed countries, which escaped the perception of individual banks. Moreover, these authorities did not impose timeously appropriate prudential requirements in this regard.

With the setting of an adverse economic, social or political environment, the 1980s have witnessed a general disaffection by foreign financiers and creditors *vis-à-vis* a large number of LDCs. The net outflow of capital from these countries has consisted of, *inter alia*, heavy servicing of foreign debt as well as capital flight and has imposed a severe constraint on their capacity to grow and to generate new wealth with which to repay their creditors. Other factors have compounded the difficulties of several LDCs. Chief amongst these factors are the deterioration of their terms of trade *vis-à-vis* the developed industrial countries (DICs) which are the LDCs major trading partners, as well as the decline of LDCs' exports following on the 1980–2 recession in DICs and its aftermath of protectionist measures. Another important factor is the real cost of servicing LDCs debt, notably through the decline in the inflation rates of creditor currencies and the rise in real interest charges of debt contracted at variable interest rates. The significance of these and other factors differs among countries. An exhaustive analysis, which is outside the scope of this chapter, would call for in-depth country case studies.

Though it is impossible to apportion responsibilities in the international debt problem, the onus of overcoming this challenge lies primarily with debtor-countries. In particular, these countries' citizens should regain confidence in their national economies to lure back the capital they have sent overseas. One cannot expect foreign lenders to provide finance to a country if the nationals themselves have no confidence in their own economy.

Solutions for debt reduction revolve around several axes, notably debt take-overs by the public authorities of creditor-countries on a bilateral or multilateral basis; the reduction of financial charges; restructuring of debt portfolios (including the extension of maturities); debt conversions and sales; liberalization of import markets in developed countries – especially those with chronic balance-of-payments surplus – in order to facilitate the import of product from debtor-countries. No lasting solution to the debt problem can, however, come without structural adjustments in LDC debtor-countries in favour of financial discipline focusing on productive spending, the elimination of waste, and the reversal of capital outflows by nationals.

LDCs have been handicapped in adjusting their economies by structural rigidities. Notable among these are the fact that their banks are often state-owned, and that they are burdened with non-banking or so-called social functions (for example, offering subsidized financial products to certain categories of borrowers). These rigidities preclude bank management both from responding readily to market forces, and from efficient and innovative performance. It is reckoned that certain structural adjustments are needed in heavily indebted countries to enable them to reduce their debt burden. Such adjustments are concerned with rendering the economy more competitive and less subject to administrative controls, price fixing, subsidies, excessive fiscal burdens, etc.

There is no uniform solution to the reduction of LDCs' debt but the parties concerned will have to design appropriate policies on a case-by-case basis. It is generally admitted that the foreign debt of the poorest developing countries, suffering from arrears with no prospect of repayment, should be converted, partially or totally, into aid, by both private lenders (through debt write-offs) and public agencies of developed creditor-nations.

One international banker believes, however, that the principle of debt forgiveness is counterproductive for most countries, notably in the case of Latin America. He cogently argues

> After realizing their losses, the creditors involved would presumably no longer be willing to take on such risks again. This would prove a fatal strategy for the debtor-country. Not only would the latter lose its creditworthiness; it would also isolate itself from the world trade system . . . Through debt-forgiveness, we cannot alter the corruption, mismanagement or simply the wrong choice of economic policy in the countries in question (Walter Seipp).

Moreover, individual banks may not have a sufficiently large capital base or earning capacity to permit a voluntary consideration of debt-forgiveness – especially when the banks' funders are not ready to share in the cost of such a measure.

In the seasoned judgement of the Netherlands Minister of Finance H. Onno Ruding, the ideal debt management forum is the International Monetary Fund (IMF), in which all parties are members –

debtor- and creditor-countries, developed and developing, big and small. Conditional financial support provided by the IMF can be an effective tool to ensure the implementation of appropriate and realistic adjustment policies in the countries concerned. Developing countries need to grow and to export in order to honour their financial liabilities. Wisdom lies in global cooperation to foster the growth of these countries and the expansion of their export trade. By avoiding egocentric policies (such as trade protectionism and restricting LDCs' access to new financial resources), the developed countries can contribute to solving the acuteness of the international debt problem. Debtor- and creditor-nations stand to gain from the reduction of the LDCs' debt burden through sustained growth and expansion of trade in a stable financial environment.

In the past few years, US and other Western banks have built up reserves to deal with the LDC debt problems. As a result, the solvency of large banks is no longer under threat, although profits can still suffer if debt repayment is limited.

PUBLIC POLICIES AND PRUDENTIAL RULES

Both the public and private sectors are concerned about the soundness and stability of the domestic as well as the international banking systems. The financial structure of banking institutions and the importance of confidence are such that the failure of a big institution can create problems for others as these problems are readily transmitted at the national–transnational level via the interlinked institutions. Governments in major Western economies have in recent years dismantled or reduced barriers to competition and innovation in their financial markets. This has enhanced the global interdependence of financial institutions, while subjecting them to the vagaries of market forces.

Various considerations have prompted public authorities to be concerned with the stability of the banking sector. Chief among these concerns are efficient mobilization and allocation of financial resources; efficient clearing and settlement of financial transactions; macroeconomic stability; and protection against systemic crises of liquidity, solvency or volatility. The above-mentioned considerations are interrelated and cannot be addressed by the sole action of private agents.

Banks have also entered uncharted waters by launching complex financial products and services to the public, sometimes without a full assessment or understanding of the potential risks associated with these innovations. Certain innovations have split the components of risks in individual financial instruments (for example, interest, foreign exchange, maturities, solvency, price fluctuation of assets, etc.) to repackage and redistribute them with a view to meeting potential investors' requirements.

Risks cannot, however, be entirely eliminated from the banking–financial system through financial innovations. One can even argue that certain types of financial innovations (for example, leveraged buy-outs, and the extensive use of junk bonds) could raise the system's risk exposure and cause the banks' assets to deteriorate. It is only through judicious macroeconomic policies – monetary and non-monetary – that systemic risks can most probably be moderated, and liquidity in the economy be improved. To respond to actual or potential volatility in financial markets, there is a tendency among industrial countries to improve communication and the convergence of policies. This has been most prominent in setting prudential rules for banks, with two overriding objectives: protecting the solidity of banking systems, and the elimination of unfair competition. In this regard, the least regulated financial centres enjoy an unwarranted competitive advantage over the more regulated ones.

The countries which appear to be moving to a higher level of convergence are those of the European Community. By the end of 1992 it is intended to give financial institutions of the twelve EC countries the freedom of doing business in that economic zone without any constraints. This single financial market, however, remains incomplete until member-governments agree to reduce the autonomy of their monetary authorities in favour of a supranational institution. The twelve European countries will probably continue to move toward greater coherence in their economic policies. Yet this is not deemed to be at the expense of the rest of the world. The Netherlands Minister of Finance, H. Onno Ruding, is opposed to the concept of Fortress Europe, that is, the creation of an inward-looking protectionist economic zone. He, like his peers in the EC, is for an open – though economically integrated – region.

The issue of whether banks can be content with self-imposed prudential rules has often been raised and discussed. It has been generally acknowledged that while internal control is imperative, independent external inspection is equally essential to cope with possible failures by management, whatever the causes. Public supervisory authorities question the ability of individual financial institutions, driven by commercial considerations, to observe single-handedly prudential control measures. A bank's drive for realizing profits could lead to relaxation of self-discipline and inadequate internal control of risks. Such a situation requires supervisory action by the appropriate public agencies in order to protect the interests of the public in general.

Some bankers consider certain prudential requirements of the supervisory authorities 'excessive'. They fear for the adverse effect on initiative and profits. Others argue that a government can protect the profitability of financial institutions by the tight regulation of their operations – especially with regard to interest rates, margins, fees, market segmentation, barriers to entry, etc. Interest rates were thus regulated in Japan until the late 1980s: they provided banks with attractive margins thanks to artificially low interest rates on deposits over long periods to the detriment of savers (Yasuo Kanzaki).

Liberalized markets boost competition and innovation as institutions respond ingeniously to the needs of customers. Bankers have often decried governmental regulations, including those relating to defining the scope of an individual bank's activities. Thus functional segmentation has been instituted in the USA and Japan: respectively by the US Glass–Steagall Act. and article 65 of the Japanese constitution – which protect investment banks and securities houses from commercial banks' competition. Concerned about the competition of commercial banks, one Japanese investment banker advocated at the International Banking Colloquium the need for a 'fire-wall' to insulate investment banking institutions from competitors! Some investment banks can, however, continue to prosper without protective measures, and despite the new capital requirements on off-balance-sheet exposures.

Geographical market segmentation has also been imposed on banks by the regulatory authorities, notably in the USA. This has often limited the territorial expansion of a bank's activities, and has thus constrained the scope for the diversification of its activities. To cope with risks encountered by banks, building-up capital in this segmented market environment can prove inadequate. In the judgement of an eminent US banker, there is in total a *surplus* of capital in the global banking system. Otherwise there is no reason why returns on capital in banking are lower than they are in other industries. The problem, of course, is that the overcapitalization is distributed among too many units. Regulators see the trees but not the forest and try to raise the capital per unit, but the real issue is one of consolidation and liquidation, it is cogently argued.

There is usually a trade-off between competition on the one hand, and safe and sound banking on the other. By ensuring an acceptable minimum common denominator to protect financial institutions from excessive risks through minimal capital adequacy ratios and through control of abuses, unfair and speculative competition could be avoided. Often bankers and supervisors are unable to gauge *ex ante* risks and to do so in time, that is, before irreparable damage is suffered. The task faced by the supervisory authorities has been that of choosing between: (i) guarding against negligence or abuse by the management, the personnel or the clientèle of a bank; and (ii) allowing sufficient freedom to banks in order to open the scope for innovation and the attainment of greater efficiency. Commenting on the fall-off of discipline in the supervision of financial markets and intermediaries, one erstwhile central bank governor (Pierre Languetin) cited the proverb 'Once danger is over, we cease imploring the saints!'

At the international level, a welcome beginning has been made in the convergence of prudential rules. This coordination has been realized in 1988 by agreement amongst the Group of Ten who cooperate within the Basle Committee on Banking Regulations and Supervisory Practices.[2] A major agreement was reached in 1988 on the measurement and assessment of minimum capital adequacy standards for transnational banking institutions; it followed in the wake of the earlier Concordats of 1975 and 1983 which allocated responsibilities to the home and host countries for improving cross-border supervisory collaboration (including recommending procedures for consolidating branches, subsidiaries, and affiliates to improve knowledge on exposure to risks of supervised institutions). The new international standards on capital adequacy have the merit of endeavouring to relate a bank's capital to the risk profile of its on-balance sheet assets and its off-balance sheet exposures. Banks will therefore have to manage judiciously both the size and composition of their business activities to comply with the risk-based capital requirements and to realize the earnings which will satisfy shareholders and other suppliers of funds. More international coordination is needed in ensuring comprehensive supervision covering *inter alia* various components of a banks' business (e.g. liquidity, position-taking, concentration of risks, country-risks, interest rate and exchange rate risks, etc.).

SAFETY NETS

The liquidation of a bank may be voluntarily decided by senior management or may be forced by business failure. The latter is often the result of inefficiency – though fraud or insider abuse can also cause bank failure. Market forces in an open competitive economy permit the fittest to survive and thrive. Weak or undercapitalized banks are likely to be displaced by dynamic capital-rich banks. Insolvent banks have to disappear – by merger, revamping with new shareholding and management, acquisitions, etc. By weeding out poor performers the banking industry will come out stronger and serve its customers more efficiently. Barring panic and a general confidence crisis, the closure of a loss-making bank is a natural sanction of a free market for the unsatisfactory or inadequate perform-ance of its management – for reasons of incompetence, fraud, em-bezzlement, etc. The solidity and stability of a banking system depend first and foremost on the competence and integrity of man-agers and the personnel, and the application of self-regulation. These qualities can be codified in the legislation and regulations which set the general prudential prerequisites for the establishment and oper-ation of a bank.

Deposit insurance is an additional safety net for the banking system, insofar as it can fend off the 'contagion' effect and preclude a chain reaction with weaker banks threatening the viability of well-run banks. Deposit insurance can thus reduce the systemic risk of bank runs and provide greater stability to the banking sector. The effec-tiveness of deposit insurance is so much greater if it is coupled with improved supervision to ascertain that prudential rules are properly observed by the insured banks. This would entail the capacity of the insurer to apply dissuasive measures and potent sanctions, such as increasing insurance premiums, buttressed by the threat of quick withdrawal of deposit insurance for unduly risky loan/investment portfolios or delinquent behaviour by the bank concerned. The ultimate penalty is the prompt closure of the insolvent bank.

Deposit insurance is faced with a number of challenges. Chief among these are questions regarding the governmental *versus* private nature of the deposit insurance institution; the advisability or non-advisability of a government subsidy (actual or contingent); the extent of deposit coverage (limited to small deposits, or comprehen-sive); the insurer's ability to assess *ex ante* banking risks; the advisability of uniform *versus* risk-related premiums, and allowing both small and bigger problem banks to default regardless of size.

US legislation has instituted a government-owned Federal Deposit Insurance Corporation (FDIC) and has chosen to give formal protection to small depositors – a maximum of $100 000 per account. By comparison, West Germany boasts of organizationally independent and self-funded deposit insurers which belong to various segments of the German banking community. Moreover, German insured commercial banks enjoy practically an unlimited deposit insurance for non-bank deposits, viz. reaching, per deposit account, up to the equivalent in value of 30 per cent of the capital base of the bank hosting the deposit account in question.

Prompted by equity considerations, the US deposit insurance system was designed originally to protect small depositors and to ease the access of small banks to the resources of such depositors. The rationale was to enable smaller banks to face up to the competition of bigger banks. Although deposits in excess of $100 000 have been excluded from the explicit official protection umbrella of the US deposit insurance system, all depositors and bank creditors in large banks which have failed have been *de facto* protected. This has contributed to make large diversified banks already deemed by public authorities to be too large to fail, safer than the small unit banks limited to a small geographic area and a few banking services.

Managers of large banks might succumb to the moral hazard of decline in discipline, in view of the implicit government guarantee provided through the safety net of the FDIC. Small banks have no such guarantee and may be allowed to fail if they become insolvent. The bias in favour of rescuing big banks – despite their bad performance – has been justified on the grounds of general stability. Such a policy is based on the argument that the failure of a big bank (in view of the size of its involvement in the national and international economies, and the extensive web of its relations) can rock the national and international economies. By comparison, the failure of a small bank is tolerable. This was clearly stated by FDIC's Chairman:

> no major industrial nation has allowed its largest banks to default because of an unwillingness to risk the consequences. The international competitive ramifications alone make it unlikely that this policy will be changed. So an insurance system designed originally to help small banks to compete with big banks now operates to

favour big banks over small banks. Alas, as Caesar lamented, 'All bad precedents began as justifiable measures' (L. William Seidman).

At the opposite end of the spectrum, some bankers and regulators – notably in Switzerland – have argued that there is no need in an open economy for circumventing market discipline or to foster inefficiencies through the creation of a deposit insurance mechanism. Deposit insurance distorts market forces, since by putting the government's credit behind the insured bank, it may tempt certain bank managers to take greater risks. The safety and soundness of banks is more effectively assured through sizeable equity and sufficient liquidity to meet the twin shocks of potential losses or a net deposit drain.

The German central bank (the Bundesbank) – similarly to the US Federal Reserve Board – has a policy of limiting direct liquidity lending against the collateral of high-quality short-term assets. Germany has nevertheless created a mixed public–private sector institution (in which both the German central bank and commercial banks participate) to provide speedily and at reasonable cost necessary funding to a solvent bank in the throes of a liquidity crunch.

Fashion or the herd instinct explains the uncritical enthusiasm or the excessive pessimism in the banks' rush to finance (or cut lines of credit to) certain countries or certain sectors. Some observers pertinently question the capacity of bankers – and for that matter other decision-makers – to make good use of knowledge on past failures or adversities. Any surge in new banking business can be a warning signal. It portends a potential substantial rise in risks in so far as it exposes banks to less familiar sets of exposures. One should also add that the present and future socioeconomic phenomena do not necessarily repeat the past experience in view of the myriad of new variables or parameters.

It has been widely acknowledged that the public authorities in the major developed countries have not allowed Black Monday (that is, the New York Stock Exchange crash of 19 October 1987 followed by similar collapses of other stock exchanges) to be irreversible, lest dire consequences affect the real economy worldwide. Central banks, in particular, introduced massive liquidity into their banking-financial systems without delay and in a coordinated manner in order to ease the impending crunch and to avoid a possible depression. However, such monetary creation is not without costs – chief amongst which are inflationary pressures.

Public authorities need to provide an optimal combination of prudential control and safety nets for banking institutions, while preserving the initiative and the responsibility of bankers – large or small. Public authorities should therefore beware of stifling initiative by imposing excessive controls, or of providing too much security to banks and their customers. Well-managed and well-performing banks should not be burdened or constrained by the mistakes and failures of incompetently or recklessly run banks. A solvent bank could be threatened with insolvency should it face a flight of deposits accruing from the 'contagious' effect of insolvent banks whose failures cause a general loss of confidence in banks. In such an event the said solvent bank needs ready liquidity. It may not, however, have assets in sufficient quantity, eligible for sale or for discount in the financial market, or for liquidity assistance from the central bank – at reasonable conditions. A liquidity crisis could put the bank in difficulty by impairing the value of assets through distress or forced sales at below-market prices, or impose on the bank costly funding.

Although it is more usual for central banks to provide liquidity funding for banks in order to avoid a liquidity crisis turning into an insolvency crisis, deposit insurance schemes have occasionally provided liquidity to the solvent but troubled bank(s) concerned, as happened with the FDIC's handling of First Republic's forty Texas banks in 1988. As eloquently stated by FDIC's Chairman, 'Deposit insurance is like a nuclear power plant. Operated properly, it is beneficial; but only appropriate safety precautions can keep it from going out of control. Once out of control, it can blow up, with great damage to the entire country.' Indeed deposit insurance allows insured institutions to borrow on the credit of the government. This structure encourages risk-taking which must be kept under control through adequate supervision and sanctions against mismanagement.

Concerted action of the monetary authorities of the major financial centres is clearly needed in periods of financial tensions. Such tensions, if left to themselves, can blow up in a general economic crisis. Credible guidelines for such international coordination in monetary policies, aimed at monetary growth without inflation, will stabilise expectations and will moderate the price volatility of financial assets. This will contribute to the proper functioning of the international financial sector. Guidelines for monetary coordination linked to prudential cooperation in the supervision of banks and financial markets, are a prerequisite for a healthy international financial system.

CONCLUSION: THE PERENNIAL NECESSITY FOR VIGILANCE

Public authorities in their varied components (the political authorities at the helm of the budget, as well as the monetary and supervisory authorities) and bankers share a common concern for a safe, sound and efficient banking–financial system operating in a relatively stable environment. All groups have to beware of accident- or crisis-prone types of policies or behaviour.

Governments have to guard against the uncontrollable slipping of macroeconomic variables. The latter include chronic budgetary or payments imbalances, inflationary pressures, volatile exchange or interest rates, etc. They have also to guard against subjecting banking activities to inflexible controls lest these thwart the dynamism and initiative of the institutions, and ultimately adversely affect their capacity to realize profits. The poor performance of the financial services industry in a country is bound to spill over other sectors of the national economy, and vice versa.

Bank management has to emphasize the importance of adequate profitability, but this should not be confused with size. For a commercial institution, profits are the first line of defence which enables it to weather possible future losses. They also offer the possibility of adding to the capital base of the institution concerned, thereby permitting a well-founded expansion in activities. An expansion of assets, with little concern for quality and for net profit margins, has grave consequences for the eventual survival of the institution. In this context, banks have to guard against the 'herd instinct' of following fashions without a rational analysis and adequate guarantees. This has led in recent years to hazardous lending to certain countries (for example, some LDC's) and to certain sectors (such as energy, real estate, farming sectors, as well as to corporate buy-outs in the USA).

Prudential regulations applying to various categories of financial institutions are disparate within one single economy, and more so at the international level. A beginning, however, has been made among major Western financial centres (within the Group of Ten) in the 1988 agreement on common capital standards for banking institutions. With a higher level of integration of banking and financial markets, there is need for national authorities to further their convergence and coordination of regulatory rules and monetary policies. This should cover notably multilateral agreements regarding: common rules of prudential control of other risks not yet covered, and the institution of a 'lender of last resort' arrangement for the global financial market, readily accessible to troubled but solvent transnational banks in the event of a liquidity crisis.

Notes

1. All citations are from contributors to this book.
2. The Group consists of Belgium, Canada, France, Germany, Italy, Japan, Luxembourg, The Netherlands, Sweden, Switzerland, the UK and the USA.

Appendix: Institutions Represented at the First and Second Colloquia by their top Policy-makers or Executives

African Development Bank	Abidjan
Al Ahli Bank of Kuwait, KSC	Kuwait
American Express Company	New York
Association Suisse des Banquiers	Basle
Banca Nazionale del Lavoro	Rome
Banca d'Italia	Rome
Banca della Svizzera Italiana	Lugano
Banca dello Stato del Cantone Ticino	Bellinzona
Banco de Bilbao	Madrid
Banco di Napoli	Naples
Banco di Roma	Rome
Banco di Sicilia	Rome
Banco do Brasil	Brazil
Bank Melli Iran	London
Bank of America	San Francisco
Bank of England	London
Bank of Ireland	Dublin
Bank of Israel	Jerusalem
Bank of Japan	Tokyo
Bank Saderat	Tehran
Banque Arabe et Internationale d'Investissement	Paris
Banque Bruxelles Lambert SA	Brussels
Banque Cantonale Vaudoise	Lausanne
Banque Indosuez	Paris
Banque Internationale à Luxembourg SA	Luxembourg
Banque Nationale Suisse	Zurich
Banque Nationale de Belgique SA	Brussels
Banque Populaire Suisse	Berne
Banque Scandinave en Suisse	Geneva
Banque Unie pour l'Orient Arabe	Geneva
Barclay's International Ltd	London
Barclays Bank plc	London
Caisse d'Epargne de Genève	Geneva
Central Bank of Iraq	Baghdad
Central Bank of Ireland	Dublin
Central Bank of Kuwait	Kuwait

Central Bank of Nigeria	Lagos
Central Bank of the Republic of Turkey	Ankara
Citicorp/Citibank NA	New York
Commerzbank AG	Frankfurt
Commission fédérale des banques	Berne
Compagnie Bancaire	Paris
Compagnie Financière Tradition/Banque Pallas	Lausanne
Compagnie Financière de Paribas	Paris
Copenhagen Handelsbank A/S	Copenhagen
Crédit Communal de Belgique	Brussels
Crédit Foncier Vaudois	Lausanne
Crédit Suisse	Zurich
Daiwa Securities Co., Ltd	Tokyo
Danmarks Nationalbank	Copenhagen
Den Danske Bank af 1871 A/S	Copenhagen
Deutsche Bundesbank	Frankfurt
Dresdner Bank	Frankfurt
Espirito Santo Financial Holding SA	Luxembourg
Federal Deposit Insurance Corporation	Washington, DC
Federal Reserve Bank of New York	New York
First National Bank of Southern Africa Ltd	Johannesburg
Générale de Banque	Brussels
Instituto Bancario San Paolo di Torino	Turin
Kleinwort Benson Ltd	London
La Caixa	Barcelona
Landesbank Stuttgart Girozentrale	Stuttgart
Les Fils Dreyfus & Cie SA	Basle
Lombard, Odier & Cie	Geneva
Midland Bank plc	London
Minister of Finance	The Hague
Mitsubishi Trust and Banking Corporation	Tokyo
Morgan Grenfell & Co. Ltd	London
Méditerranée Investors Group SA	Luxembourg
National Westminster Bank plc	London
Nederlandsche Middenstandsbank NV	Amsterdam
Oesterreichische Laenderbank	Vienna
Oesterreichische Nationalbank	Vienna
Privatbanken A/S	Copenhagen
Reserve Bank of Australia	Canberra
S.G. Warburg & Co. Ltd	London
Sanwa Bank Ltd	Tokyo
Saudi American Bank	Riyadh
Saudi Arabian Monetary Agency	Riyadh
Schroders plc	London
Société de Banque Suisse	Basle
South African Reserve Bank	Pretoria
Sparekassen SDS	Copenhagen
Swiss Commodities & Futures Association	Lausanne

Tetra Pak Finance & Trading	Lausanne–Pully
The Hongkong and Shanghai Banking Corporation	Hong Kong
The Nikko Securities Co., Ltd	Tokyo
The Royal Bank of Canada	Toronto
The World Bank	Washington, DC
Trustee Savings Bank of Scotland	Edinburgh
Union Bank of Finland	Helsinki
Union Suisse des Caisses Raiffeisen	St-Gall
Union de Banques Arabes et Françaises	Paris
Union de Banques Suisses	Zurich
United Bank for Africa Ltd	Lagos
Vereins- und Westbank AG	Hamburg
Westpac Banking Corporation	Sydney

Index